GROWTH, INDUSTRIALISATION AND NEW ECONOMIC REFORMS IN INDIA

By the Same Author

Essays on Political Economy
Developmental Problems and Policies in India

About the Author

Prof. B. Satyanarayan (*b.* 1938) has been working in the University for more than 35 years holding various positions. He is presently working as a Senior Professor of Economics in the Department of Economics, Osmania University. He is simultaneously holding the position of Director/Coordinator, Special Assistance Programme (Sponsored by the University Grants Commission), Department of Economics, Osmania University, during the last six years. Earlier, he worked as Head of the Department of Economics and Chairman, Board of Studies, Osmania University.

He has to his credit more than 100 research papers published in a number of academic Journals. Professor Satyanarayan has undertaken and successfully completed nearly a dozen research projects, sponsored by the Government of India, U.G.C., Planning Commission, Government of Andhra Pradesh etc. He has recently completed a major research project on "Regional Cooperation among SAARC countries with Special Reference to Trade Prospects" Sponsored by the UGC, New Delhi. He had the privilege of being invited as a Visiting Professor by the Illinois Institute of Technology, Chicago, USA (Stuart School of Business) for a period of 3 months during July-October 1994. His name has been published by the Biography International (1992) and Marqui's "Who's Who in the World" (1999). He has authored and edited nearly ten books on various aspects of Development Economics.

GROWTH, INDUSTRIALISATION AND NEW ECONOMIC REFORMS IN INDIA

PROF. B. SATYANARAYAN

Co-ordinator/Director
Special Assistance Programme
Department of Economics,
Osmania University, Hyderabad

CONCEPT PUBLISHING COMPANY, NEW DELHI-110059

ISBN 81-7022-893-X

First Published 2001

Published and Printed by

Ashok Kumar Mittal
Concept Publishing Company
A/15-16, Commercial Block, Mohan Garden,
New Delhi-110059 (India)
Phones : 5648039, 5649024
Fax : 091-11-5648053
Email : publishing@conceptpub.com

PREFACE

The present volume consists of the extension lectures delivered by the eminent economists/scholars who have been invited under the auspices of the Special Assistance Programme (Now it is known as Department of Special Assistance), Department of Economics, Osmania University, sponsored by the University Grants Commission. These lectures were spread during the period from 1994 to 1998. We are able to utilise the publication grant sanctioned under the DSA Funds. Our thanks are due to all the Visiting Professors/Scholars who have readily agreed to spare the written matter and send the material for necessary publication.

The Advisory Committee of the DSA has been kind enough to have agreed for the publication of all the extension lectures.

PROF. B. SATYANARAYAN

ACKNOWLEDGEMENTS

At the outset, I wish to thank the University Grants Commission, New Delhi for providing the publication grant. I wish to thank Prof. D.C. Reddy, the Vice-Chancellor and Chairman of the Advisory Committee of the Department of Special Assistance. I wish to express my thanks to Prof. Pannalal, the Registrar and Prof. P. Jaya Prakash Rao, Dean, Development and UGC Affairs, Osmania University and their staff who have helped us in releasing funds. I am also thankful to Prof. V. Ramakishtayya, former Vice-Chancellor, Prof. M. Bhagwanth Rao, former Registrar and Prof. S. Pullaiah, former Dean, UGC Affairs, Osmania University, who have extended their helping hand in completing the task on hand. I also wish to thank all the members of the Advisory Committee of the DSA for their valuable suggestions from time to time.

Finally, I wish to thank all the members of the faculty who cooperated wholeheartedly in the publication of the present volume, particularly the successive Heads of the Department of Economics, Osmania University, viz., Prof. H. Venkateshwar Rao, Prof. M. Narasimhulu, Prof. K. Chakradhar Rao and Prof. V. Suguna. I also thank all the members of the Research and the Administrative Staff who have helped me in completing the publication of the present volume.

Date : 31st March, 1999
Hyderabad-7

PROF. B. SATYANARAYAN

CONTENTS

LIST OF CONTRIBUTORS

P.R. Brahmananda

Former Director, Bombay School of Economics, Bombay University, Mumbai.

A.V. Gokak, IAS

Secretary to Government of India, Formerly with the Department of Programme Implementation; and Presently with The Department of Chemicals and Fertilizers, New Delhi-110001

M. Gopalakrishna, IAS (Rtd.)

Formerly Chairman and Managing Director, Rural Electrification Corporation Ltd., New Delhi and Presently Director, Institute of Public Enterprise, O.U. Campus, Hyderabad-7.

Ashok Mathur

Professor of Economics, Centre for the Study of Regional Development, School of Social Sciences, Jawaharlal Nehru University, New Delhi-110 067

Late Prof. K.N. Reddy

Formerly Professor, National Institute of Public Finance and Policy, New Delhi-110067

D.U. Sastry

Former Professor and Senior Fellow, Institute of Economic Growth, Delhi-110007

S.K. Thorat

Professor of Economics, Centre for the Study of Regional Development, School of Social Sciences, JNU, New Delhi-67

INTRODUCTORY REMARKS

The Chapter entitled "Energy Scenario and the Indian Economy" by Shri M. Gopalakrishna says that there is a strong linkage between energy use and growth of the GDP in any country. Roughly 50 per cent of India's GDP is directly or indirectly the result of energy. India's average per capita consumption of power is only around 314 kWh. It is a very low figure when compared to 5000 kWh of the developed world. The author records that India's consumption in terms of Kgs of oil equivalent is 242 against the world's average of 1421 Kgoe. The Kgoe of the developed countries ranges between 5000 to 8000. In the current energy scenario in India there is a wide disparity in the matter of use and nature of consumption of energy between the urban areas and rural areas. It may be noted that while India has 16 per cent of world's total population, it has just around 2 per cent of total world's energy. India is well endowed only in respect of coal. Our oil and gas resources are very meagre.

While we were in a position to add 4000 MW of power annually during the Seventh Five Year Plan, it dropped considerably to around 3000 MW per year. This happened due to low investment and reduced efficiency. The author feels that the present energy problem in the country is because of Government's excessive reliance on private sector's entry into the power sector which of course did not materialise. The energy shortage at the national level is around 9.2 per cent. It is felt that the Government has given priority to generation rather than distribution network as far as privatisation is concerned. The author feels that a combination of both the activities within a definite time frame work be a better proposition. The energy problem should have a short term, a medium term and a long term component. There has to be a balanced investment in hydel, thermal and renewable energy resources as well as transmission. The author says that we should emulate Israel in water and energy use efficiency.

The author has also dealt with the generation of Nuclear Power.

According to him, although the capital cost is relatively more and the safety requirements more stringent, the generation cost is relatively more attractive when compared to other modes of power generation. A section is devoted to discuss the performance of State Electricity Boards. In the long run, it is observed, this country will have to build hydel projects, nuclear and thermal projects and also go in for decentralised grid supply wherever it is possible.

The Chapter entitled "Some Theoretical Considerations in Reform of Rural Institutions in India" by Professor S.K. Thorat makes an attempt to highlight the recent theoretical developments in the institutional economics with a purpose to identify the possible framework or starting points for reforms of rural institutions in India. Within the neo-classical framework, two broad approaches have emerged to overcome the limitations of mainstream economics. It includes transaction and information costs theory on the one hand and the school of collective action on the other. As a matter of fact, there is a controversy—one school says that institutional change depends on technical change and another says that technical change depends on institutional change, the latter being governed by other independent variables. Technological determinism formed the essential base of Marxist writings. Prof. Pranab Bardhan seems to have argued that the neo-classical institutional economists focus their attention on allocative efficiency of institutions but ignored the distributive aspects of the institutional change. He also highlights the role of ideology and states which the Neo-classical Institutional Economics has ignored.

According to Prof. Thorat, although the state during the last five decades has spent huge sums of money on rural development, the success is insignificant. He observes that the failures of the states and local institutions are in the areas of land reforms, and providing the public goods like irrigation, education, health, infrastructural facilities like roads, power, credit and extension service including the administration of various programmes for the poor such as IRDP and EGS. The programmes are usually administered by distant, uncoordinated bureaucracy which is insensitive to the needs of the people and often little reaches the intended beneficiaries of the programmes. This problem seems to have been realised by the Government. The Approach Paper on the Ninth Five Year Plan observes: "In view of the lessons from experience, it has become necessary to introduce the necessary correctives to reverse many of the unsustainable trends in programme/ project formulation and implementation. This will be a central priority of the Ninth Plan".

The Approach Paper also suggested the following policy measures in general and in particular for social sector programmes:

(i) A genuine push towards decentralisation and people's participation will be given.
(ii) Reorientation and integration of all village level schemes under the Panchayati Raj to avoid thin spread and wastage of resources.
(iii) The existing schemes whose delivery costs are disproportionately high or which fail to make the desired impact should be considered for reorientation and discontinuation.
(iv) Monitoring and Evaluation of programmes will have to be made more effective and purposeful.
(v) Institutional changes to bring in transparency in implementation and operation of programmes.
(vi) Build in sustainability of outputs and benefits and maintenance of public facilities as a necessary component of project/ programme formulation.

The Chapter entitled "New Economic Policy and Its Impact on Employment and Poverty of the Scheduled Castes: Some Observations" by Prof. S.K. Thorat assesses the impact of the far-reaching economic reforms initiated by the Government in response to a major economic crisis in early 1991 on economic situations of Scheduled Castes in India. This is done by looking at the trends in few important aspects, namely: (a) employment/unemployment; (b) by examining some of the theoretical issues underlying the new economic policy, in as much as they relate to the specific social and economic situation of Scheduled Castes in India. The New Economic Policy (NEP) comprises of "Stabilisation" and "of Structural Adjustment" programmes which were initiated to overcome the crisis in two areas : (a) External debt crisis; and (b) Fiscal deficits (Public debt crisis). The important elements of Structural Adjustment Programme (SAP) are to shift resources:

(i) From non-traded goods to traded goods sector and with in latter form import substituting activities to export activities; and
(ii) Away from Government Sector to private sector.

The author discusses the impact of New Economic Policy (NEP) on the overall employment situation in the country. A section is devoted to discuss the unemployment situation of Scheduled Castes taking statistics from Five Year Plan Documents. The impact on employment under Reservation is also discussed in detail. The Poverty Ratios are presented as estimated by the Expert Group Method. The author feels that the caste based discrimination in so far as it excludes or reduces the access of scheduled caste persons to various factor markets i.e., labour, land, capital, information and social service sector, it has implications on the earning capacity, employment and income of the scheduled castes. In that sense, it is inhibitive to economic growth and income distribution.

Finally, the author says that the increase in productivity of public expenditure requires a meaningful restructuring of public sector to raise its efficiency and productivity. It is argued that there is no unique relationship between ownership and performance. The efficiency of an enterprise is determined more by compilation in the market structure and competence in the management than by nature of its ownership.

Prof. D.U. Sastry in Chapter entitled "Fixed Investment" has analysed the determinants of financial variables. The role of accelerator and financial variables is studied. The inter-dependence between fixed and inventory investment is also analysed. To start with, the author makes an overall review of all the Indian studies in the field—by authors like Krishna Murthy, Sarkar, Patnaik, Swamy, Bagchi, Siddharthan, Divatia and Athawale, Jameson etc.

The author is of the opinion that public investment activity and import substitution policies have provided stimulus to the private sector in India. Apart from providing physical climate through infrastructure, public investment stimulates activity in atleast two ways: (i) through the supply of capital and current inputs; and (ii) through direct and indirect demands generated by the Government spending. The author says that Inventory is an important charge on funds. It is nearly one-third of the total use of funds for the corporate sector in India. In a shortage economy, inventories, particularly raw materials, could constitute a priority item on the use of funds. Raw materials and goods-in-process inventories constitute two-thirds of the aggregate inventory holdings for the organised manufacturing in India. The conclusions arrived at by the author are as follows:

1. The analysis brings out the importance of accelerator in the explanation of fixed investment. However, when there is

extreme form of controls inclusive of price and distribution, the results indicate the absence of the effect of accelerator as in the case of sugar and cement;

2. Financial flow variable, internal and external are found to be significant determinants of fixed investment. External finance seems to have relatively larger impact on fixed investment;
3. The age of equipment as measured by depreciation reserves has not shown by and large, the replacement effect on fixed investment;
4. The results point out that fixed investment and inventory investment are competitive.

On the basis of Ordinary Least Squares (OLS) method, the author has derived the result which shows that the accelerator, financial variables and inventory investment are crucial determinants of fixed investment in the Indian private corporate sector.

The Chapter entitled "Capital Surrogates and Production Function" by Prof. D.U. Sastry deals with the Cobb-Douglous and Constant Elasticity Production Functions for the period 1949-70. The elasticity of output with respect to capital and labour have been estimated and comparisons made for Maharashtra, Tamil Nadu and for All-India. It was found that the estimates of elasticity output with respect to capital vary according to capital measure. Elasticity of output with respect to capital surrogates. As between capital surrogates, elasticity of output with respect to total energy consumption is somewhat higher as compared to elasticity of output with respect to electricity consumption.

The author has found that the implied elasticity of output with respect to labour is high in Maharashtra when compared to Tamil Nadu. It could be due to difference in the quality of labour. The higher wage rate and higher wage share in Maharashtra is consistent with higher elasticity of output with respect to labour. Given the differences in product mix between the two regions, it would appear that efficiency of labour is higher in Maharashtra whereas efficiency of capital is higher in Tamil Nadu.

The author concludes that capital surrogates such as electricity consumption and total energy consumption have definite advantages as they help in overcoming some of the difficult problems of capital measurement. As between the two capital surrogates his analysis suggests obvious preference to total energy consumption. It is from both conceptual and statistical point of view the composite measure of total energy consumption seems to be a more meaningful surrogate to capital in production analysis.

The Chapter entitled "Theories of Agricultural Development: Trends and Perspectives" by Prof. S.K. Thorat says that any one sector is a part of an interdependent system represented by the country's economy and what it does is not fully attributable to it but is contingent upon what happens in other sectors of the economy. Against this background, the author is of the opinion that any meaningful economic theory of agricultural development should incorporate the following interrelated parts:

(i) An analysis of the role of agriculture in economic development;
(ii) An analysis of the economic nature of traditional agriculture; and
(iii) An analysis of the economic process of modernisation of agriculture.

The author says that the factors which influence output are divided into two categories:

(a) Traditional inputs; and
(b) New production process resulting from new technology that alters input-output relationship.

The level of use of inputs is a function of :

(a) The total stock available;
(b) The percentage utilisation of the stock.

The Chapter entitled "Expenditure on Repairs in Selected Indian Industries: An Exploratory Study" by Prof. D.U. Sastry makes an attempt to analyse the expenditure on repairs in selected Indian industries. Expenditure on repairs includes maintenance of the capital also. The author deals with a number of factors which influence the expenditure on maintenance and repairs, such as the intensity with which capital assets are used, age of the used capital assets etc. The author has arrived at three important conclusions. They are as follows:

(i) There is a clear and unmistakable evidence of positive role of capacity utilisation on the expenditure on repairs;

(ii) The influence of age of the capital stock on repairs expenditure is observed in a large number of industries;

(iii) The impact of retained profits on the expenditure on repairs is somewhat limited.

Prof. K.N. Reddy in his brief Chapter relating to "Government Role and the Efficiency of Policy Instruments" deals with the relationship between the role of the Government and efficiency of policy instruments. According to him gap often exists between Government goals and the availability of fiscal instruments which are necessary to pursue those goals. The author comments that while the evidence available points to a greater need for Government action in developing countries as compared with industrial countries, it is the latter that exhibit a much larger role for the Government when that role is measured by levels of taxation and public spending. He found that, on an average, the level of taxation and public spending, measured as a share of GDP, is atleast twice as large in industrial countries as in developing countries. The author also deals with instruments like "Quasi-fiscal regulations" such as rent controls and "Quasi-fiscal activities" such as borrowings from commercial banks etc.

Prof. P.R. Brahmananda in his Chapter "Fifty Years of the Indian Economy after Independence" has dealt with the problem of population growth and food supplies during 1950's, 1960's, 1970's, 1980's and 1990's. He says that but for PL-480 Assistance, India would have had a succession of famines in late 1950's and 1960's. Then he goes on giving the population growth rates for all the individual States in India. Wherever, population controls are adopted, the population is under control. In States like Bihar, Madhya Pradesh, Rajasthan, the population growth rate is very high. The author has nicknamed them as BIMARU States, meaning "sick". The author says that the Indian economy has now reached an explosive state of regional dualism. The BIMARU States have a heavy concentration of below the poverty line people. The author is of the opinion that the Ninth Plan Approach Document also does not realise the importance of population explosion.

Turning to capital-output ratio, the author says that the capital-output ratio which was of the order of 1:2.5 during the First Five Year Plan, has gradually risen to about 1:5.0 during 1990's. This shows that the Indian economy has become not only capital-intensive but a high-cost economy. Likewise, the author observes that the net savings to net income ratio has risen from about 9 per cent in the First Plan to about

17.5 per cent during 1995-96, although the gross savings are anywhere around 24-25 per cent. As far as agriculture is concerned, Prof. Brahmananda says that the growth rate of agricultural production in the post-Independence period has been lower than that in non-agriculture. He also adds that there is a significant growth of casual employment in agriculture. This is due to mechanisation, hidden evasions of ceilings, substitution of family labour against outside labour, the unreality of minimum wages etc. According to him, emergence of rural poverty is a direct consequence of adoption of wrong strategy in the Indian economy.

So far as industrial growth rate is concerned, it was 5.71 per cent during the period from 1950-51 to 1983-84 when compared to 7.13 per cent during the period from 1983-84 to 1996-97. According to the author, the enhanced rate of industrial growth is due to the process of liberalisation which has stated in the Indian economy from 1980's onwards. Only seven States in India after Independence have managed to double their per capita real income during the 34 years span for which data are available in the post-Independence period. These States are: Punjab, Haryana, Orissa, Maharashtra, Gujarat, Karnataka and Manipur.

The Chapter entitled "Poverty Alleviation in India: Its Various Facets" by Shri A.V. Gokak deals with the conceptual problems relating to poverty both internally and externally. According to him, poverty in India could be explained by a multiplicity of causes such as unequal distribution of land, lack of employment opportunities and the price factor specially inflationary pressure which affects essential commodities. As per the estimates of the Planning Commission rural poverty is reported to have fallen from 54 per cent in 1972-73 to around 21 per cent in 1993-94. He deals with various strategies which have been adopted in India to reduce the incidence of poverty since Independence.

The author then goes on discussing the strategies which have been developed by the policy-makers for poverty alleviation in this country. Broadly, they are as follows :

1. Public Distribution System;
2. Wage Employment;
3. Integrated Rural Development Programme.

Discussing about the families below the poverty line the author feels that they require different degrees of assistance depending upon how below they are below the poverty line. Just as geo-physical conditions below the earth are different at various depths, so also the socio-economic conditions of the families which are below the poverty line also vary a great deal. The poorest of the poor may require a different kind of package altogether. They may for instance, require a second dose of assistance after the initial assistance. It is also felt that the repayment schedule may have to be drastically revised.

According to the author, the concept of poverty itself will have to undergo a radical change. It may not be viewed in terms of income alone but also in terms of access to various social services. In India itself, the approach to poverty based on the food intake i.e. in terms of the consumption of 2300 calories of food per day by an individual is giving way to another approach based on certain minimum standard of living, which is called the Minimal Standard of Living Approach. The new trend is in line with the recent international trends. The author is of the view that famines in this country are a thing of the past since food production has increased substantially.

Prof. Ashok Mathur in his Chapter entitled "Work Participation, Gender and Economic Development: A Quantitative Anatomy of the Indian Scenario", analyses forces which influence the degree of participation of population in economic activity in a developing economy. In the first stage, the relationship between economic development and work participation is examined. The core of the analysis is based on a cross-sectional study of 306 districts of India, using a composite index of development. The entire analysis is conducted separately for males and females on the one hand, and the rural and urban segments on the other. The oft-referred to inverse relationship between female work participation and economic development emerges to be true in initial stages of development in the rural segment. In the second stage, the role of key socio-economic and demographic factors in addition to that of development, has been investigated using a recursive multi-equation regression model. Finally, the author keeping in mind the crucial role of education in this context, work participation is analysed in terms of ten disaggregated educational categories.

1

ENERGY SCENARIO AND THE INDIAN ECONOMY

M. GOPALAKRISHNA

Energy and its Role in Growth of National Income

Energy in layman's language is *Shakti*. There is a Sanskrit saying that "if *Shakti* flows through the body, it becomes *Shivam* or auspicious. When it does not, it becomes *Shavam*", or dead. It is much like electricity, which, when it courses through a conductor, becomes a live wire and if it does not, it becomes dead or dud. Energy is, therefore, a life force—a basic input—one which imparts vigour and dynamism, the driving force—the prime mover of the economy—a part of the basic infrastructure. It determines the status of the economy as its use is an important indicator of the economy.There is a strong linkage between energy use and the growth of the GDP. Roughly 50 per cent of India's GDP in one way or the other is directly or indirectly the result or effect of the function of energy in growth, in output and in development of the economy. Hence, improvement of the growth of the economy through better energy availability and management is very important national issue.

In a rapidly changing world we have to develop our ability to accurately 'gauge' the requirements of change, to 'engage' the elements of change as partners and to effectively 'manage' the requirements of change.Therefore, the gauging, engaging and managing of energy for the purposes of development of the economy are really the most critical aspects, which need attention. Only when the rate of growth of energy is higher than the rate of growth of the GDP, a certain level of GDP growth can be sustained in developing countries. We are today in India, at a stage, where we have to and ought to keep a minimal sustained rate of growth of availability and demand for energy to trigger development, to improve productivity, to increase production and more importantly create jobs and ensure that income levels go up for sustainable level of savings for future capital formation.

Energy Use Patterns—Disparities and Future Needs

India's average per capita consumption of power is only around 314 kWh. It is a very low figure when compared to 5000 kWh of the developed world. India's consumption in terms of kgs of oil equivalent is 242 against the world's average of 1421 kgoe. The kgoe of the developed countries ranges between 5000 to 8000. So we are far below in respect of energy usage, though, allowance has to be made for our climatic conditions, large population and relatively limited needs. Our investment in power must, therefore, ensure that our energy requirement is met in full, its use helps in raising living standards and that it can achieve a critical mass that triggers off a continuous chain reaction of self-sustaining development. In the current energy scenario in India there is a very wide disparity in the matter of use and nature of consumption of energy between the urban areas and rural areas. In urban areas, 75 per cent of the households have electricity, while in the rural areas, only 31 per cent of the households have electricity. In urban areas, there is predominance of commercial energy use whereas in rural areas, non-commercial energy is mostly used for cooking and lighting purposes and much less for income generating of productive purposes. The predominant use of commercial energy is by way of widespread electric power consumption by agricultural pumpsets. With growing incomes in the rural areas from agriculture and small industry and services sector, we can expect a very rapid growth in the demand for power for domestic consumption.

Energy Use Efficiency for Sustainable Development

We often hear glib talk that India is a very rich country with a lot of natural resources. This is true in relation to the magnitude of resources but it is meagre in relation to its huge population. We have to link the physical resource availability with the human resources. We have to also examine whether human resources are consuming the physical resource capital or whether they are adding value or ensuring sustainability of these resources and thereby contributing to advancement of the economy. This distinction, should be clearly understood. It is very important to perceive in proper perspective the fact that India has 16 per cent of the world's population but does not have 16 per cent of the world's total energy resources. Probably it has just around 2 per cent. India is well endowed only in respect of coal, albeit of high ash content, accounting for 13 per cent of the world's coal resources. However, our oil and gas resources are low at hardly half a per cent each of the world's resources. We have to therefore more intensively and extensively explore and judiciously exploit our resource base in energy. We have to also consider measures to ensure energy security with proper utilisation of the resources while conserving and improving energy use efficiency.

It is high time that we look for energy resources not only within the country or its offshore prospective areas but also outside the country by suitable joint ventures and alliances. The need for tapping all available sources of energy to augment energy supply also becomes important. Our R&D and technological efforts must be directed to optimally use the solar insolation in the country alongwith all other renewable energy sources like hydel, biomass, wind, geo thermal, ocean thermal energy etc. We should simultaneously encourage energy use efficiency and energy conservation as a long term State policy. Unless we simultaneously practice demand management while making strenuous exploration efforts and press into service all renewable and non-conventional energy sources, the energy availability scenario over the next 15 to 20 years may not be very optimistic in relation to our economic needs.

Financing Energy Development and Judicious Investments

The propensity to save raises the capacity for internal resource generation which is very important for the Indian economy. How well one invests and secures returns is the function of input to output which determines continuous investment and supports internal resource generation. With the creation of a good investment climate, long term policy to control inflation and appropriate incentives, it is possible to garner more resources from all over the world and within the country for the energy sector. At the same time, we must articulate, integrate and properly intervene and secure a match between the requirements of energy, its utilisation, economic use and profitability of investments.

Investment in Power Generation in the Five Year Plans

Inadequate Funding after Seventh Five Year Plan

Ever since planning began in the country, roughly 20 per cent of the total investment has gone into the energy sector. We have to examine, whether this investment has really given the expected returns. Conceding that there is also a need for equity considerations, we have to examine whether we have priced energy in the manner in which internal resource generation is made possible. At a time when we were doing reasonably well on the energy front in the Sixth and Seventh Five Year Plans, the order of investment in the power sector started declining. While we were in a position to add 4000 MW of power annually in the Seventh Five Year Plan, it dropped very considerably to around 3000 MW per year at a time when there was a need to double the quantum of capacity installation in generation. This unfortunately happened at a time when inadequacy of energy warranted more investment and better efficiency. The net result was a situation of inadequacy compounded by inefficiency in energy management. This has been one of the major causes of the problems on the energy front.

Eighth Plan—Inadequacies of Liberalisation Policy

At the time when the Eighth Five Year Plan was formulated, an additional capacity of 50,000 MW was envisaged representing an annual capacity addition of 10,000 MW. The target was subsequently scaled down to 30,000 MW for the Eighth Plan. The progress during the first 4 years has not been satisfactory. We will probably be able at best to add 18,000 MW capacity. It is no wonder that we are faced with the situation of chronic shortage of power. To a large extent, the current shortage situation was accentuated by the policy of the Government of relying excessively on private sector entry into the power sector which did not materialise. Budgetary support to the central public sector utilities and the State Electricity Boards, should have been continued to secure immediate additions to capacity while the private sector could have supplemented the efforts of Government over the medium and long term. In the absence of a good legal and policy framework with an independent regulatory body and tariff clarity, private sector entry was far fetched but a tantalising mirage. In the euphoria of liberalisation and foreign direct investment, we appear to have put all the eggs in a dubious basket of private sector investment for public needs and concluded that the entire additional capacity requirements of the next 5 years could be met primarily and in very substantial measure from the private sector investment. If it does not materialise, which is very likely, we may be in for a long summer as well as winter of energy shortages and discontentment. This is indeed a sad indictment on our planning, political will, administrative skill and executive abilities.

The purpose of energy policy should ensure that energy availability not only meets the demands of the economy, but must be ahead of the needs of the economy. The energy shortage at the national level is around 9.2 per cent.The peaking shortage at 18 per cent is twice the energy shortage. If we look at the Southern region, the shortages of both energy and peaking are very high. Andhra Pradesh is no exception. Andhra Pradesh has no doubt improved the hydel-thermal mix in the recent past but given the vagaries of the monsoon, it has to plan for quicker installation of additional thermal capacities with more reliable output of energy.

Power Shortages—Inadequacies in Existing System

Low PLF at Generating Stations

Plant availability in terms of capacity utilisation has very serious economic implications. There are large number of plants operating with as abysmally low Plant Load Factor (PLF) of around 25 to 40 per cent. Most plants are operating between 45 to 60 per cent. A few are operating at acceptable levels of above 68 per cent. In most PPAs, the minimum prescribed PLF is 68.5 per cent. It means that PLF in India has been very poor. Due to the unscheduled and unplanned plant outages, atleast 500 to 600 MWs of power capacity is being lost annually in a critical shortage situation. The lack of renovation and modernisation, poor maintenance—whether predictive or preventive—have been responsible for the sorry state of affairs. If investments already made have not given us the anticipated benefits, should we not ponder over the situation and consequences of future investment which may be of the higher order of 5 to 6 times more than in the past? Can a poor country like India afford this sub-optimal use of scarce resources?

High Transmission and Distribution Losses

Another problem is our high transmission and distribution losses. In developed countries, it ranges between 5 to 10 per cent. In India, this figure is roughly 21 per cent. Can we, a poor country afford this loss and wastage of precious energy produced at high cost? If we reduce the loss by one per cent, we will save roughly 800 MW. Thus, with better managerial inputs and without any further investment, we can conserve a capacity of about 1300 MW annually which is being wasted now. We are also losing around 5 to 6 per cent by way of theft and pilferage. In effect, power produced with great effort is being fraudulently enjoyed by anti-social persons who should be penalised under the law.

Energy Mix—Planning for the Future

Coal—Conserving Resources

The available sources of energy and its mix is an important consideration. India has abundant deposits of coal. Our energy policy for the present or in the near future, has to therefore depend on coal resources till alternate energy sources become available. We should plan plants of economic size at pithead itself with good arrangements for ash disposal and protection of ecology and better transmission facilities. We should encourage location of industries which are energy intensive near the pithead station, so that the transmission and distribution losses could be cut sharply.

Oil and Natural Gas—Collaborations for Exploitation

India does not unfortunately, have adequate resources of either oil or natural gas. Gas is however relatively more abundant than oil. We have to do a lot more of intensive exploration and exploitation for oil resources. Given the slow pace of our exploration efforts and the time lags involved, it appears that we may have to import an increasingly larger quantum of oil to tide over our energy shortage. Imports subject us to the forces of worldwide demand-supply situation and fluctuations in price. With our poor foreign exchange resources, we might not be able to import all our requirements. In this situation, we have to consciously foster joint-ventures, strategic alliances, partnerships and linkages by which we can join hands with competent foreign oil companies to explore oil and gas worldwide to secure regular oil supplies. We have been talking for a long time about the Southern Gas grid and the Oman gas pipeline but nothing much has happened. We should not count the chicken before the eggs are hatched. Unless we have control over the sources of energy, whether within the country or abroad, we cannot have security of oil supplies.

Hydro Electric Power Potential—Need for Advance Planning

We have an estimated 80,000 MW of hydel potential in the country. Bulk of the potential is in the North Eastern and Himalayan Region while some quantum is available in the Central Region. A hydel project needs atleast 5 years of serious pre-project planning by way of geological and soil investigation, environmental studies, displacement and rehabilitation matters, cost benefit exercises etc. before we can take informed decisions. We need to build up a shelf of well-investigated projects. The capital cost of hydel projects is high and the gestation period long but is based on a renewable source. The operational cost is low, maintenance requirements minimal and is an excellent arrangement for peaking support. Therefore, a continuous programme of hydel investigation and execution of projects in time is imperative.

Nuclear Power—Our Alternative to Dwindling Resources

We have good resources to set up and sustain nuclear power generation within the country. Though the capital cost is more and the safety requirements stringent, the costs of generation make it quite attractive. We ought to also devote more attention to nuclear power. In short, we should plan and fix the time frame for the thermal, hydel and nuclear power generation. At the same time, we must stress on innovation and modernisation. We should also utilise the new and renewable energy sources, whether it be wind energy or solar energy or biomass energy. R&D inputs would be required and economically viable local grid concepts developed. We must integrate all sources of energy and have a holistic perspective plan of energy. Moreover, we should not forget the high order of investment needed for transmission and distribution. In fact, generation, transmission and distribution arrangement will have to be properly dovetailed.

Performance of State Electricity Boards

Weak Financial Base

The State Electricity Boards are criticised, often unfairly, for poor performance though such performance is the result of external or remote control decisions. The State governments should, in all fairness subsidise the cost of power which is to be supplied at lower than actual cost of generation and distribution as a policy directive for socio-economic reasons. Unfortunately, the burden of Government policy has to be borne not by Government but by the Electricity Boards as most States do not pay the subsidy due to the Electricity Boards. As the financial position of many governments is not sound, they have managed to transfer their fiscal burden to the Electricity Boards. The Electricity Boards which have turned sick have in turn started transmitting their sickness to their customers and suppliers. Even the lender financial institutions are not being spared! Due to the creeping sickness, financial institutions, suppliers and capital markets are applying quarantine at a time when more money is needed by SEBs. The annual loss incurred by SEBs on this account is approximately around Rs.15,000 crores per annum. If the Rs.15,000 crores were available annually to SEBs, it would have formed the seed money for mobilising resources for much needed investment. We would have generated much more money and with rationalised tariffs primed our engines for growth. Unfortunately this has not happened.

Woes of Cross-Subsidisation of Tariff

The Electricity Boards have been able to absorb losses of the order of Rs. 8000 crores by way of cross-subsidisation annually. But Rs. 7000 crores still remain as loss. The scenario of consumption has in the meantime, changed cosiderably. 60 per cent of the consumption was earlier accounted for by industry. Now, the national average has come down to 35 per cent. Agriculture at one time accounted for 10 per cent at the national level, it has now come upto 30 per cent. In several States which are agriculturally developed, it is in the range of 40 to 50 per cent. While industry, once accounting for 60 per cent could easily cross-subsidise 10 per cent of agriculture, industry which now accounts for 35 per cent is unable to cross-subsidise agricultural sector which accounts for 30-50 per cent of consumption. Industry with 35 per cent consumption contributes 60 per cent of the total revenues of the Electricity Boards; agriculture with 30 per cent consumption accounts for only 5 per cent of the revenues of the Board. This disparity is clear and glaring. Unless this disparity is corrected, by a suitable mechanism, there is no point in blaming the Electricity Boards for the ills externally imposed on them.

Captive Generation by Large Consumers—Impact on SEBs

Some SEBs are already facing the loss of big corporate customers. 48 per cent of the corporate requirements of power is likely to be met by captive generation. This figure is going up which means that the future health of the Electricity Boards will to some extent be dependent on reversing this trend. That would depend on how aggressively they will add new capacities at low cost. We have to expedite ongoing projects and even small projects. Human resource development is the most important area for attention. Unless our engineers are able to effectively manage their resources, bring attitudinal change and a change in favour of increased productivity, it would be very difficult to achieve our goals. We have to provide proper environment where economics is separated from politics as good politics may oftentimes be bad economics.

Realities—Need for a Rational Tariff Structure

It is quite clear that we have to contend with energy shortage for the next 10 to 15 years. We have to concentrate on reducing the energy shortage and meet the needs of power for productive use by proper demand management. We have to look carefully at the intensity of use of energy, value addition, employment creation and evolve tariff policies that foster energy conservation and use efficiency. If necessary other policies may also have to be modified in tune with this requirement.

At times, people talk glibly that separation of generation, transmission and distribution will work wonders. To my mind whether, generation, transmission and distribution is vertically integrated or horizontally decentralised, is not the real issue. The real problem is one of improving efficiency, modernisation, energy conservation, energy pricing, customer orientation. The fixation of proper tariff, billing and collection is a crucial issue. The single reform needed at this juncture is tariff rationalisation. We have to consider the cost at the customer's point for fixing the tariff and eliminate cross-subsidisation to the maximum extent as soon as possible. If subsidies are to be provided, Government must compensate the SEBs like any other bulk consumers.

Energy Policy for the Power Sector

The policy framework for power would certainly have to ensure a steep and rapid increase in generation capacity. At the same time, there has to be an annual accretion and fine tuning of that annual accretion with more productive investment in less energy intensive uses where the value addition is most advantageous. We also have to look at tariff rationalisation and cost based pricing for all categories of consumers. The restructuring of the SEBs is also important and must take into account situational factors and ground realities. OSEB has recently undergone restructuring. It is already running into some unanticipated problems. The problem is with regard to distribution. There is not much visible impact of privatisation of distribution. No one is willing to come forward, to undertake distribution in rural areas and prefer urban areas with HT consumers and high load density. Unless universal metering is done, and the concept that one has to pay for the electricity used is brought home to the farmer, we have a long and tortuous way ahead of us. In fact, the whole exercise of restructuring is predicated on constitution of regulatory authorities, to hold the scales even between Electricity Boards, private utilities and the consumers. The regulatory authorities are yet to be constituted and come to grips with problems. We have probably started the privatisation exercise from the wrong end. Instead of commencing privatisation with the distribution network, we have given priority to generation which bustles with quite a few problems. May be a combination of both activities within a definite time frame would have been a better proposition.

Short, Medium and Long-Term Power Policy

The energy policy must have a short term, a medium term and a long term component. There has to be balanced investment in hydel, thermal and renewable energy resources as well as transmission. A lot of detailed investigations has to be done to plan for the future. Increased budgetary support to the public sector undertakings has to be earmarked till private sector enters the field in a visible manner and shows results. Whether in the Central PSEs or State Electricity Boards, a more aggressive policy of joint ventures should be followed so that funds could be mobilised and additional investment made for mutual benefit. The energy use efficiency and energy conservation principles are important.

In a short term policy of one to three years, renovation and modernisation, tariff revision with improved collection, T&D loss reduction, energy intensive use, captive generation and co-generation as well as fuel policy are important.

In the medium term, liquid fuel and gas based generation deserves attention. The restructuring of the SEBs in line with local requirements must be pushed through. Unless that is done, the energy situation will become more difficult. Regulatory bodies must be placed in position along with streamlining of the distribution network and rationalisation of the tariff. System Improvement and standardisation bring the advantages of better equipment efficiencies. We are at present operating our motors, drives and pumps at low levels of efficiency with avoidable loss of 30 per cent. We have to really look at the quality of the appliances also which is extremely important.

In the long term, we will have to build hydel projects, nuclear and thermal projects, we have to plan for bulk transmission of power and also go in for decentralised grid supply wherever possible. Even for rural electrification power at high voltages must be stepped down where needed and utilised. The quality of the transformers should be improved to ensure that energy dissipation and particularly no load losses are reduced.

Watershed Management—Conserving the Life Blood of Rural India

In rural areas conservation of water is as important as conservation of power particularly where the level of groundwater exploitation is nearing saturation point. South India has by and large utilised or has plans to fully utilise the irrigation and hydel potential of its rivers. In fact, claims for more water and impending water shortages have accentuated the river water disputes. The same is also true in case of ground water potential. Andhra Pradesh, Karnataka, Tamil Nadu and Maharashtra, have all utilised nearly 100 per cent of the groundwater potential. In fact, they are over-exploiting the groundwater potential. In future, water shortages will become more acute. This highlights the need not only for energy conservation, but also for water conservation. We must link energy use and water use in a combined tariff policy which will help conserve both these scarce resources. We must regulate water use to bring about better efficiencies in agricultural production. Japan uses much less water and produces much more yields of crops than India. When a shortage of both water and energy is looming, we surely ought to take a hard look at the optimal power needed to draw water and water requirement per acre of land? We should emulate Israel in water and energy use efficiency. To meet considerations of equity; we could price the bare requirements consistent with efficiency of usage at reasonable prices. Any excess use of water or power beyond the prescribed norms should attract a penal rate of charge. If conservation and efficiency norms are enforced judiciously, our people can also respond and meet the challenge.

Perspective of the Ninth Plan and Beyond—Capacity Addition

Additional capacities have to be brought on stream in double quick time to meet the growing power demand. The Government have estimated an additional capacity requirement of 52,463 MW for the Ninth Plan and 44,640 MW for the Tenth Plan. We have to install about one lakh MW of additional capacity in the next 10 years or 10,000 MW every year. To provide for all contingencies, line losses and actual availability at user end, we may have to plan for 15 to 20 per cent above the target. We have to assess and arrange for investment required. Assuming that inflation will be under control over the next 10 years, equipment costs would not rise unduly, duties would be low and favourable conditions will exist or can be created, the most conservative estimate of investment needed will be Rs. 50,000 crores per annum for generation and another Rs. 50,000 crores for transmission and distribution. This is undoubtedly a large investment which calls for a high order of resource mobilisation within the country and abroad. We have to make it more worthwhile for investors to invest in energy. Creating a conducive and enabling environment will, therefore, be the most important task. An economy will grow when there is an inflow of technology, of investment and access to the market and reasonable returns on investment. We must secure all these contributing factors to achieve our objective.

Since an annual capacity of 10,000 MWs has to be set up, the share of the public sector and the private sector becomes relevant. The public utilities i.e., the SEBs have a historical cost of assets and are able to supply power at much lower cost than new plants. The capital cost of new plants would be much higher. Their operating costs would also be high. Very recently, the World Bank Consultants made a study of UPSEB and found that even at today's current level of operations, unless the average price of power is Rs. 3.40 paise per unit, UPSEB is unlikely to break even. We have to devise a combination of improved functioning of existing units and more efficient new units at least cost to be able to supply power at reasonable prices. The fixation and collection of economic tariff is the crux of the problem that has to be solved.

CREDIT Rating—The Need of the Hour for the Power Sector

The six letters of the word CREDIT has a lot of relevance for the power sector. If we are 'able' to gain credit, we will achieve creditable results. The letters should stand for :

C-	Customer focus Capacity addition Conservation of energy Collection of dues Co-ordination Cooperation
R-	Reality of the situation Resource management Right action Re-structuring Regulation
E-	Efficiency Economy Equity Ecology Energy use

D-	Demand management Development Direction Decision
I-	Initiative Innovation Image Investment Improvisation
T-	Tariff Timing Transmission Transportation Transparency Truthfulness Trust

If we remember these attributes, I am sure that there will be an attitudinal re-orientation leading to a sea-change in the power sector. The public do deserve a better deal and we do owe a duty to them and to society to make India 'energetic' and 'powerful'. We should empower ourselves to provide energy to millions and electricity to all.

2

SOME THEORETICAL CONSIDERATIONS IN REFORM OF RURAL INSTITUTIONS IN INDIA

SUKHADEO K. THORAT

Introduction

The inefficient and inequitous functioning of institutions governing economic life in rural India has been increasingly recognised as the key constraints to broad based economic growth. This point has been particularly brought in to the focus after the involvement of bureaucracy and other organizations in rural development. The late recognition about the significance of economic institutions, (as crucial as that of technological, economic and other factors) was due to the fact that the institutional framework has been taken for granted in mainstream economics and often many of the central positions are stated with a false assumption of institutional neutrality. It is only after the early 1960's that mainstream neo-classical economists have relaxed the assumption of institutional neutrality and recognised the role of economic institutions in economic growth. Since the early 1960's number of economists have addressed to this issue, and this development led to the emergence of a whole school of neo-classical writers, who developed a well articulated endogenous theory of institutions and traced the changes in economic history to changes in institutions. In the recent literature this body of writings has been identified as what is known as "Neo-classical Institutional Economics (NIE)".

It must be mentioned that Marxists have a well-known endogenous theory of institutions. The criticism, by Marxists and other institutional economists in this respect have been valuable in raising the general awareness of institutions presumption in economics.

The NIE which has emerged in early 1960's highlights the shortcomings of (traditional) neo-classical paradigm and provide original insights into the evolution of economic institutions, economic functions which the institution performs, explain the new forms that institutions take and their relation with economic development. These are some of the vital questions which forms the themes of NIE.

In this chapter, I intend to make a modest attempt to highlight the recent theoretical developments in the institutional economics with a purpose to identify the possible framework or starting points for reforms of rural institutions in India. The reason why such effort is necessary that, in the discussion on the institutional reform in India, the policy framework is often articulated in a fairly loose manner without recognising the relevant underlying theoretical considerations.

What are Economic Institutions ?

Institutions are usually defined as the rules of society or organizations that facilitate coordination among people by helping them form expectations which each person can reasonably hold in dealing with others. (Ruttan, 1989). They reflect the conventions that have evolved in different societies regarding the behaviour of individuals and groups relative to their own and that of others. In the area of economic relations, institutions have a crucial role in establishing expectations about the *rights* to use resources in economic activities and about the *partitioning of income streams,* resulting from such activities—institutions provide *assurance* respecting the action of others and give order and stability to expectations in the complex and uncertain world of economic relations. Like formal organizations (such as labour unions and employers organizations, bureaucracy), markets too, be they stock exchange, land, labour, credit, or product markets, are institutions because they embody rules and regulations, formal or informal which governs the exchange and economic relations. "Contracts", explicit or implicit, are also institutions in so far as they lay down *rules* which govern specified activities involving people who are parties to such contracts. Similarly cultural rules and codes of conduct, norms, values and institutions in so far as they too can constrain the relationship between different individuals or groups.

In the main stream neo-classical economics, the institutional framework is taken for granted and many of the Central propositions are sometimes framed with an unrealistic assumption of institutional neutrality. The simple laws of market supply and demand are often applied without being fully conscious of the complex institutions on which "contracts" in actual markets crucially depend. In the real world, market exchanges consume resources and property rights are costly to enforce. Thus, the institutions are not costless, but consume resources.

Economic Role of Institutions

In the last two decades, however, three different approaches or theories of institutions have emerged—which mainly include, Transaction and Information Cost Theory, the Collective Action School, and of course the Marxian Approach.

The Marxian School has a well known indigenous theory of institutions. In the Marxian system, the economic structure of society (which in this theory provides the foundation of its legal and political institutions) consists of property relations, and it corresponds to the level of development of productive forces (which includes all means of production and technology). The central driving force behind institutions is thus the forces of production. Changes in the forces of production particularly technological change produce over time some tension between the existing structure of property rights and productive potential of economy, and it is through class struggle that this tension is resolved in history with emergence of new institutions relating to property rights, land ownership, tenancy and labour relations. The main criticism of Marxist analysis however is that it cites some of these production relations as institutional obstacles to development in poor agrarian economy, overlooking the microeconomic rationale of the very formation of these institutions. There is also a tendency to equate some of the pre-existing relations mechanically with "feudal" or "semi-feudal" mode of production, ignoring how in the real world the same institutions (say, share cropping) adopt themselves to the development of the forces of production (with numerous cases of capitalist share—tenant farmers—as for example in Punjab or more widespread cases of cost-sharing and other forms of landlord-tenant partnership in adoption of new technology of HYV in agriculture).

Within the neo-classical framework, have emerged *two* broad approaches to overcome the limitations of mainstream economics. It includes transaction and information costs theory on the one hand and the school of collective action on the other.

The first strand originates from a famous paper by Coarse (1960) which led to development of a whole school of neo-classical writers on property rights and transaction costs. These writers developed a well articulated indigenous theory of institutions and trace changes in economic history to changes in the institutional ground rules. To begin with, the neo-classical assumption of institutional neutrality is dropped and it is asserted that real world market transactions or exchanges consume resources, enforcement of property rigths and contract also cost. In the transaction cost theory, the general hypothesis is that, institutions are transaction cost-minimising arrangements which may change and evolve, with changes in the nature and sources of transaction costs and means for minimising. Thus, the transaction cost and the institutions that evolve to minimise these costs are the key to the efficient performance of the economies. These costs include those of information, negotiation, monitoring, coordination and enforcement of contracts. It is in the nature of transaction costs that they arise not from the production of good but from their transfer from one to another. The key proportion in the poverty rights approach associated with the Coarse (1960) is that when the transaction costs are absent, the initial assignment of property rights does not matter from the efficiency point of view because rights can be voluntarily adjusted and exchanged to promote increased production. But when transaction costs are positive and substantial the allocation of property rights is critical.

The existence of property rights and rules governing contracts helps reduce conflict and facilitates co-operation. Both results in the reduction of transaction costs and thus allows the productivity gains of large-scale and improved technology to be realized.

The other strand grew out of the theory of "Imperfect Information" particularly of Akerlof and Stiglitz. This theory of institutions is closely related to that of transaction cost theory since information cost constitutes an important part of the former. It provides a more rigorous and sharply defined frame-work for analyzing institutions as a substitute for *missing market* in an environment of pervasive risks, incomplete markets, information assymetry and moral hazard. Since this environment in some respects is particularly acute in developing countries, the recent literature in development economics has seen a number of attempts to model related to share-cropping and other forms of tying, credit rationing, interlinkage between credit and land lease, labour hiring and output sale transactions and others. The "information approach" has been found quite useful in the analysis of agrarian institutions. In general, transaction and information cost approach has proved to be particularly useful for the analysis of contractual choice.

The third general approach which is distinct from transaction and information cost approach concerns collective action and the elimination of free rider problem. The theory of collective action not only provides explanations for the behaviour of individuals which can result in non-cooperation but also deal with the identification of conditions under which cooperation can be achieved. This theory has been concerned with public or collective goods not only of physical character such as pollution, highway, parks and the like but also with issues such as higher wage rates, higher price, tariff or quota, regulations, a lower tax rate or a farm policy. The main theme under this approach concerns emergence of group interests and organizations and the relationship between these interest groups and the State. It is mainly explained through the theory of rent seeking, which primarily concerned with the means that interest groups use for getting what they want.

While the two main approaches, namely, the analysis of transaction and information costs and contractual choice on the one hand and analysis of collective action and pressure groups on the other have developed separately, nevertheless many issues in these approaches are complementary. There are important similarities in the framework and axiom upon which they are based. For example, as in the analysis of transaction costs, collective action is analyzed from the point of view of self-interest and bounded rationality including opportunism. Secondly, both transaction costs and collective action are affected by the same factors. Castes, ethnicity and family loyalty may affect the contractual relations among members of economic organisation by reducing transaction costs, but also may either facilitate collective action by their members by helping to solve the free-rider problems which plunge such action by increasing the transaction costs of change. Thirdly, since the role of Government is emphasized in both transaction costs and collective action theories. They have to be inter-related and complementary. On the one hand, Government's decisions affect the transaction and information costs of different economic agents and thereby their choice of organizational forms the type of contract (for example, tenancy laws, wage legislations and ceiling laws), on the other hand, different agents or groups have incentive to organize themselves, in such a way as to influence the Government decisions in the protection of their interests. Since in this sense, collective action can be said to begin where contractual choices based on the principles of transaction costs leave off, the two perspectives are obviously complementary. Both have a lot to do with explaining institutions and changes in the process of institutional change.

Process of Institutional Change

In order to perform essential role, the institutions must be stable for an extended time period, but institutions like technology must also change if development is to occur. A clear understanding of the mechanism through which the existing institutions undergo change and how new institutions emerge has continued to elude economists.

Researchers in this area have tended to take one or the opposite view, namely, that institutional change depends on technical change or technical change depends on institutional change, the latter being governed by other independent variables. Technological determinism formed the essential base of Marxist writings. Although Marx stressed a dialectical relationship between changes in the mode of production (technical change) and in production relations (institutional change) he believed that the mode of production provides more dynamic source of change in social organisation.

Technological determinism has been a dominant theme with the work of American Institutional School as well. The institutional innovation or change has been viewed as a lagged response to the rising economic value of man and growth of productivity. In the field of development economics, primary emphasis is placed on the new income streams released by technical change as an important source of institutional change.

The other view point maintains that institutions rather than technical change is the dynamic source of economic development. North attributed the major western economic growth to the changes brought about by the process of population against increasing resource scarcity in the institutions which govern property rights. The neo-classical economic historians believed that the relative factor price changes fuel the main motivate force for institutional change in history (primarily by inducing the development of property rights to the benefit of owners of more expensive factors of production). In particular, demographic change altering the relative prices of labour to land lead to the incentive for redefining property rights on land and rearrangement of labour relations. North, Hayami and Ruttan give several examples from European and Asian History suggesting that rise in the prices of land relative to labour led to more control over land, elimination of commons and a change to a system based on either owner operatorship of land by proprietor or by use of wage labour by capitalist land owner. In other, situations, when wages have increased relative to the value of land, the institutional changes occurred that gave the peasant or free holder greater control over the use of his own labour. In the situation of raising. economic value of men, there has been a move from a state of slavery (or its variants in bonded or attached labour) which denied man the opportunity or incentive to invest in himself to a situation where both private an public investment in the human agent in terms of both the promotion of health and education have become institutionalized. Similarly, some argued that the new income streams released by technical change do represent an important source of institutional change. It would set in motion attempts by individuals to reallocate their personal resources and to organise and initiate collective action for the purpose of redefining property rights and production relations so as to achieve greater equity in the sharing of new income streams.

Institutions and Equity

In his critics, Pranab Bardhan (1989 and 1996) argued that the neo-classical institutional economists focus their attention on allocative efficiency of institutions but ignored the distributive aspects of the institutional change. The Marxists however, emphasised how institutional change depends on consideration of surplus appropriation by dominant class. The emphasis on the effect of an institutional change on control of surplus by a particular class also suggests that the question of efficiency improving institutional change cannot really be separated from that of redistributive institutional change, particularly when issues of collective action, class capacity, mobilisation and struggle are important. A shift in the focus of attention from efficiency aspects of an institution to the distributive aspects confronts with the question of "concept of power".

In this context in recent Marxist theoretical models in economics, Bardhan (1989) identifies two distinct forms of power relations.

Roemer (1982) traces the primary focus of capitalist power in unequal distribution of property where as Bowler (1985) traces it to political structure of control and surveillance at the point of production. Both these stands of Marxist theory serve a reminder that Transaction Cost (TC) and Imperfect Information Theories (IIT)—demonstrating constraints for efficient working in terms of T.C. and moral hazard, it underemphasized that a more democratic organization of the work process and more egalitarian distribution of assets might reduce significantly informational constraints.

Bardhan (1989) also highlights role of ideology and the States which the NIE ignored. Marxists assign theory of ideology and state a central place in theory of History and institutional change. Although we do not have good theory of the formation, maintenance and institutionalization of ideology, yet we have norms, customs and enforced code of conduct shaped by different ideologies which in one case bring some order and in other situation bring conflict—in the latter it is the minority which suffers in the process of institutional change.

As regards the role of the States—it is either conceived as body looking on behalf of "dominant class or a passive respondent to rent seeking behaviour of various interest groups and lobbies. Barden drew important distinction between top political leadership (which takes general decisions) and hierarchy of agents, the bureaucracy and argued that latter may form a pressure group and mechanism to seek favours. It follows the goals that are much narrower than set by the State.

Ninth Five Year Plan Approach towards Institutional Reform

Even when the State in the last five decades has spent vast sums of money in rural development, there has been a significant failure on this fronts. The failures (or partial success) of the States and local institutions has been in the area of land reforms, and of providing public goods like irrigation, education, health, infrastructural facilities like roads, power, credit and extension service and administration of various programme for the poor such as IRDP & EGS. The programmes are usually administered by distant, uncoordinated bureaucracy which is insensitive to the need of the people and often little reaches the intended beneficiaries of the programmes.

The "*Approach Paper on the Ninth Five Year Plan* " recognized this problem in the following manner.

> "For realisation of intended plan objectives, the quality of design and the manner of implementation of programmes/projects are as important as the availability of resources. Our past experience has been that many programmes fail to deliver the results because of failures in implementation. Time and cost overruns

in infrastructure and investment projects have been widespread and substantial. Many development programmes have also not had the desired impact on the well-being of the poor because of inadequate administrative planning and implementation. An area of priority of the Ninth Plan is to improve project implementation and delivery mechanisms and to ensure that intended benefits actually reach the people. No new programmes or projects should be launched without paying sufficient attention to these aspects". (Approach paper, 1997, p. 115).

It further observes—

"In view of the lessons from experience, it has become necessary to introduce the necessary correctives to reverse many of the unsustainable trends in programme/project formulation and implementation. This will be a central priority of the Ninth Plan".

On accountability, it observed—

" Lack of accountability of the implementing agencies either to the Government or to the people has been the single major cause for misappropriation of funds in development programmes. It is well known that implementing agencies and programmes managers can get away easily with time and overruns or non-fulfilment of targets by attributing these to factors beyond their control. In many cases they are indeed justified as most programmes leave too many loose ends at the planning stage. Nevertheless, several cases of mis-appropriation of funds meant for anti-poverty programmes have also come to light....". This happened primarily because of lack of people's participation; in the implementation of programmes, the lack of transparency in the operation of schemes and inadequacy of the monitoring mechanism. Suitable institutional reforms, for involvement of the people and grass-root level non-Government agencies in formulation and implementation are needed to overcome these problems" (Page 120).

The Approach Paper suggests the following policy measures in general and in particular for social sector programmes, (Page 122).

- A genuine push towards *decentralisation and people's participation will be given*. Through institutional reforms a conducive environment for the people's participation will be created for strengthening the Panchayati Raj and the different models of people's institutions.
- Reorientation and integration of all village level schemes under the Panchayati Raj to avoid thin spread and wastage of resources.
- The existing schemes whose delivery costs are disproportionately high or which fail to make the desired impact should be considered for reorientation and discontinuation.
- Monitoring and Evaluation of programmes (M&E) will have to be made more effective and purposeful. The Centre, States and the grassroots level organisations/institutions would all have to be involved to ensure the effectiveness of M & E.
- Institutional changes to bring in transparency in implementation and operation of programmes. For this purpose, avoidable barriers to full flow of information must be removed.
- Build in sustainability of outputs and benefits and maintenance of public facilities as a necessary component of project/programme formulation.

The Ninth Five Year Plan thus puts emphasis on the cost-minimisation, accountability and transparency in the policy measures relating to the working project and implementation.

It also emphasises on the people's participation, particularly through decentralized working of Panchayat Raj institutions, by bringing an element of openness and democratic working. However, the document does not spell out changes in the working rules of various institutions which are supposed to bring reduction in transaction cost, promote accountability, bring transparency and more democratic working.

Further, in order to assure people's participation through Panchayat Raj institutions it does not suggest measures to overcome severe problems for realising successful collective action in highly socially and economically segmented Indian society. There is also a complete lack of awareness of measures to make information more accessible to the people which is awefully lacking in several areas.

The theoretical insights acquired through a review of major theoretical writings in earlier section indicates that institutions could play effective role in economic growth if they are cost effective, equitable in terms of access and are fairly just in the distribution of income gains from economic activities. The equitable access to informations (about the economic opportunities offered by the market and government's, interventions) transparency and accountability in the working makes the institution efficient and equitable in seeking access.

In this context a significant reform of various rural institutions in India is necessary.

(a) The working rule of rural bureaucracy and various other organisation and bodies needs to be changed in such a manner that its working become more cost-effective (reduce transaction cost). These should cover all institutions, related to factor and product markets, and others involved in implementation of several development programmes.

(b) A major reform is necessary in the area of information to the rural people. These include information about all markets, particularly employment, credit, technologies, education and several other areas. More transparent system will help in making information open to people. Therefore, there is need to bring reforms on this front. Giving more programmes to Panchayats as well as provision of informations to them will promote access of information to people at local level.

(c) The theories regarding collective actions and Marxian perspective bring out clearly that in socially and economically segmented and unequal society, and at time socially conflicting interest groups behaviour, the rural organizations and bodies are generally controlled and used by powerful groups. The reforms or regulating provisions which will provide effective participation and also ensure due share to the poor and deprived social groups is, therefore, absolutely necessary.

3

NEW ECONOMIC POLICY AND ITS IMPACT ON EMPLOYMENT AND POVERTY OF THE SCHEDULED CASTES: Some Observations

SUKHADEO K. THORAT

Introduction

This Chapter intends to assess the impact of the far reaching economic reforms initiated by the government in response to a major economic crisis in early 1991 on economic situations of Scheduled Castes in India. This is done by looking at the trends in few important aspects namely (a) employment/unemployment, (b) poverty, (c) employment under the reservation, and (d) by examining some of the theoretical issues underlying the new economic policy in as much as they relate to the specific social and economic situation of Scheduled Castes in India.

The new economic measures were initiated in July 1991. An attempt to measure the impact of on going economic reforms is faced with difficulty as only five years (July 1991 to July 1996) have passed since reform has been initiated. The assessment has become more difficult in the case of Scheduled Castes as the relevant data on the employment, poverty and other indicators are not available for the years under reforms. The employment and consumption statistics (on the basis of which poverty ratios are estimated) and information on the incidence of wage labour and other aspects for Scheduled Castes are available up to 1987-88. Therefore, impact of new economic measures on the economic situation of Scheduled Castes can at best be understood indirectly, by looking at trends in some variables and directly in the case of only few variables.

Why New Economic Policy (NEP)

The NEP comprising Stabilization and of Structural Adjustment programmes was initiated at least initially as a response to overcome the crisis in two areas: (a) external debt crisis, and (b) Fiscal deficits (Public debt crisis).

The external debt crisis which surfaced in early 1991 brought India closer to default in meeting its international payment obligations. The balance of payment crisis (which roughly means that receipts from foreigners were less than payment to foreigners) was the result of policy of liberalisation of trade regime beginning with the mid-1970's and 1980's which encouraged imports disproportionately in relation to export earning, the gap being met from financed by borrowing abroad, ultimately leading to a debt trap. The current account deficit double from an annual average of $ 2.3 billions (1.3% of GDP) in the first half of the 1980's to an annual average of $ 5.5 billions (2.2% of GDP) in the second half of 1980's.

This was sustained by continuous increase in external debt which increased by more than two and half times in a decade from $ 23.8 billions at the end of 1980-81 to $ 62.3 billions at the end of year 1990-91. The debt service burden also rose from 15 per cent of export earnings in 1980-81 to 30 per cent of export earnings in 1990-91. What is more important is that the external resources were used mainly for consumption and much less for investment purpose. Due to the end of any further external support, by early 1991 the foreign reserves dropped to a level that would not have paid for imports even for fortnight.

The fiscal deficit or crisis (the gap between government spending and receipts) was also in making for a while and it was also accumulated through the 1980's. The fiscal deficit was met by borrowing at home mounted steadily leading to accumulation of internal debt. The fiscal deficit grew as the internal debt of government rose from Rs. 485 billions (35 per cent of GDP) at the end of 1980-81 to Rs. 2830 billions (54 per cent of GDP) at the end of 1990-91 and interest payment on debt almost double from 10 per cent to 19 per cent. Like the external borrowing the public borrowing was also mainly used for consumption purpose and less for investment purpose and latter did not earn a rate of return which was not high enough to finance interest payment on entire borrowing.

The external and internal debt reaching the unsustainable level. By mid-1990s the room for manoeuvre to live either on borrowed money or on borrowed time had been completely used . (Bhaduri and Nayyer, 1996)

Crisis Management Response

In tune with theoretical framework of IMF and World Bank the government introduced programmes of (a) Stabilisation, and (b) Structural adjustment.

The Stabilization Programme (SP) has a main objective of balance of payment at least in short-run by reducing deficit on current account and to curb inflation but the issues relating to employment and poverty receive passing attention. The main instrument for "Stabilization" are fiscal policy and monetary policy, both are applied in a manner so as to reduce the level of aggregate demand. In addition, the devaluation of domestic currency is used to improve balance of payment (by making the country's goods cheaper relative to foreign goods). This package of policies was used under which there was a sharp reduction in fiscal deficit of government, a tight money policy and substantial devaluation of the rupee in two investments in July 1991.

The Stabilization Programme (SP) was accompanied by Structural Adjustment Programme (SAP). The essence of Stabilization is to compress demand and hope that reduce demand will mostly reduce the prices rather than output and employment .The SAP on the other hand is recommended for promoting supply (assuming that demand squeeze will not have adverse effect on supply response).

The main elements of SAP are to shift resources :

(i) from non-traded goods to traded goods sector and within latter form import substituting activities to export activities;
(ii) away from Government Sector to private Sector; and
(iii) apart from such reallocation of resources, the SAP seeks to improve resource utilisation by:
    (a) increasing the degree of openness of economy.
    (b) and changing the structure of incentives and institutions in favour of private initiative and against the State.

The general economic philosophy is to rely more on market forces, dismantle controls, as far as possible by relying more on prices and reduce the public sector in the hope that the vacuum will be filled by the private sector. The underlying assumption is that industrialization based on State intervention leads to inefficient allocation and utilisation of economic resources. In tune with this theoretical presumption the Government of India had initiated several structural policy changes in beginning with July 1991 which include: (i) the industrial sector; (ii) the trade regime; (iii) foreign investment; (iv) foreign technology; (v) the public sector; and (vi) financial sector.

Theoretical Foundation of NEP and Its Limitations

The theoretical foundation of the "SP and SAP" is based on the economic proposition relating to what economist called "price adjustment or mechanism". The argument runs like this. "A reduction in the Government deficit would correspondingly reduce the trade deficit by making the Indian goods more price competitive in world market. That is reduction in the government expenditure along with tight money policy will reduce the aggregate demand and thus the domestic prices relative to foreign price. And this is supposed to promote exports (or reduce imports) and thereby reduce trade deficit. Thus, reduction in fiscal deficit is supposed to reduce the trade deficit through lowering of prices of exportable goods.

But there is an alternative proportion based on "quantities or output and incomes rather than prices." The alternative proposition is that as the general expenditure is reduced through decline in government expenditures and tight money policy, the purchasing power in the economy falls (leading to reduction in the aggregate demand) to begin with directly in the government sector and then indirectly in private sector for producer and worker who supply to meet the demand from the government. It is argued that the decline in the purchasing power could be something like three times the original reduction in the government deficit. This fall in purchasing power and shrinking of market at home for selling goods typically brings a loss of income and employment all around and increase in poverty. It is thus falling income and purchasing power which reduces imports until the trade deficit is reduced again to match the reduced government deficit.

This is the "Income Adjustment proposition" and plausibility of it has been established in many countries. Evidence is now irrefutable that substantial reduction in the government deficit reduce the trade deficit very significantly through a reduction in the level of economic activities i.e. employment and output rather than simply reducing the rate of inflation in the country attempting stabilization. It may reduce the trade deficit only at a great social cost by reducing output and employment drastically (Bhaduri and Nayyer, 1996). It is this line of evidence we seek to present in the following analysis in the Indian context.

NEP and its Impact on Employment

The wage labourers (both in agriculture and non-agriculture) constitute the large segment of poor in the country. Their income and consumption level is thus determined by the level of employment and the wage rate, any change in these variables also bring a change in their income level. The contraction in public expenditure, consequent upon the reduction in aggregate demand will bring the reduction in employment level and increase in unemployment rates. The statistics on unemployment rates during pre- and post-reform period support this observation

(a) The usual status data shows that there has been an increasing trend in unemployment rate between 1977-78 and 1990-91 for male and female both in rural and urban areas, (the only exception being the drought year of 1987-88). (Table 3.1). For

TABLE 3.1: Unemployment Rates

Year	Rural				Urban			
	Male		Female		Male		Female	
	Usual Status	Weekly Status	Usual Status	Weekly Status	Usual Status	Weekly Status	Usual Status	Weekly Status
1977-88	2.2	3.6	5.5	4.1	6.5	7.1	17.8	10.9
1983	2.1	3.7	1.4	4.3	5.9	6.7	6.9	7.5
1987-88	2.8	4.2	3.5	4.4	6.1	6.6	8.5	9.2
1989-90	1.6	2.6	0.8	2.1	4.4	4.5	3.9	4
1990-91	1.3	2.2	0.4	2.1	4.5	5.1	5.4	5.3
1992	1.6	2.2	1.2	1.2	4.6	4.6	6.7	6.2
1993-94	2	3.1	1.3	2.9	5.4	5.2	8.3	7.9

Source : (a) S.P. Gupta, EPW June 3, 1995.
Consumer Expenditure & Employment Survey, NSS 1992.
(b) NSSO, 5th Quinquennial Survey, 50th Round (July 1993-June 1994).

instance the unemployment rate for male based on usual and weekly status increased from 1.3 per cent and 2.2 per cent in 1990-1991 to 2.0 per cent and 3.1 per cent in 1993-94. Similarly for female the rates increased from 0.4 per cent and 2.1 per cent in 1990-91 to 1.30 per cent and 2.9 per cent respectively in 1993-94. There was also all round increase in unemployment of male and female in urban areas. This increase in unemployment rate in post-reform period (i.e. between 1990-91—1993-94) should be understood against the trend of decline between 1972-73 and 1990-91).

(b) The decline in employment rate occurred mainly in secondary and tertiary employment in the rural sector. The percentage of male worker in secondary and tertiary sector, has declined between 1990-91 and 1993-94. This has reversed the steady increasing trend observed right from 1977-78 to 1990-91 both in secondary and tertiary sector. In the case of female workers the ratio declined between 1990-91 and 1991-92 in secondary sector but showed some recovery in 1993-94 . Yet it was much below the level achieved in 1987-88 and (10.00 per cent) and 1989-90 (12.4 per cent). In the case of tertiary sector the decline in post reform period was quite clear. i.e. a decline from 7.00 per cent in 1990-91 to 5.6 per cent in 1993-94. (Table 3.2).

(c) Thus the impact of new economic measures was mainly on rural-non-farm sector and urban sectors. Obviously there was a reverse movement of worker from rural-non-farm sector to agriculture. This is very well reflected in the increase in the percentage of male worker in agriculture from 71.10 per cent in 1990-91 to 74.1 per cent in 1993-94 and 84.9 per cent to 86.2 per cent for female. This declining trend in secondary and tertiary sector however, come under check between 1992 and 1993-94 due to reversal of cut in public expenditure in rural areas.

(d) The rate of growth of employment in organised sector of the economy (public and private taken together) dropped from more than 1.7 per cent per annum in late 1980's to 1.2 per cent in 1991-92 and 0.6 per cent in 1992-93.

(e) Within the organized industrial sector in the post-reform period the employment in private sector either remained stagnant or increased marginally but the same has declined in public sector enterprise from 2.2 per cent per annum in pre-reform period,

TABLE 3.2: Percentage Distribution of Usually Working by Broad Group of Industry : Rural

Year	Male				Female			
	Primary All	Secondary All	Tertiary All	Casual Labour Principal Status	Primary All	Secondary All	Tertiary All	Casual Labour Principal Status
1977-78	80.6	8.8	10.5	27	88.1	6.7	5.1	40
1983	77.5	10	12.2	29.9	87.5	7.4	4.8	42.2
1987-88	74.5	12.1	13.4	32.1	84.7	10	5.3	40.2
1989-90	71.7	12.1	16.2	30.9	81.4	12.4	6.1	39.9
1990-91	71	12.1	16.9	31.7	84.9	8.1	7	41
1992	75.7	10.4	13.9	31.4	86.2	7.8	6	41.6
1993-94	74.1	11.2	14.7	—	86.2	8.3	5.6	—

Source : (a) S.P. Gupta, *EPW*, June 3, 1995.
Consumer Expenditure & Employment Survey, NSS 1992.
(b) NSSO, 5th Quinquennial Survey, 50th Round (July 1993-June 1994).

(i.e., 1981-1990) to 1.2 per cent in post-reform period (i.e.1990-1992).

This discussion clearly indicates that it is the rural non-agricultural and urban informal employment which has suffered the most. It is well known that growing public expenditure was in the past mainly responsible for rapid employment growth in rural non-agricultural sector in the 1980's. The reduction in public expenditure and the consequent reduction in aggregate demand could not but adversely affect employment in rural non-farm sector and urban-informal sector. It may be noted that the rural non-farm employment in India has been growing at much faster rate between 1977-78 and 1987-88 than the agricultural employment. The percentage share of rural non-farm employment in total employment increased from around 14 to 17 per cent and in rural employment from 17 to 22 per cent between 1977-78 and 1987-88. And this has been a major factor for reducing poverty between 1977-78 and 1987-88.

The recent statistics on employment by NSS for the year 1993-94 confirmed the above observations (Table 3.3).

(a) The annual (compound) growth rate of employment for usual (principal + subsidiary) in non-agriculture reduced from 3.83 per cent per annum during 1977-78/87-88 to 1.52 per cent per annum for male and from 5.17 per cent per annum to 0.17 per cent per annum for female in rural areas.
(b) This has occurred due to decline in several non-farm activities for male which include mining and quarrying, manufacturing, utilities trade, transport, finance and construction. The most severe downfall was in construction where the growth rate was in negative (–1 per cent per annum).
(c) In the case of rural-female a major decline occurred in the same sectors. But there was a sharp fall in employment in construction sector. (–15.74 per cent per annum).
(d) In agriculture sector there has been an increase in the employment of rural male worker.
(e) In urban areas the major decline has occurred for female worker in mining and quarrying, manufacturing, construction and agriculture.

TABLE 3.3: Percentage of Workers by Industrial Categories—Rural (Male) 1991

Category	Scheduled Caste				Scheduled Tribe				Others			
	1961	1971	1981	1991	1961	1971	1981	1991	1961	1971	1981	1991
Cultivator	42.9	34.94	36.7	33.11	68.46	63.63	62.52	61.28	63.74	59.27	58.44	54.74
Agri-Lab	32.83	50.24	46.82	49.27	19.57	28.48	26.72	27.89	12.12	19.19	18.3	20.14
Agriculture	75.73	85.18	83.52	82.39	88.03	92.11	89.24	89.9	75.86	79.26	76.74	74.88
Non-Agri.	24.27	14.82	16.48	17.61	11.99	7.89	10.76	10.81	24.14	20.74	23.26	25.12

TABLE 3.4: Size Distribution of Ownership Holding by Size Class

	Scheduled Caste		Scheduled Tribe		Others		All	
Size Class	1982	1992	1982	1992	1982	1992	1982	1992
Landless	12.61	13.34	17.11	11.5	10.18	9.85	11.33	11.25
Marginal	72.41	72.91	43.26	54.9	52.2	53.95	55.32	60.63
Small	8.4	7.85	17.36	17.54	16.09	13.58	14.7	13.44
Semi-Medium	4.52	3.86	14.27	11.39	12.05	10.08	10.78	9.28
Medium	1.8	1.83	7.07	4.02	7.66	11.48	6.45	4.54
Large	0.26	0.21	0.93	0.65	1.82	1.06	1.42	0.88
Total	100	100	100	100	100	100	100	100

Unemployment Situation of Scheduled Castes

The Scheduled Castes constitute a significant section of the poor in India. A look at some of the variables of economic level of living bring out this fact quite clearly.

In 1991, of the total rural workers about 82 per cent were engaged in farm activities and the remaining 18 per cent in non-farm activities. This division for Non-SC/ST was 75 per cent and 25 per cent respectively. In other word the occupational pattern of SCs was much less diversified as compared to Non SC/ST. Further within agriculture, the percentage of wage labour among SCs was nearly 50 per cent. Only 33 per cent of them were cultivators. Reverse was, however, true for non-SC/ST, as much as 55 per cent worked as cultivation and only 20 per cent works as wage labour in agriculture. In fact the Scheduled Caste agricultural labour constitute 33 per cent of the total male agricultural labours in the country, although their share in total male population was only 18.50 per cent.

Thus a small proportion of Scheduled Castes household owned or cultivate some land. Among them also as many as 73 per cent were marginal farmers with average of less than 2.50 acres of land. Another 13 per cent were landless households. So nearly 86 per cent of Scheduled Castes households in 1991 were landless and near landless households (Table 3.5).

The high incidence of landlessness and near landlessness among

TABLE 3.5: Some Features of Rural Labour Households of Scheduled Castes in India

Category & Years	Percentage of Rural Labour Household	Percentage of Rural Labour Household with Land	Percentage of Rural Labour Household without Land	Total
1. Scheduled Caste				
1964-65	—	42.3	57.7	100
1974-75	57.41	44.4	55.6	100
1977-78	63.18	42.6	57.4	100
1983	62.55	37.77	62.23	100
1987-88	63.14	75.54	24.46	100
2. Scheduled Tribe				
1964-65	—	46.2	53.8	100
1974-75	31.03	51.3	48.7	100
1977-78	43.11	52.7	47.3	100
1983	44.05	50.04	49.96	100
1987-88	49.60	83.09	16.91	100
3. Non SC/ST				
1964-65	—	44.30	55.70	100
1974-75	26.65	52.27	47.73	100
1977-78	28.88	53.17	46.83	100
1983	29.14	46.33	53.67	100
1987-88	31.16	80.92	19.08	100

Source : Rural Labour Enquiry, Report, NSSO, Delhi.

SCs population creates an enormously high proportion of wage labour among them. The information generated by successive Rural labour Enquiries throw additional light on the incidence of wage labour among Scheduled Castes in rural areas (Table 3.6). In 1987-88 (the latest Rural labour Enquiry survey), of the total SC rural household as high as 63.14 per cent, were wage labour households . This proportion was quite high compared to 31.16 per cent among others. Further nearly 63.14 per cent of wage labour household among Scheduled Castes owned some land and the remaining 24.2 per cent were without any land. Thus, a substantial section of land owning household among the Scheduled Caste also resort to wage employment due to the smallness of the land that they owned. In fact it was

TABLE 3.6: Unemployment Rate: Percentage of Unemployed (age 5 years and above) According to Usual, Current Weekly & Daily Status : Rural

Category	Year	Male				Female			
		Usual Principal Status	Usual Status	Current Weekly	Current Daily	Usual Principal Status	Usual Status	Current Weekly	Current Daily
Scheduled	1987-88	1.30	0.90	—	—	1.40	1.10	—	—
Caste	1983	1.14	0.76	3.22	7.16	0.50	0.23	2.16	4.23
	1977-78	1.23	—	2.93	6.73	2.58	—	1.90	4.09
Scheduled	1987-88	0.80	0.40	—	—	0.80	0.60	—	—
Tribe	1983	0.49	0.34	1.47	3.29	0.18	0.80	1.21	2.57
	1977-78	0.52	—	1.57	3.31	1.22	—	1.23	2.37
Others	1987-88	1.70	1.10	—	—	0.48	0.70	—	—
Non SC/ST	1983	1.49	1.03	2.15	4.03	0.43	0.29	0.91	1.72
	1977-78	1.57	—	2.15	3.90	1.53	—	0.97	0.97

Source : Employment Survey, NSS.

observed that nearly 75 per cent of wage labour household with land belongs to the marginal farmers owning land less than 1.49 acres.

This discussion indicate that nearly 63 per cent of Scheduled Castes households has to resort to wage employment to earn major part of their income. Obviously the economic well-being of them would depend on the employment opportunities both in farm and rural non-farm sector under the new economic regime.

TABLE 3.7: Employment in Rural Non-Farm Sector : Percentage of Rural Non-Farm Workers to Total Rural Workers

Category	1977-78	1983	1987-88	1990-91	1992-93	1987-88/ 1992-93
General						
Male	19.3	22.20	25.5	29.00	24.30	–4.70%
Female	11.80	12.20	15.30	15.00	13.80	–9.80%
Scheduled	—	—	24.56	—	23.40	—
Caste	—	—	17.37	—	15.66	—

Source : Employment Survey, NSS.

Note : Figures for 1992-93 are based on interpolation.

Table 3.7 presents the unemployment rates for SC and others for the year 1977-78, 1983-84 and 1987-88 (the latest year for which the data is available). We observed some important feature concerning the unemployment situation of Scheduled Caste vis-a-vis the others. In the case of unemployment rate based on usual status there is no significant difference in the unemployment rate between the SCs and others. In fact the unemployment rate of SCs is slightly lower than that of others. This has been the case in earlier years as well. This is not surprising as the NSS treat a person to be usually employed if he or she worked for more than 180 days in a year. Since Scheduled Caste workers have limited alternative other than wage employment their participation in the work around the year would be certainly higher than others. However no sooner we move on to the unemployment rate based on current weekly status and current daily status the picture changed completely. The unemployment rate for SCs turn out to be much higher than the other group. For instance in 1977-78 and 1983- 84 the unemployment rate (base on daily status) of SC male worker was 6.73 per cent and 7.16 per cent respectively. These rates were significantly higher compared with 3.90 per cent and 4.03 per cent for others respectively. Similar gap exists for female labour too. The same must be true for the year 1987-88 (NSS does not provide the data in weekly and daily status after 1983-84).

There are other features which needs to be emphasised. First the unemployment rate (based on usual status) was higher in the age group of 15-29 years (5.50%) followed by those in age group of 10-14 years (3.67 %) (Table 3.8). Secondly besides the persons in productive age group (i.e. 15-29 years and 30-59 years) the children of age less than 14 years and the aged persons above 60 years also participate in the work due to economic compulsion. The participation rate was 16.30 per cent and 42.15 per cent for persons in the age group 10-14 years and above 60 years respectively. Third feature is that little less than one-fourth (i.e 23 %) of workers were engaged in rural non-form activities (Table 3.8). And fourthly the SCs account for about 22 per cent of total unemployed in the country. This share varies between 31% to 36% for persons in the age group above 30 years. The share was obviously much higher than their share in total population (Table 3.9).

TABLE 3.8: Age-wise Distribution of Scheduled Caste Worker—1987

Status	5—9	10—14	15—29	30—44	45—59	60 above	All
Agriculture	76.7	1648.9	12104.4	10406.1	6680.2	2179.8	33091.4
Non-Agri.	15.3	327.2	3653.8	3215.6	1767.5	449.9	9429.6
Total	92.0	1976.2	15758.3	13616.9	8450.8	2636.1	42537.5
Unemployed in ('000)	0	75.5	918.9	299.5	136.16	38	1468.1
% share in total unemployed	0	27.61	18.96	30.35	35	35.88	21.91
Labour force in ('000)	92	2051.7	1667.7	13923.4	8586.9	2674.1	44005.6
% in Agriculture	83.37	83.43	76.81	79.05	82.69	1.42	3.36
% in Non-Agri.	16.63	16.53	23.62	20.09	17.31	42.15	41.44
Unemploy-ment Rate	0.00	3.67	5.50	2.15	1.58	1.42	3.36
Participation Rate	0.06	16.30	61.89	76.95	73.80	42.15	41.44
Total Unemployed worker in ('000)	0	272.8	4946.5	986.7	388.1	105.9	6699.94

Source: Employment Survey, NSSO, 1987-88.

TABLE 3.9: Represenıation of Scheduled Caste in Government Jobs

Year	No. of SCs	Percentage	% Change
1956	121754	14.98	—
1957	253308	13.87	-17.3
1958	215940	12.38	-17.3
1959	223124	12.12	3.22
1960	228497	12.42	2.35
1961	235968	12.4	3.17
1962	267001	12.62	11.76
1963	283208	12.83	5.58
1964	298369	13.17	5.08
1965	311425	13.28	4.19
1966	316073	13.38	1.47
1967	334744	13.39	5.58
1968	341010	13.18	1.84
1969	359943	13.62	5.26
1970	291874	13.09	-23.32
1971	360042	13.34	18.93
1972	370584	13.48	-2.84
1973	340938	13.99	-8.7
1974	395453	13.67	13.79
1975	408879	13.84	3.13
1976	421685	14.18	4.69
1977	441463	14.61	1.64
1978	448713	14.81	4.23
1979	467712	15.12	4.89
1980	490592	15.64	-0.08
1981	490194	15.19	6.27
1982	520994	16.67	2.9
1983	536037	16.35	-1.21
1984	529573	16.03	7.13
1985	567356	16.32	-2.85
1986	551161	15.95	-0.78
1987	555471	16.18	-2.08
1988	543905	16.3	4.54
1989	568600	16.41	3.78
1990	590108	16.97	6.54
1991	628709	17.2	3.87
1992	604347	17.12	-2.91

This factual account of unemployment situation of the Scheduled Caste up to 1987-88 does not help us to estimate the direct impact of NEP on their employment. But it certainly tells a story that since there has been a decline in the growth rate of employment in rural-non-farm sector (particularly for female worker), urban informal sector, in public sector and near stagnation in the growth rate of employment in organised private sector, it must have affected more severely the employment of sechduled caste as they mainly depend on wage paid employment. Close to a quarter of them are engaged in rural-non-farm activities. And any fall in that sector must have severely affected their employment and income particularly of the worker in the age group of 15-19 years and 45-59 years where the ratio of employment in rural non-farm sector is higher than the average for scheduled caste.

We do not have the actual statistics no non-farm employment of scheduled caste for post-reform period i.e. after 1990-91. However, we can work out in a somewhat crude way the magnitude of decline by using the rate of decline observed for general population. The percentage of general non-farm male workers decline from 25.5 per cent in 1987-88 to 24.30 per cent in 1992 and for female from 15.30 per cent to 13.80 per cent respectively. The ratio decline by 4.70 per cent in five years period for male and by 9.80 per cent for females (This has certainly reversed a strong increasing trend observed during pre-reform period). In 1987-88 about 25 per cent of SC male and 17.39 per cent of SC female were engaged in rural non-farm activities. At this rate of decline the percentage of SC male and female worker in rural non-farm must have declined to 23.40 per cent and 15.66 per cent respectively in 1992-93.

The decline in employment in rural non-farm and urban informal sector was obviously the outcome of curtailment in the government expenditure. It is well known that growing public expenditure was in part mainly responsible for rapid employment growth in the rural non-farm sector in 1980s.

This evidence in favour of decline in employment in rural non-farm sector is indirect as it is based on the trends in general population. But there is more direct evidence which clearly supports decline in the absolute as well as ratio of Scheduled Caste employees in public sector i.e. recruitment in government services and public sector undertaking. The banking sector where the process of reform has been slower than the government and public sector undertakings the decline was not yet visible.

Impact on Employment under Reservation

Due to privatisation some sectors had cut in Government expenditure and also slowing down of public sector of the employment of scheduled castes and scheduled tribes has been reduced after 1991. Table 3.10 presents the relevant data on employment of scheduled caste in the public sector. The data in fact, support this assumption at least for trends in employment of SCs in government services and public sector undertakings after 1990. It is observed that during the pre-reform period i.e. between 1956 and 1990 there has been a steady increase in the employment of SCs in Government services. The absolute number as well as the percentage of SCs/STs in government jobs and services improved until 1990.

TABLE 3.10: Representation of Scheduled Caste in Public Sector Undertaking

Year	No. of SCs	Percentage	% Change
1970	40640	7.24	—
1971	59108	9.26	45.44
1972	103416	12.7	74.96
1973	198273	16.89	91.72
1974	218142	16.39	10.02
1975	236810	17.25	8.56
1976	275362	17.47	16.28
1977	283248	16.45	2.86
1978	300405	17.29	6.06
1979	317401	17.44	5.66
1980	318204	17.08	0.25
1981	335441	17.23	5.42
1982	338347	17.25	0.87
1983	267043	18.08	8.48
1984	371625	18.1	1.25
1985	395922	18.94	6.46
1986	399382	18.86	0.95
1987	414539	19.42	3.8
1988	423879	19.5	2.25
1989	428491	19.57	1.09
1990	432890	19.54	1.03
1991	365421	16.98	15.59
1992	369834	17.74	1.21

After the July 1990 the new measures have led to decline in the employment of SCs in Government services and jobs. The absolute number of SC employees has gone down from 6.28 lakh in 1991 to 6.04 lakh in 1992. There was also decline in the percentage share of SC employees between 1991 and 1992.

Identical trends is observed in employment of SCs in public sector undertakings. Since the beginning of the reservation in this sectors there has been a considerable improvement both in absolute numbers and percentage share between 1970 and 1990. However, the representation varied across types of services. The representation of SC was much below the required quota in grade 'A' and 'B' services. There was a concentration in Grade 'C' and 'D' jobs. As result of the new measures however, the recruitment of SCs has gone down substantially (Table 3.11). The absolute number of Scheduled Caste employees in public sector undertakings has declined from 4.32 lakh in 1990 to 3.69 lakh in 1992. Their percentage share has also declined from 19.54 per cent in 1990 to 17.74 per cent in 1992. This decline has occurred more prominently in 'B', 'C' and 'D' grade jobs. Thus the burden of the fallen employment has fallen on the relatively poor among the scheduled castes.

TABLE 3.11: Estimate of Rural Headcount Ratio: Expert Group Method, India (in Percentage)

	Rural		Urban	
Year	General	SC	General	SC
1973	56.4	—	—	—
1977	53.1	64.6	47.4	54.3
1983	45.6	58.07	42.1	56.52
1986	38.3	—	—	—
1987	39.1	49.95	40.1	46.98
1989	34.4	—	38.4	—
1990	35.01	—	37.1	—
1992	44.02	—	37.6	—
1993	37.5	—	—	—

In public sector banks, the negative trend in employment of SCs have not yet set in.

The analysis indicates that the reservation policy has helped the SCs in getting access to jobs in Government services, public sector undertakings and public sector banks. At least at the aggregate level their recruitment has been in proportion to their share in population. But after 1990, i.e. after the introduction of the new economic measures which are aimed at privatisation and reduction in the role of Government, the employment of SCs has declined both in absolute numbers and in proportion. The new measures, thus have reversed the positive trends set in since 1956.

Impact on Poverty

Table 3.12 presents the poverty ratio as estimated by Expert Group Method. It shows that generally rural poverty has steadily declined during pre-reform period, from 56.4 per cent in 1973-74 to 34.4 per cent in 1989-90 but after 1990-91 poverty level increased sharply during the first 18 months of the reform period from 35 per cent in 1990-91 to 44 per cent in 1992-93. This upward trend was reversed as poverty declined marginally to 37.5 per cent in 1993-94. Thus the post-reform trends in rural poverty do not suggest any improvement, the initial impact of stabilization/ structural adjustment package was adverse particularly in rural areas.

Two different explanations are offered for increase in rural poverty during post-reform period. Tendulkar and Jain (and others) attribute sharp increase in rural poverty between 1990-91 and 1992-93 not to reform *per se* but to fall in agricultural output by 2 per cent between 1990-91 to 1991-92 due to bad monsoon and to higher post-reforms inflation. Sen (1996) however, differs with Tendulkar and Jain. Sen argued that the decline in poverty till during 1980's (up to 1987) was mainly due to significant improvement in rural-non-farm employment (as agricultural employment growth has been quite sluggish) which drove real wages up and caused poverty to decline. The non-agricultural growth led to a betterment in the condition of labourers during the 1980s. And in turn, this was largely due to increase in government expenditure and due to the availability of government cheap credit to the small scale industries. The onset of stabilization and structural adjustment programme has led to large decline in rural non-farm employment pushing millions of self-employed and casual rural non-agricultural workers to agriculture, thus reducing per worker income in agriculture. Thus, Sen believes that the massive increase in rural poverty by over 60 millions people in the first

TABLE 3.12: Percentage of Persons below Poverty Line by Household Type for each Social Groups—1987-88

Category	Self Employed in Agriculture	Self Employed in Non-Agri.	Agriculture Labour	Non-Agri. Labour	Others	All
SC	41.26	41.6	59.77	46.49	29.98	50.05
ST	52.51	47.22	68.28	59.02	23.11	51.32
N-Buddhist	37.51	29.56	65.63	43.33	38.31	55.12
Others	27.68	31.42	53.3	34.45	19.26	34.37
All	31.59	36.58	57.51	43.62	21.87	39.06

Urban	Self Employed	Regular Wage Earner/ Service	Casual Labour	Others	All
SC	61.48	43.69	73.45	56.84	56.98
ST	47.29	43.09	76.81	49.49	51.51
N-Buddhist	36.06	45.08	87.77	33.61	53.92
Others	43.14	25.26	70.11	32.21	37.21
All	44.34	28.25	71.49	37.96	40.12

Source: Employment Survey, NSSO, 1987-88.

18 months of reforms was to a very large extent a direct result of stabilization structural adjustment policies. The decline in rural poverty between 1992-93 and 1993-94 supports this assumption as there was a restoration of public cuts and with the result rise in rural non-farm employment both of male and female. (only exception being share of female in tertiary sector.)

Where do the Scheduled Castes stands in this situation? The poverty ratio are available for SCs only for the year 1983 and 1987-88 and therefore like employment/unemployment we cannot know the trends after 1987-88.

Table 3.12 presents the poverty ratios, total and by household types for rural and urban areas for the SCs and others. In 1987-88 half of the SC population was below poverty. The ratio was as high as 55.12 per cent for the neo-Buddhists. The poverty level was indeed high compared to 39.06 per cent among the other group (i.e. non-SC/ST). The incidence was 60 per cent in the case of agricultural labour followed by 50 per cent non-agricultural labour. The ratio was relatively lower for person engaged as self-employed in agriculture and self employed in non-agriculture sector (about 41 per cent each). However this was much higher than the other groups.

In urban areas the poverty ratio among SCs was higher than their counterpart in rural areas (57 per cent). By comparison this was much higher compared to other group (i.e. 37.21 per cent). The incidence was quite high among the casual labour in urban areas (73.45 per cent). The incidence was also particularly high among the casual labour of neo-Buddhists group (87.77 per cent).

In 1987-88 around quarter of the poor people in the country belongs to Scheduled Castes. The absolute number work out approximately to 49.41 millions persons, out of the total of 213.10 millions poor persons in the country in 1987-88. In 1993-94 there were about 244.86 millions poor persons in rural area. If we assume that the poverty ratio of SCs did not change much or if at all changed it may have declined only marginally. Under this assumption then the 25 per cent of 244.86 millions work out to about 55.15 millions persons. This means there was an addition of about 5.7 to 6.0 millions poor people in rural area among SCs in a period of five years i.e. between 1987-88 and 1993-94.

Besides there is an addition to urban poor as well. In 1987-88 the urban poor belonging to SC constitute about 16 per cent of the total poor in the country which comes to a total of about 11.16 millions persons. Assuming that the urban poverty among SC also remained constant or declined only marginally the absolute figures of urban poor belong to Scheduled Castes and neo-Buddhist roughly comes 12 to 13 millions. Thus in 1993 the tentative number of total poor among the Scheduled Castes could be somewhere between 65 to 68 millions persons.

Privatisation, Market and Caste Based Discrimination

One of the important aspects of NEP is a move towards privatisation. The general economic philosophy is to depend more on the market forces, thus minimise the public sector and fill the vacuum by private sector. The underlying presumption is that economic organisation based on State intervention leads to inefficient allocation and utilisation of economic resources. There is a whole lot of discussion regarding State failure *versus* market failure with regard to their economic role. The problem is posed in terms of choice between State failure and market failure, or in terms of complementary role of the State and the market rather than as a substitute.

In the context of mega move towards privatisation (not only in areas of production, infrastructure, but also in large number of social services as much as education, power, communication etc.) and their channelisation through market, the issue of market failure became important. In the shift towards marketisation the Economists talk about market failure referring to the economic situations such as presence of monopoly/oligopoly or what is called "imperfect markets", externalities, public goods and merit goods. They also refer to what is called "information failure" of the market. There are other perhaps even more important market failures. For example, reliance on market often generates inflation, unemployment and increase poverty and income inequality, (Bhaduri and Nayyer 1996).

While these market failures are discussed, not much is being talked about the market failures that specifically relates to the scheduled castes. The scheduled castes not only suffers from the various market failures referred above and quite surely more extensively than others, additionally they suffer from the market failures which arose out of the caste and untouchability based discrimination (and hence from the lack of access) in factors and product market. The Economists have barely began to talk about this but perhaps not realised the serious implications for the scheduled castes, in the context of privatisation and withdrawal of the State as well as the planning process under the NEP.

But before we discussed the nature of market failure associated with caste based discrimination let us try to understand the imperfection observed in factor market in general. We take an example of labour market as it is important for the scheduled castes. Does the recruitment in the private organised sector indicate efficient and equitable working of labour market ?

Discussing about the working of labour market institution in India, Papola (1992) made some important observations. Discussing the role of Employment Exchange (EE) (which increased from only 75 in 1947 to 850 by 1991) Papola observed that the "EE has been responsible for bringing about some change in the system of recruitment in the organised sector : from chaotic and highly personalized, blatantly unfair system towards a degree of orderliness, impersonal methods and fairness". The effectiveness of EE has been rather limited in total industrial employment as notification of vacancies by employees through EE declined from 70 per cent to 83 per cent between 1947-53 to 55 per cent in 1980's.

Thus, not all vacancies are notified through EE and informal channel or recruitment are common. Predominance of the informal or particularistic modes of recruitment is found to be common in Indian factories, Studies on Pune, Bombay, Ahmedabad and Coimbatore clearly brings out that "contact and influence dominate the scene". The important results of these studies are as follows :

(a) In over two-third cases, the worker got information about availability of the jobs from friends, relatives and neighbours. Employment Exchange were the sources for 1.5 per cent persons in Bombay, 10.6 per cent in Coimbatore, 20 per cent in Ahmedabad, and 25 per cent in Pune who had registered with employment exchange. Newspaper advertisement provide information about their jobs to 1.5 per cent in Bombay, 2.2 per cent in Pune, and 10.6 per cent in Coimbatore.

(b) Jobs were secured on the basis of recommendation or introduction by friends, relatives and persons of the same region and caste, (generally employees of the same factory) 67 per cent of cases in Pune, 61 per cent in Ahmedabad, Bombay and Coimbatore, Placement through EE accounted for 2 per cent of jobs in Pune and Ahmedabad.

This reveals that informal channels are predominantly used in about 60 per cent of the cases because they turn out to be efficient from the point of view of employer but are highly iniquitous from the point of employees.

Where do the scheduled castes stand in this situation? The access to employment market to the scheduled caste persons in the private organised sector is likely to be much lower. Given the high level of recruitment in this sector through "informal channels" and given the inadequate access to the network of opportunities for the scheduled caste due to powerlessness, the discrimination in their case on general count might be of a high order. However, besides the high probability of general discrimination, the scheduled caste suffered in the private employment market specifically due to discrimination based on the caste and untouchability.

There is likely to be very little disagreement in pointing out the role of caste and untouchability as one of the most important sources of discrimination and segmentation. Caste untouchability based discrimination is the most obvious form, which is used as strategy of exclusion from certain labour markets and jobs.

That discrimination leads to segmentation has been amply proved by the nature of their occupation. There are limited number of studies which tried to examine the caste-untouchability based discrimination in the labour market. But there are very few attempts which examine the caste-untouchability based discrimination in other factor market such as land market (in purchase and leasing of land) capital market, information, trade, and in access to social services such as housing education, sanitation etc.

The statistics, on land ownership, employment/unemployment wages, credit do provide some evidence in favour of caste-based discrimination and segmentation in private sector. The official statistics presented in the earlier section do indicate that the incidence of landlessness is higher among the SCs as compared to non-SC/ST. Similarly the proportion of agricultural labourer in 1991 was 50 per cent among SCs and only 20 per cent among non-SC/ST. The percentage of cultivator among them was 33 per cent but 55 per cent among Non-SC/ST. The magnitude of marginal farmers among them was 73 per cent. This was quite high compared to 50 per cent among other. Due to high landlessness and near landless the incidence of wage labour household among them was nearly 63 per cent but only 31 per cent among others. So segmentation in employment in the case of SC workers was quite clear as large section of them are concentrated in unskilled manual labour in rural areas.

The statistics on wage rate from Rural labour Enquiry revealed the possible presence of discrimination in the payment of wages. The daily wage paid to SC labour in agriculture was relatively lower compared to other labour in 8 States in 1964-65 and 1973-74, in 4 States in 1983-84 and in 9 States in 1987-88. Similarly the wage paid to SC labour was lower in rural non-farm activities in 8 States in 1964-65, in 12 States in 1973-74, in 15 States in 1983 and in 7 States in 1987-88. (Das Minakshi 1996).

The discrimination in employment is reflected in higher unemployment rate among them. The unemployment rate (based on current Daily status) in 1977-78 and 1983-84 of SC male work out to 6.73 per cent and 7.16 per cent compared to only 3.90 per cent and 4.03 per cent for other respectively. Similar gap has been observed in the case of access to social amenities (Kundu 1994).

Caste-based Discrimination: Implication for Growth and Discrimination

The caste based discrimination in so far as it excludes or reduces the access of scheduled caste persons to various factor markets i.e. labour, land, capital, information and social service sector it has implications on the earning capacity, employment and income of the Scheduled Castes. In that sense it is inhibitive to economic growth and income distribution. (Kannan 1994) It is inhibitive of the objective of distribution because discrimination and segmentation exclude people in having access to employment and other income earning assets. This leads to exclusion from opportunities for maximization of income and economic welfare in private sector.

This is in fact is the base for reservation policy for scheduled castes/ scheduled tribes in India in only one segment of organised sector i.e. public sector jobs. This constitutes however, only around 3 per cent of total employment . The move for privatisation on large scale will reduce even this small component in future and will further expose the scheduled castes to the discrimination in private sector.

The growth implication of discrimination in labour market and other factor market are not as easily appreciated as argument based on distribution. (Kannan 1994). The policies aimed at economic growth could be adversely affected by discrimination and segmentation mainly (a) by reducing effective demand in the economy due to lack of purchasing power with discriminated groups (and hence inadequate stimulant for output growth); and (b) by lack of qualitatively better human resources with good education and skill due to pre-market discrimination particularly in access of education. This would affect the productivity and production as only limited number of human resources are available for production purposes. In so far as affirmative action provide opportunities to discriminated group (although on a limited scale) to develop capabilities and skill it helps the productivity in the country to raise further.

Thus the caste based discrimination and segmentation in factor markets in organised private sector are incompatible with the objective of growth and distribution which are pursued under large scale privatisation as part of NEP.

Role of the State

Given this type of market failure what is indeed required is more State intervention and not less to make the access to labour, land, capital markets and access to various social services more open to the discriminated groups. In fact the economic role of the States in fact has to be redefined in the view of the known situation of market failure and State failure. There is a view which contradict the position that Government should not participate in economic organisation because (a) the government has no money and (b) the public sector organisation are generally used resources inefficiently.

Bhaduri and Nayyer argued that large scale government spending is in fact essential and such spending either by way of borrowing or deficit financing will be non-inflationary and sustainable of long as (a) the real rate of growth of the economy (or investment money) greater than real rate of interest at which government borrows, (b) government spending is directed to economic and social infrastructure facilities, (c) government not only spend effectively but also mobilise resources effectively.

They argued that the rate of growth of economy in real form will be higher than real rate of interest if (a) government spending are shifted from consumption to investment, (b) government's public investment should be in the creation and development of physical infrastructure in particular power, transport, communication, irrigation and also in social consumption, such as education, health, etc.

The increase in productivity of public expenditure therefore requires a meaningful restructuring of public sector to raise its efficiency and productivity. It is argued that there is no unique relationship between ownership and performance. The efficiency of an enterprise is determined more by compilation in the market structure and competence in the management than by nature of its ownership. Thus it is essential to expose public sector firms to compilation in the market. Similarly it is crucial to provide the management of public sector enterprises with an autonomy, and follow it up with an accountability.

REFERENCES

Bhaduri, A. and Nayyer D. (1996). *The Intelligent Persons Guide to Liberalisation*, Penguin.

Chadha, G.K. (1996), "Gender Differences in some Aspects of Non-form Employment in Rural India" Paper for the IEG-ISLK Seminar.

Das, Minakshi, (1996), *Employment Wages and Earnings Across Social Groups in India*, M. Phil thesis, CSBD/JNU, Delhi.

Gupta, S.P. (1995), "Economic Reform and Its Impact on Poor", *EPW*, June 3, 1995.

Gwartny, J.D. (1970), "Discrimination and Income Differences", *The American Economic Review*, June 1970.

John, H. Kannan, K.P. Garry Rodgers (1990), *Urban Labour Market Structure and Jobs Access in India: A Study of Coimbatore*, IILS, Geneva.

Kannan, K.P. (1994), "Labour Institutions and Economic Development in India: Some Exploratory Hypothesis", *IJLE*, January-March, 1994.

Kundu, A. (1995), *In The Name of the Poor : Access to Amenities*, Sage, Delhi.

Nayak, R.K. (1995), *New Economic Policy and Its Impact on Reservation*, Research Project by National Institute of Social Work and Social Sciences, Bhubaneshwar.

Papola, T.S. (1992), "Labour Institutions and Economic Development: A Case of Indian Industrialisation", in Papola and Garry Rodger (Edt.) *Labour Institutions and Economic Development in India*, ILTS, Geneva.

Sen, Abhijit "Economic Reform Employment and Poverty: Trends and Options", *EPW*, Special No. Sept. 1996.

Thorat, S.K. (1993), "The New Economic Measures and Its Impact on Reservation", in Arun Kumar, *Alternative Budget, People's Group*.

Thorat, S.K. (1992), "Dalit Reality: An Analysis from Economic Perspective", The Gurukul Institute, (Madras), "*Dalits and Women*".

4

FIXED INVESTMENT

D.U. SASTRY

In this Chapter, it is proposed to analyze the determinants of fixed investment expenditures. The role of accelerator and of financial variables are considered. Among the financial variables, retained earnings and external finance have received attention. The inter–dependence between fixed and inventory investment is also analyzed. It may be useful to give a brief account of the econometric studies on fixed investment in India before proceeding with the analysis.

Review of Indian Studies

There have been some attempts in recent years to study the determinants of fixed investment for India.[1] Most of the studies relate to the private corporate sector. Some are time series and others are cross–section studies.

Among the time series studies[2] Krishnamurty's investment functions are aggregative in character covering the entire private sector for the period 1948–61. Capacity utilization, profits, and long–term rate of interest are found to be of some importance in determining private investment in machinery and equipment. The studies of Divatia and Athawale and that of Swamy and Rao are aggregative and relate to the corporate sector. These studies cover the period 1955–70 and 1954–70 respectively. Divatia and Athawale conclude that a combination of accelerator and profits can explain gross capital formation adequately. The study by Swamy and Rao attempts an integrated treatment of the flow of funds and their uses. They infer that accelerator, flow of funds, internal as well as external and capital intensity are significant determinants of corporate fixed investment. The attempt by Krishna and Krishnamurty focuses attention on public investment as a determinant, among others, of corporate fixed investment. The period covered is 1950–66. Public investment could be viewed as a surrogate for aggregate demand. They infer that public investment expenditures is an important determinant of corporate investment. The macro econometric models for India contain global investment functions and an appraisal for these can be found in the survey by Desai.[3]

The study by Sarkar examines bivariate relationship of investment with change in sales, legged profits and interest rate for several individual industries for the period 1950–65. Finite distributed lag models in sales change and in profits are also tried. The results suggest that profit–investment relationship is more pronounced than investment–sales relationship. Interest rate is found to be generally of no importance. Jameson's paper covers twenty–five individual industries in the corporate sector and relates to the period 1951–66. The paper emphasizes the user cost variable and concludes that it has a significant impact on the rate of investment in most of the industries. Kanbur's work on Fertilizer Corporation of India relates to the period 1960–69. The variables considered are sales and liquid assets. The results are not satisfactory although the coefficients have the appropriate signs. The study by Rama Rao and Anjaneyulu on the cotton textile industry relates to the period 1952–69. They have an investment equation in a model integrating output, utilization of capacity and investment. Sales and capital stock at the beginning of the period are significant determinants of fixed investment. Patnaik's study for the period 1950–65 relates to some individual industries and to the aggregate corporate sector as well. The study suggests that the rate of investment and the rate of profit are closely related, but this relationship is obscured by the operation of special factors in certain years; the inclusion of dummy variables to take account of such special factors goes a long way towards explaining investment movements.

The studies are at constant prices except that of Swamy and Rao, Sarkar and Patnaik. All the studies relating to corporate sector, except that of Kanbur, have made use of consolidated balance sheet data published periodically by the Reserve Bank of India.

One of the earliest cross–section studies[4] in the field of corporate investment in India is by Bagchi. His study is cross–section analysis across twenty–seven industries covering such diverse activities like tea plantations, electricity supply and shipping. The unit of analysis is industry. Yearly cross–sections have also been tried. The consolidated balance sheet data of public limited companies published by the Reserve

Bank of India have been used. Investment equations, one with sales change and another with profits separately using yearly averages for the two periods, 1952–55 and 1957–59 have been estimated. The broad conclusion of the study is that profits after tax has a more powerful influence on the level of investment than changes in sales. Patnaik estimates a simple cross–section relationship using average data for the three samples of Reserve Bank of India series with industry as unit of analysis. No significant relationship is found between the rate of investment and the rate of profit.

The study by V.K.Sastry is a major attempt to analyze investment, dividends, external finance and their interdependence for the corporate sector. The study is based on individual balance sheets of public limited companies and includes firms all the way from mining, manufacturing to public utilities with varying capital intensities. The analysis relates to yearly cross–sections for the period 1955–60. The variables in the fixed investment equation are accelerator represented by sales change, profits, dividends, liquid assets, debt equity, the flow of external finance and depreciation reserves representing the age of equipment. Both the ordinary least–squares and the two–stage least–squares estimates are presented. The least–squares estimates suggest that accelerator, profitability and the flow of external finance are the prime factors influencing investment expenditures. The two–stage least–squares estimate further reveal that dividends has a significant negative impact on investment suggesting competitiveness between dividend payments and investment expenditures. This study as well as the studies of Bagchi and Patnaik ignore inter–industry differences.

The studies by Krishnamurty and D.U. Sastry and that of D.U.Sastry are individual industry studies. Both the studies make use of individual company balance sheet data of public limited companies. The study of Krishnamurty and D.U.Sastry analyzes investment, dividends and external finance behaviour for the chemical industry on the basis of annual cross–sections for the period 1962–67. An attempt is made in this study to appraise the importance of accelerator, retained earnings and the flow of external finance in the analysis of fixed investment. The analysis reveals that accelerator hypothesis has some validity in the explanation of investment. Financial variables are of significance. Retained earnings exerts its influence on investment when the supply of funds is limited on account of poor profits. The impact of external finance is felt on investment when money–capital markets are tight. The study by D.U.Sastry on the capital goods industry relates to the period

1957–67. Both cross–section and time series approaches have been used. Within the cross–section analysis several variants viz., single year cross–section, two year aggregate, three year aggregate and pooled cross–section have been tried. The cross–section results lend support to the importance of retained earnings and external finance in investment decision. The accelerator does not seem to have any impact. Time series results of individual companies confirm the importance of financial variables. In a large number of companies, current sales seems to have an impact on investment. Time series results are subject to the limitations of short series and simple specification. The cross–section studies, by and large, have not displayed temporal stability of the coefficients.

Siddharthan analyzes the investment behaviour of firms belonging to two conglomerates, the Tatas and the Birlas in a cross–section study based on balance sheet data for the period 1963–72. The rate of growth of assets is explained by average profitability and its variability, growth rate of sales and of non–production expenditure. The results suggest that the growth rate of sales and of non–production expenditure are important determinants. However, in the short–run profitability appears to be important in the case of oligopoly and competitive firms. The analysis further reveals that the behaviour of conglomerate firms differs in different markets viz., monopoly, oligopoly and others.

The financial variables considered in these studies do not include new equity. The reason perhaps is non–separability of new equity from summary balance sheets that have been generally used in cross–section studies. However, new equity is not a major component of the total flow of funds in India.

All the cross–section studies are at current prices. The cross–section studies except that of Bagchi attempt to correct for heteroscedasticity by deflating the variables by a size measure. In the studies of V.K. Sastry and that of Krishnamurty and D.U. Sastry different size measures have been used to deflate different variables in the equation so that some of the deflated variables acquire economic meaning. The specific examples are deflation of sales change by sales (rate of change of sales), investment by capital stock (rate of change of capital) and debt by networth (debt equity ratio). This has not been an uncommon practice in the literature. In so far as different size measures are well correlated, deflation by different size measures may not be inappropriate from a statistical point of view. However, the use of different size measures for different variables in an equation cannot retrieve the original specification.

The time series studies of Divatia and Athawale, Jameson, Swamy and Rao, and Rama Rao and Anjaneyulu are in the framework of capital stock adjustment models. The cross–section studies generally attempt the analysis in the same framework, and use finite distributed lags in sales. Except the study of Krishnamurty and D.U.Sastry where the specification of the lag structure is considered in some detail, others confine only to one or two lags. Both the cross–section and time series studies except one use the ordinary least–squares estimation procedure.

TABLE 4.1: **Distribution of Correlation Coefficients between Sales Changes of Different Lags**

Size Class r_{ij}	Cotton textiles	Jute	Sugar	Paper & Paper board	Chemicals	Engi–neering	Cement
0.00–0.10	6	5	2	7	1	7	5
0.11–0.20	3	2	3	3	3	2	3
0.21–0.30	1	2	4	—	2	1	2
0.31–0.40	—	—	1	—	2	—	—
0.41–0.50	—	1	—	—	1	—	—
0.51–0.60	—	—	—	—	1	—	—

Note : $/ r_{ij} /$: Correlation coefficient between $\frac{\Delta S(t-i)}{K(t-1)}$ and $\frac{\Delta S(t-j)}{K(t-1)}$ for $i \neq j$

Apart from the studies reviewed above, some work has begun to emerge in the area of short–run investment forecasting. Paul and Rangarajan have recently made a serious attempt to explore systematically the forecasting ability of various bodies of data, such as consents for capital issues, flow of funds and the data available with term lending financial institutions, for the corporate sector.[5]

Earlier work in the area of corporate investment in India is limited, inadequate and unsatisfactory in many respects. Except for a couple of studies, others are rather superficial. In most of the studies the specification is naive, in some inter–industry differences are ignored and in others the results are generally weak. The conclusions therefore are not definitive. However, these studies indicate that apart from accelerator which is of some importance, financial variables (profits/

retained earnings and external finance) are important determinants of private corporate investment in India.

The distinctive features of the present study are : (a) an analysis of investment at the industry level for several industries using firm level data, (b) consideration of a detailed lag structure of accelerator, (c) an analysis of competitive nature of fixed and inventory investment, and (d) a study of inter–dependence of investment, dividends and external financing decisions at the industry level.

Framework of Analysis

In the analysis of investment behaviour, two broad approaches are discernible.[6] The first approach centres around the accelerator and the second relates to the profit hypothesis. Within each there are several variants. However, over the years, the exclusiveness of these two approaches has somewhat blurred. Some variant of profits is brought into the context of accelerator model to account for constraints imposed by the supply of funds in an imperfect market. Cost of capital is another variable around which some controversy centres. It is the flexible accelerator hypothesis with financial variables that has received considerable attention.[7] Investment behaviour in this study is analyzed in the context of flexible accelerator model with financial variables.

The accelerator hypothesis rests on technical relationship between output and capital stock. The production relationship that is generally assumed is of the Leontief type barring some recent studies.[8] The flexible accelerator hypothesis implies that adjustment of capital stock to desired level is not instantaneous. There are time lags between changes in demand and adjustment of capital stock to the target level. Such lags arise on account of technological, expectational and institutional factors. On account of these, alignment of capital stock to the equilibrium level is a gradual and time–taking process. Technological lags are essentially of a long–run nature. In the short–run, expectational lags are relevant which are related to the market demand. Entrepreneurs would like to assess whether changes in demand are transitory or of a permanent character before deciding to expand capacity. Lags can also arise due to institutional constraints which are of particular importance in the Indian context. The special institutional considerations present in the Indian scene are industrial licensing and controls. The licensing procedures for capacity expansion, raising of funds, sanction of foreign exchange for import of capital goods and their procurement introduce lags between decisions to invest and capital expenditures. There is a general scarcity of capital. Imports of capital goods are constrained by foreign exchange scarcity. Domestic capacity of capital goods is also limited. On account of such scarcities, procurement lags get lengthened. The supply constraints that are usually present in capital scarce economies, unlike in the developed economies where they may operate only in boom periods, would lengthen lags between changes in demand and capacity expansion. It is because of the presence of various kinds of lags, current changes in sales induce investment in future. Likewise, current investments are induced by past changes in sales.

The presence of controls, in addition to lengthening lags, may also constrain the accelerator in so far as they interfere with the market mechanism. The way in which licensing of capacity constrain the accelerator may be briefly indicated. Demand increases lead to requests for capacity expansion. Requisitions for new capacity are scrutinized by licensing authorities in the light of plan priorities and requirements, apart from others. The capacity sanctioned induce investment expenditures with the usual lags. To the extent sanctioned capacity is less than the requested capacity, the link between investment and demand gets weakened. On the other hand, requested capacity may be more than what is genuinely required as dictated by market considerations. Under conditions of general scarcity, planning and priorities, firms may apply for more capacity than is genuinely required as they may expect cuts on their requests. Other reasons such as the desire to pre–empt targeted capacity to preserve their monopoly/oligopoly position may also exist.

It has been suggested that accelerator models may not be so relevant for developing economies as there are ample opportunities for investment and Government supported investment promotion.[9]

These considerations along with institutional interference with market mechanism and supply constraints discussed earlier might interfere with the operation of the accelerator. Whether these factors completely snap the relationship between demand and investment expenditure is an empirical question.

The acceleration principle applies to new investment only. It is not possible to separate new investment and investment due to replacement from balance sheet accounts. There is need, therefore, to introduce a variable in explaining gross investment to account for replacement demand. Replacement demand can be accounted for either by using stock of capital on the assumption that replacement demand is proportional to capital stock or by depreciation reserves. Following Meyer and Kuh depreciation reserves has been used to reflect replacement demand in this study.[10] The basic reason for such a practice is that firms with older stock of equipment in an industry are likely to have a greater proportion of capital stock written off as compared to firms with newer equipment. Depreciation reserves is the cumulative sum of annual depreciation provision that is set aside by firms. Depreciation provision is a financial entity governed by tax laws and institutional practices. As such, it may not adequately reflect actual capital used. However, in so far as firms within an industry have broadly the same accounting practice, depreciation reserves could reflect the average age of equipment.

In the analysis of investment behaviour, financial variables, internal flows, external finance and cost of borrowing are considered as important determinants. The importance of financial variables arises on account of market imperfections. Internal finance is usually represented by retained earnings. The rationale for considering internal funds is that the supply of funds schedule raises at the point where internal funds are exhausted. This implies that the cost of internal finance is lower than external funds. It is further argued that the cost of institutional or bond finance is lower than the cost of equity.[11] As opposed to this view, others argue that cost of finance is independent of the financial structure of the firm.[12] Firms may also prefer internal financing because of the risk associated with borrowed capital. The fear of loss of control through equity financing and dilution of return on equity may also favour internal financing.[13]

Internal finance is considerably more convenient and allows the firm to retain control. Enterprises in India are family (industrial house) controlled and may have preference for internal finance as opposed to equity as the former would enable continuance of such control. Furthermore, the preference for internal funds may increase now in view of the recent changes in policy enabling term lending public financial institutions to convert loans into equity.

Although firms may have preference for internal financing they often seek outside funds for financing their investment plans. It is argued that firms resort to external finance if the desired rate of growth is higher than that is permitted solely by their own funds. However, there are limits to the availability of internal funds. The limit is set by their long–run dividend policies. If profitable opportunities for investment exists than could be met by their own funds, firms draw on external sources. Even if investment is not marginally profitable, firms in an oligopolistic world may seek external finance to protect their market share. The time taken to align actual capital stock to the desired level depends on the speed of adjustment. Given the growth objectives of the firm, the speed of adjustment may be faster for those firms which use external finance than for those firms which deliberately restrict to internal funds alone, in so far as the speed of adjustment is influenced by financial conservatism.[14] On these considerations, flow of external finance is considered as an important variable.

Another dimension of loan financing is cost of borrowing. The lending rates of public financial institutions and of banks in India have been below their shadow rates on account of regulation and control by public authorities. There are quantitative controls on credit, short and long. It seems, therefore, appropriate to argue that availability of funds is more relevant than the rate at which firms can borrow.

Public investment activity and import substitution policies have provided stimulus to the private sector in India. Apart from providing physical climate through infrastructure, public investment stimulates activity in at least two ways: (i) through the supply of capital and current inputs, and (ii) through direct and indirect demands generated by Government spending. Import substitution policies, by creating a sheltered market, have also provided stimulus to the development of industry. Doubts could be raised as to the relevance of past experience in explaining such investment which is stimulated by Government spending and import substitution policies. As these forces have been gradual and spread over a number of years, they should get reflected in the lag structure. To the extent there are abrupt changes, year specific dummies could enable in isolating such factors. It could also be argued that the stimulus provided by Government policies do not entirely get reflected in terms of market signals. Year specific dummies could help to capture the effect of such forces.

The tempo of Government investment slowed down due to diversion of resources to defence needs after Sino–Indian conflict in 1962. The declining trend in public investment, more or less continued in later years due to the suspension of foreign aid consequent on Indo–Pakistan conflict in 1965 and a three–year plan holiday after 1966. The easy phase of import substitution having reached a plateau in the early sixties almost coincided with the slowing down of public investment. While import substitution policies affected the machinery industries in particular, the decline in public investment affected all industries, but the engineering sector was particularly hit.

A reference was made earlier to the constraints imposed by the scarcity of capital goods and foreign exchange. The supply of current inputs can also impose a constraint. There is some evidence to suggest that the availability of raw materials was not a serious bottleneck until about mid–sixties in the case of agriculture based industries. Foreign exchange availability does not also seem to have been generally a constraint after 1962, thanks to liberal Government policies towards foreign collaboration. The availability of finance did seem to constrain investment when capital goods imports were more freely available.[15]

Specification

In the specification of the investment function in the present study, the time structure has been represented by finite distributed lags in sales. Five sales change variables—one current and four lagged—have been used to represent the accelerator. Some survey results suggest that the time taken between the initiation of a project including licensing and its completion is about 3–4 years on the average.[16]

Gross retained earnings is an important financial variable considered in the analysis. Gross retained earning is defined here as profits net of dividends and taxes but gross of current depreciation. The other financial variable is flow of net debt. Debt includes current and non–current liabilities. Current liabilities are an important source of funds. The justification for the inclusion of short–term funds in the fixed investment equation lies in the fact that substitution possibilities may exist at the margin between different sources of funds as there is no exact specificity between sources and uses.[17] Some items on the current liabilities side are netted out with corresponding items on the current assets side of the balance sheet so that net availabilities are represented. Trade dues and tax provision are net figures. All of these funds may not be fully available for investment as a part of it may go to meet liquidity requirements. Debt therefore, is netted out for financial assets, i.e., cash, bank balances and marketable securities. The flow of net debt represents the flow of external finance. External finance excludes equity. As noted earlier, new equity constitutes less than 10 per cent of the total flow of funds for most of the industries covered in the analysis.[18] It is not possible to derive new issues from summary balance sheet accounts used here.

Inventory is an important charge on funds. It is nearly one-third of the total use of funds for the corporate sector in India.[19] In a shortage economy, inventories, particularly raw materials, could constitute a priority item on the use of funds. Raw materials and goods–in–process inventories constitute two–thirds of the aggregate inventory holdings for the organized manufacturing in India.[20] Short–term borrowings are generally influenced by inventory requirements. As argued earlier, specific sources of funds cannot be exclusively associated with specific uses as there may be substitution between various sources. Inventory requirements may be met not only by short–term borrowings but also by retained earnings. To obtain a correct appraisal of the flow of funds, internal as well as external, inventory investment ought to be included as an explanatory variable in the fixed investment equation. Even if only long–term borrowings and retained earnings are included in the equation, there is a need to include inventory investment to get a correct appraisal of the effect of retained earnings on fixed investment, as retained earnings could finance inventory investment. The age variable represented by depreciation reserves is included to account for replacement demand.

All variables are in current prices. It is a pooled cross–section analysis involving flow and stock variables, both current and lagged. There is need for price deflation. But the problem of obtaining appropriate deflators for firms with capital stock of various vintages and of different product mix that change over time, is formidable. All variables have been deflated by capital stock. This procedure may help to correct for heteroelasticity which is a common feature in cross–section analysis. Dummy variables are introduced to account for year specific effects as several cross–sections have been pooled. The year specific dummies help in isolating the influence of special factors that do not get reflected in economic variables present in the function. The exact identification of year specific effect with any single factor is difficult. The year dummies represent changing environment. It was observed earlier that all firms included in the sample do not have the same accounting year. Dummy variables representing quarters in which they close accounts have been introduced to account for such differences. The equation allows for intercept changes but not for slope changes. There could be variation in the effect of explanatory variables on investment from year to year.

The same sample is used in the analysis of inventory investment, dividends and external finance, and their interaction. The procedure followed with respect to size deflation and use of dummies is also the same. The entire cross–section analysis is at current prices. The specification of the fixed investment function is as follows:

$$\frac{I(t)}{K(t-1)} = a + \sum_{j=2}^{4} b_j Q_{jt} + \sum_{t=2}^{T} c_t Y(t) + \sum_{r=0}^{4} d_r \frac{\Delta S(t-r)}{K(t-1)} + e \frac{IN(t)}{K(t-1)} + f \frac{RENT(t)}{K(t-1)} + g \frac{FNDE(t)}{K(t-1)} + h \frac{DR(t-1)}{K(t-1)}$$

Where,

$I(t)$	=	gross fixed investment in year t.
$K(t-1)$	=	gross fixed assets at the beginning of year t.
Q_{jt}	=	dummy variable representing accounts closing quarter.
$Y(t)$	=	dummy variable representing year t.
$\Delta S(t)$	=	sales change in year t.
$IN(t)$	=	inventory investment in year t.
$RENT(t)$	=	gross retained earnings in year t.
$FNDE(t)$	=	flow of net debt (external finance) in year t.
$DR(t-1)$	=	depreciation reserves at the beginning of year t.

Among the omitted variables which are relevant to the analysis of fixed investment, mention may be made of capacity utilization which is an important variable. Capacity data at the firm level are not available. Even at the industry level, the available published data on installed capacity are suspect. In an earlier study on chemical industry,[21] an attempt was made to introduce a capacity measure based on peak output–capital ratio method[22] for each firm but did not yield satisfactory results. Variables like liquidity and durability are often considered in cross–section studies. Gross retained earnings may partly account for liquidity.

Analysis of Results

In this chapter, the results obtained by the method of ordinary least–

squares (OLS) are discussed. The effect of accelerator is captured by a finite distributed lag model with five sales changes, one current and four lagged. It is not unusual in this approach to find that different sales lags are correlated among themselves.[23] The sum of individual sales change coefficients reflects the long–run effect of sales on investment. Another way of capturing the long–run effect of sales on investment is to consider the average of sales changes over different lags. This procedure presumes equal weight to sales changes of various lags. The results of the two sets of equations, one with five sales changes individually, and the other with the average of five sales changes along with other variables are presented in Table 4.2. The F-tests for the contribution of different sets of variables are also presented.

TABLE 4.2: Fixed Investment: Pooled Cross–Section Results (OLS) (with intercept dummies for accounts closing quarter and for year)

Dependent Variable: I(t)/K(t–1)

Regression Coefficients				
Industries	*Cotton Textiles* 1961-67		*Jute* 1962-67	
No. of Companies	(165)		(30)	
Variables	Eq 1	Eq 2	Eq 1	Eq 2
S(t)–S(t–1)/	0.0922*		0.0599*	
K(t–1)	(0.9894)		(2.9583)	
S(t–1)–S(t–2)/	0.0445*		0.0419*	
K(t–1)	(2.3063)		(2.3343)	
S(t–2)–S(t–3)/	0.0705*	0.2976*	0.0753*	0.2772*
K(t–1)	(3.4971)	(5.6366)	(3.5871)	(5.0821)
S(t–3)–S(t–4)/	0.0450*	5 year	0.0595*	5 year
K(t–1)	(2.0016)	average	(2.9877)	average
S(t–4)–S(t–5)/	0.0231		0.0595*	
K(t–1)	(1.0466)		(3.3692)	
Sum of Sales change coefficients	0.2753*		0.2961*	
	(5.1874)		(5.0593)	
IN(t)/K(t–1)	–0.0759*	–0.0774*	–0.5488*	–0.5414*
	(3.7515)	(3.8215)	(7.0391)	(7.0786)
DR(t–1)/K(t–1)	0.3061*	0.3053*	–0.0463	–0.0468
	(10.9993)	(10.9647)	(0.7841)	(0.8025)
FNDE(t)/K(t–1)	0.5207*	0.5124*	0.5750*	0.5716*
	(19.3079)	(19.1079)	(10.9388)	(11.2887)
RENT(t)/K(t–1)	0.3173*	0.3326*	0.4690*	0.4988*
	(7.7109)	(8.1953)	(5.9075)	(6.8404)

TABLE 4.2 (Contd.)

Regression Coefficients

Industries	*Cotton Textiles* 1961-67		*Jute* 1962-67	
No. of Companies	(165)		(30)	
Variables	Eq 1	Eq 2	Eq 1	Eq 2
Constant	–16.4355*	–15.9975*	3.2353	2.5317
	(7.5720)	(7.4189)	(0.7642)	(0.6257)
R^2	0.342	0.338	0.646	0.643
$\bar{R}^2$	0.332	0.330	0.609	0.615
Sample Size	1155		180	
F-Value due to :				
(i) Equality of Sales coefficients	1.7279		0.3453	
(ii) Quarterly Dummies	4.0284*	4.0181*	0.4576	0.6200
(iii) Yearly Dummies	0.2877	0.5740	1.8305	1.9529**
(iv) Sales	7.9414*	32.7190*–	5.5830*	26.9690*
(v) FNDE(t) & RENT (t)	205.4468*	203.2024*	61.0932*	66.4929*

Industries	*Sugar* 1961-69		*Paper & Paper Board* 1962-70	
No. of Companies	(41)		(11)	
Variables	Eq 1	Eq 2	Eq 1	Eq 2
S(t)–S(t–1)/ K(t–1)	0.1146**		0.3367*	
	(1.6700)		(3.9181)	
S(t–1)–S(t–2)/ K(t–1)	0.0780		–0.0400	
	(1.0951)		(0.3520)	
S(t–2)–S(t–3)/ K(t–1)	0.0783	0.3734	0.0479	0.7241*
	(1.0348)	(1.6178)	(0.4252)	(2.4075)
S(t–3)–S(t–4)/ K(t–1)	0.0220	5 year	–0.0296	5 year
	(0.2917)	average	(0.2856)	average
S(t–4)–S(t–5)/ K(t–1)	0.0533		0.1696	
	(0.7299)		(1.5894)	
Sum of Sales change coefficients	0.3462		0.4846	
	(0.4510)		(1.6120)	
IN(t)/K(t–1)	0.0387	0.0268	0.5941*	0.7020*
	(0.2962)	(0.2085)	(1.9800)	(2.3120)

TABLE 4.2 *(Contd.)*

Regression Coefficients				
Industries	*Sugar* 1961-69		*Paper & Paper Board* 1962-70	
No. of Companies	(41)		(11)	
Variables	Eq 1	Eq 2	Eq 1	Eq 2
DR (t–1)/K(t–1)	0.0301	0.0234	–0.0212	0.0286
	(0.1251)	(0.0979)	(0.2478)	(0.3258)
FNDE(t)/K(t–1)	0.0693	0.0645	0.4853*	0.4559*
	(0.6467)	(0.6050)	(6.5297)	(6.0058)
RENT(t)/K(t–1)	–0.4229	–0.3450	0.1169	0.0694
	(0.9970)	(0.8468)	(0.3447)	(0.1997)
Constant	5.5181	3.6080	0.2363	–5.5552
	(0.3287)	(0.2180)	(0.0344)	(0.7970)
R^2	0.036	0.034	0.699	0.650
$\bar{R}^2$	–0.016	–0.007	0.622	0.582
Sample Size	369		99	
F-Value due to :				
(i) Equality of Sales coefficients	0.1815		3.2151*	
(ii) Quarterly Dummies	0.8326	0.5298	0.2591	0.8590
(iii) Yearly Dummies	0.8413	0.8907	1.4396	1.6400
(iv) Sales	0.6878	2.9235**	3.8352*	5.8570*
(v) FNDE(t)	0.7059	0.6577	22.6744*	19.2114*

Industries	*Chemicals* 1962–67		*Engineering* 1962–67	
No. of Companies	(40)		(62)	
Variables	Eq 1	Eq 2	Eq 1	Eq 2
S(t)–S(t–1)/ K(t–1)	0.0084		0.0388*	
	(0.3962)		(3.1997)	
S(t–1)–S(t–2)/ K(t–1)	–0.0150		0.0326*	
	(0.6156)		(2.4327)	
S(t–2)–S(t–3)/ K(t–1)	0.0826*	0.1133*	0.0181	0.1284*
	(2.8548)	(3.0713)	(1.2458)	(3.5329)
S(t–3)–S(t–4)/ K(t–1)	0.0424	5 year	0.0135	5 year
	(1.2926)	average	(0.0566)	average
S(t–4)–S(t–5)/ K(t–1)	0.0039		0.0172	
	(0.1098)		(1.2514)	

TABLE 4.2 *(Contd.)*

Regression Coefficients				
Industries	*Chemicals* 1962–67		*Engineering* 1962–67	
No. of Companies	(40)		(62)	
Variables	Eq 1	Eq 2	Eq 1	Eq 2
Sum of Sales change coefficients	0.1223* (2.5421)		0.1202* (3.2122)	
IN(t)/K(t–1)	–0.3078*	–0.3016*	–0.4653*	–0.4650*
	(5.0848)	(4.9700)	(9.5795)	(9.6129)
DR (t–1)/K(t–1)	–0.2045*	–0.2025*	–0.2572*	–0.2669*
	(3.4991)	(3.4373)	(5.2052)	(5.4607)*
FNDE(t)/K(t–1)	0.3697*	0.3569*	0.4992*	0.4991*
	(9.4120)	(9.1380)	(14.0590)	(14.0983)
RENT(t)/K(t–1)	0.4672*	0.4504*	0.5744*	05998*
	(5.2382)	(5.1248)	(6.2831)	(6.7014)
Constant	15.7813*	16.0039*	18.7960*	19.4413*
	(4.2206)	(4.3126)	(6.4692)	(6.8188)
R^2	0.426	0.404	0.557	0.554
$\bar{R}^2$	0.382	0.370	0.536	0.538
Sample Size	240		372	
F–Value due to :				
(i) Equity of Sales coefficients	2.1367*		0.6010	
(ii) Quarterly Dummies	0.7735	0.7584	3.2541*	3.3207*
(iii) Yearly Dummies	0.6188	0.6067	1.5523	2.0886*
(iv) Sales	3.6355*	9.4795*	2.9927*	12.4530*
(v) FNDE(t) & RENT(t)	48.3449*	46.0721*	110.0649*	112.5177*

Industries	*Cement* 1962–68	
No. of Companies	(11)	
Variables	Eq 1	Eq 2
S(t)–S(t–1)/K(t–1)	–0.1721	
	(1.1087)	
S(t–1)–S(t–2)/K(t–1)	0.0733	
	(0.4296)	
S(t–2)–S(t–3)/K(t–1)	0.0804	0.0511
	(0.4197)	(0.0983)
S(t–3)–S(t–4)/K(t–1)	–0.0815	5 year
	(0.4165)	average
S(t–4)–S(t–5)/K(t–1)	0.1202	
	(0.6302)	

TABLE 4.2 *(Contd.)*

Regression Coefficients

Industries	*Cement* 1962–68	
No. of Companies	(11)	
Variables	Eq 1	Eq 2
Sum of Sales change coefficients	0.0203 (0.0384)	
IN(t)/K(t–1)	–0.0116 (0.1941)	–0.0205 (0.3542)
DR (t–1)/K(t–1)	0.0646 (0.3512)	0.0889 (0.4922)
FNDE(t)/K(t–1)	0.6134* (2.9957)	0.6263* (3.0921)
RENT(t)/K(t–1)	0.7486 (0.9833)	0.7578 (1.0592)
Constant	–7.2847 (0.7422)	–7.2719 (0.7709)
R^2	0.315	0.270
$\bar{R}^2$	0.118	0.119
Sample Size	77	
F–Value due to :		
(i) Equity of Sales coefficients	0.9854	
(ii) Quarterly Dummies	0.0430	0.0432
(iii) Yearly Dummies	1.1262	1.2082
(iv) Sales	0.7751	neg
(v) FNDE(t) & RENT(t)	4.4788*	4.7897*

Note : Figures in parenthesis denote 't' values.
* Significant at 5%
** Significant at 10%
Neg : Negligible
All variables are in percentages except dummy variables.
The coefficients of quarterly and yearly dummies are not reported here to save space.

The explanatory power (R^2) of the two equations is fairly good in paper and paper board, jute, engineering, chemicals and cotton textiles and ranges from 30 to 70 per cent. In cross–section analysis, especially with deflated variables, high explanation is not a commonly observed feature. The explanation corrected for degrees of freedom (R^2) does not differ very much for the two equations except in the case of paper and paper board where the sample size is relatively small. In the case of the cement industry, the explanation offered by the two equations is around 30 per cent, but the adjusted explanation is around 12 per cent. Cement has a relatively small sample size. The equations have not fared well in the case of the sugar industry as the explanation is near zero. The nature of the results both in terms of their magnitudes and statistical significance as between the two variants does not diverge in any significant way for almost all the industries.

Quarterly dummies generally are not significant. As a group they do not significantly contribute to total explanation barring cotton textiles and engineering. Most of the yearly dummies are not significant except in the case of engineering. In the case of engineering, all the yearly dummies are significant and negative. This result may be reflecting the slowing down of public investment activity and of import substitution. In jute, sugar, paper and paper board and cement, yearly dummy is significant only for one year. As a group, yearly dummies contribute significantly to the explanation in jute and engineering and that too in the case of average sales variant.

Both the equations have done remarkably well in the textile group. The individual sales change coefficients are all of the right sign. They are all significant in the case of jute. In cotton textiles all the sales change coefficients are significant except the last one. The coefficient of average sales change in the second variant is significant and positive for both the industries. The long-run effect of sales as revealed by the sum of sales change coefficients and the coefficient of average sales change agree closely for the textile group. The long-run impact of accelerator is about the same for these two industries.

The individual sales change variant in the chemical industry did not fare too well as far as sales change variables are concerned. The coefficient of the second lag sales change is alone significant. One coefficient is negative but not significant. In the other equation, the coefficient of the average sales change is positive and significant, and is quite close to the sum of the individual sales change coefficient. In engineering, all the sales change coefficients are positive with the first two being significant. The average sales change coefficient is positive and significant in the other equation. The sum of individual sales change coefficients and the average coefficient are very close to each other, contributing factor for the low value of the accelerator coefficient which is common to both the industries may be that they are relatively more dependent on imported equipment as compared to other industries

Long–run Accelerator Coefficients and Average Capacity Utilization

Industry	Long–run Sales Coefficient		Average Capacity Utilization*		Whether affected by 1966–68 drought and/or recession
	Eq 1	Eq 2	Per cent	Period	
Cotton textiles	0.2753	0.2976	90.4(i) 90.3(ii)	1961–67 1961–67	Very mildly affected
Jute	0.2961	0.2772	88.5	1962–67	Severely affected
Chemicals	0.1223	0.1133	88.5	1962–67	Not affected
Engineering	0.1202	0.1284	77.8(a) 81.9(b)	1962–67 1962–67	Severely affected
Paper & paper board	0.4846+	0.7241	91.0	1962–68	Not affected
Sugar	0.3462+	0.3734+	87.7	1961–68	Very severely affected
Cement	0.0203+	0.0511+	88.1	1962–68	Mildly affected

Note : (i) Cotton spinning (ii) Cotton weaving
(a) Capital goods (b) Metal based industries

+The coefficients are not significantly different from zero
*Estimates of capacity utilization are drawn from the R.B.I. study.

considered in the analysis. The accelerator may not reveal its full impact under constraints imposed by foreign exchange scarcity on investment.

The accelerator coefficients do not seem to have been affected by under–utilization of capacity in other industries. The average capacity utilization has been around 90 per cent in these industries. Although capacity utilization in jute was high around 90 per cent on the average, the decline over 1965–67 of the order of 12 to 16 per cent points could have affected the results. The sugar industry was also badly affected with a steep decline in capacity utilization from 100 per cent in 1966 to 65 per cent in 1967 and in 1968. This could be another contributory factor for the weak results.

Given the scaling factor $K(t-1)$, the constant term with dummies shows the net effect of capital stock at the beginning of the year on investment which is expected to be negative. The constant term in the regression is significant and negative in cotton textiles, significant and positive in chemicals and engineering. Considering together the coefficient of dummies and the constant term, capital stock at the beginning of the year has a negative impact in every year on investment in cotton textiles and a positive impact in chemicals and engineering. In so far as the allotment of scarce foreign exchange for import of maintenance equipment and raw materials is based on production capacity, it may be profitable for firms to create new capacity even when the existing capacity is not fully utilized. In such cases, the lagged capital stock variable could show a positive effect. However, the effect of lagged capital stock may get confounded with different sales lags as both could represent delayed response of capital stock to the desired levels.

The results establish the importance of financial variables in the investment analysis. The contribution of external finance and retained earnings to the explanation is significant for all the industries except in the case of sugar. Both the flow of external funds and retained earnings show their impact on investment in cotton textiles, jute, chemicals and engineering. The impact of external finance as revealed by its coefficient is larger than retained earnings in cotton textiles and jute, while its impact is smaller in chemicals and engineering. Paper and paper board and cement present a different picture. The results for these two industries indicate the importance of external finance only. In sugar, none of the financial variables is significant. External finance seems to have relatively larger impact than retained earnings on fixed investment.

The analysis suggests substitution between fixed and inventory investment as revealed by a significant negative coefficient of inventory investment in cotton textiles, jute, chemicals and engineering. Paper and paper board shows complementarity between the two components of investment. In cement and sugar, no significant substitution is indicated.

The age of equipment as measured by depreciation reserves indicates either no impact or significant negative impact on investment in all the industries except in the case of cotton textiles. The regression results corroborate well with simple correlation of age with investment except in the case of jute (Table 4.3). In the case of jute, although the simple correlation of age with investment is strongly negative, this is not reflected in the regression results due to high correlation of age variable with other explanatory variables. The results reveal 'senility effect' i.e., negative impact of age on investment in chemicals, engineering and also

TABLE 4.3: Correlation of Age [DR (t–1)/K(t–1)] with other Variables

(Per cent)

Industry	$\frac{I(t)}{K(t-1)}$	$\frac{1}{5}\sum_{r=0}^{4}\frac{\Delta S(t-r)}{K(t-1)}$	$\frac{PNT(t)}{K(t-1)}$	$\frac{RENT(t)}{K(t-1)}$	$\frac{FNDE(t)}{K(t-1)}$
Cotton Textiles	0.2261*	–0.0548**	–0.0017	–0.0227	–0.0544**
Jute	–0.3640*	–0.4182*	–0.2942*	–0.3085*	–0.0890
Sugar	0.0027	0.0579	0.1794*	0.1348*	–0.0478
Paper & Paper board	0.0734	–0.4156*	–0.2290*	–0.3386*	0.2201*
Chemicals	–0.2749*	0.0348	–0.0553	–0.0278	–0.1226**
Engineering	–0.3378*	–0.1181*	–0.1480*	–0.1864*	–0.1731*
Cement	–0.0330	–0.1008	–0.2377*	–0.2608*	–0.2033**

Note: * Significant at 5%

** Significant at 10%

jute. No impact of age on investment is suggested in sugar, paper and paper board and cement. Cotton textiles is the only industry showing 'echo effect' i.e., positive impact of age on investment. The 'echo effect' theories of investment suggest that older the existing stock of capital, larger will be the investment demand due to replacement.

The results, by and large, lend no support to the 'echo' theories of investment. However, it is argued that the true cross–section relationship between age and investment is negative[24]. Firms with aged equipment face a vicious circle of lower efficiency, lower sales, lower profitability, lower internal flow of funds, relative inaccessibility to external funds and hence lower investment compared to firms with newer equipment. Thus, older firms continue to grow old. This tendency applies to firms whether they belong to a growing or a declining industry. The vicious circle could be broken by strong outside forces. It may be observed that a cross–section test of 'echo effect' is only partial. A complete test would require time series verification also.

The correlations of age with sales change, profits, retained earnings and the flow of net debts are, by and large, negative (Table 4.3). Significant negative values dominate in jute, engineering and paper and paper board. Jute and engineering have shown negative impact of age on investment. In chemicals, the correlation of age with other variables is low and non significant. This suggests firms with older equipment do not suffer from low sales, low profits and low retained earnings. The explanation for significant negative impact of age on investment has, therefore, to be sought elsewhere. The sample for chemicals includes companies belonging to pharmaceuticals also which have foreign participation and control. The results may be reflecting partly their conservative investment policies of foreign owned companies.

The absence of the 'echo' effect in most of the industries covered in the analysis could also be ascribed to macro economic factors and to the policies of the Government. Restrictions on imports and controls on investment may contribute to slow modernization of industries which depend on imported capital equipment in industries like chemicals and engineering. The Government pricing policies based on the 'cost plus' formula, which exists in many industries like sugar and cement, yielding an assured rate of return may leave no incentive for modernization because even high cost output can be sold in the face of buoyant markets. On the other hand, there may be Government policies aimed at modernization as in case of priority industries like industrial chemicals and capital goods and as also in export oriented industries like jute. In the ultimate analysis, the final outcome depends on the balance of various forces.

Conclusions

1. The analysis brings out the importance of accelerator in the explanation of fixed investment. However, when there is extreme form of controls inclusive of price and distribution, the results indicate the absence of the effect of accelerator as in the case of sugar and cement.
2. Financial flow variable, internal and external, are found to be siginificant determinants of fixed investment. External finance seems to have relatively larger impact on fixed investment
3. The age of equipment as measured by depreciation reserves has not shown, by and large, the replacement effects on fixed investment.
4. The results point out that fixed investment and inventory investment are competitive.

In brief, the OLS results reveal that accelerator, financial variables and inventory investment are crucial determinants of fixed investment in the Indian private corporate sector.

NOTES

1. A detailed survey of some studies is available in V.R. Panchamukhi, A Survey of Econometric Studies in the Fields of Production, International Trade and Money and Banking," in *A Survey of Indian Econometric Literature*, in, N.S. Iyengar and N. Bhattacharya.
2. K. Krishnamurty, "Private Investment Behaviour in India: A Macro Time Series Study." *Arthaniti*, January, 1964; M.G. Kanbur, *Investment Behaviour in the Fertilizer Industry in India*, University of Birmingham, July 1970 (mimeo); D. Sarkar, "Capital Formation in Indian Industry: An Empirical Application of Investment Theories," *Economic & Political Weekly*, Review of Management, February, 1970; V.V. Divatia & A.G. Athawale, *Corporate Investment Behaviour in India—An Empirical Study*, paper presented to the Indian Econometric Conference, December, 1972, (mimeo); Kenneth, P. Jameson, *Economic Policy and Private Manufacturing Investment in India*, University of Notre, Dame, (unpublished); Dalip, S. Swamy & V.G. Rao, *The Flow of Funds in The Indian Manufacturing Sector*, paper presented to the

Indian Econometric Conference, January, 1974 (mimeo); K.L. Krishna & K. Krishnamurty, "Investment Functions for the Corporate Sector," in Towards *An Econometric Model of the Indian Economy*, Part III, Report submitted to the Indian Council of Social Science Research, February, 1974 (mimeo); T. Rama Rao & D. Anjaneyulu, *An Econometric Model of the Indian cotton Textile Industry*, a study prepared in Department of Statistics, R.B.I. (mimeo); Prabhat Patnaik, *Private Corporate Industrial Investment in India, 1947-67; Factors Affecting its Size, Cyclical Fluctuation and Sectoral Distribution*, unpublished doctoral dissertation, University of Oxford, (undated). This study is basically non-econometric. However, some simple equations have been tried.

3. M.J. Desai. "Macro Econometric Models for India: A Survey", *Sankhya*, Series B, Vol. 35, Part II, 1973.

4. A. K. Bagchi, "Investment by Privately Owned Joint Stock Companies in India," *Arthaniti*, July, 1962; V.K. Sastry, *Dividends, Investment and External Financing Behaviour of the Corporate Sector in India*, unpublished doctoral dissertation, University of Pennsylvania, 1966 ; K. Krishnamurty & D.U. Sastry, "Some Aspects of Corporate Behaviour in India—A Cross–Section Analysis of Investment, Dividends and External Finance for the Chemical Industry, 1962–67," *Indian Economic Review*, October, 1971; D.U. Sastry, *Investment Behaviour in the Indian Capital Goods Industry*, Institute of Economic Growth, Delhi, E 22/73 (mimeo); N.S. Siddharthan, *Investment Behaviour of Conglomerate Firms*, Institute of Economic Growth, Delhi, E/ 39/74,(mimeo).

   The effect of development rebate and other tax concessions on fixed investments has also received some attention recently. *See*, V.V. Somayajulu, *Tax Incentives and Other Determinants of Corporate Investment Behaviour in Indian Industries, 1965–66 through 1970–71—An Economic Analysis*, Paper presented at the Indian Econometric Conference, January, 1975.

5. Samuel Paul & C. Rangarajan, *Short–Term Investment Forecasting*, Macmillan India 1974.

6 For exhaustive surveys of the literature refer: J.R. Meyer & E. Kuh, *The Investment. Decision*, Harvard, 1957; E. Kuh, *Capital Stock Growth: A Micro–Econometric Approach*, North–Holland, 1963; R. Eisner & R. Strotz, "Determinants of Business Investment," in *Impacts of Monetary Policy*, Commission on Money and Credit, Prentice–Hall, 1963; D.W. Jorgenson, "Econometric Studies of Investment Behavior: A Survey, *The Journal of Economic Literature*, December, 1971.

7. In recent years, the neo–classical model of Jorgenson has come into prominence.

8. *See* for instance, D.W. Jorgenson, "The Theory of Investment Behavior," in *Determinants of Investment Behavior*, Ed., R. Ferber, N.B.E.R., 1967; and other works of Jorgenson on investment; R. Eisner and M.I. Nadiri, Investment Behavior in the Neo–classical Theory," *Review of Economics and Statistics*, August, 1968; C.W. Bischoff, "Hypothesis Testing and the Demand for Capital Goods,"*Review of Economics and Statistics*, August,1969; C.W.Bischoff, "The Effect of Alternative Lag Distributions," in *Tax Incentives and Capital Spending*, Ed., Gary Fromm, North–Holland, 1971.

9. L.R. Klein, "What Kind of Econometric Model for Developing Economies,"

The Econometric Annual of the Indian Economic Journal, Vol. XIII, No. 3, 1965–66.

10. J.R. Meyer & E. Kuh, *op. cit.*, p. 68.
11. J.R. Meyer & E. Kuh, *op. cit.*; J.S. Duesenberry, *Business Cycles and Economic Growth*, McGraw–Hill, 1958; E. Kuh, *op. cit.*, pp. 26–44.
12. F. Modigliani & M.H. Miller, "The Cost of Capital, Corporation Finance and the Theory of Investment," *American Economic Review*, June, 1958.
13. E. Kuh, *op. cit.*, p. 24.
14. E. Kuh, *op. cit.*, p. 38.
15. Prabhat Patnaik, *op. cit.*, Chapters 4-6.
16. "Time-lags in the Implementation of Industrial Projects and Return on Investment," and "Time-lags in the Implementation and Return on Investment of Medium Sized Industrial Projects," *R.B.I. Bulletin*, March, 1968 and January, 1969 respectively.
17. There appears to be some suspicion that in the corporate sector funds meant for working capital like bank borrowings are used for creating non–current assets. *See Report of the Study Group on the extent to which Credit Needs of Industry and Trade are likely to be inflated and How Such Trends could be checked*, Chairman; V.T. Deheja, R.B.I., 1969.
18. An exception to this is the case of paper and paper board. New issue which was only 14 per cent of the flow of external sources in the first half of the decade, 1961–71, increased to 54 per cent in the second half. *See*, Chapter 2, Table 2.4.
19. L.C. Gupta, *The Changing Structure of Industrial Finance in India*, Oxford, 1969, p. 25.
20. K. Krishnamurty & D.U. Sastry, *Inventories in Indian Manufacturing*, Institute of Economic Growth, Academic Books Ltd., Bombay, 1970, p. 21.
21. K. Krishnamurty & D.U. Sastry, "Some Aspects of Corporate Behaviour in India—A Cross-section Analysis of Investment, Dividends and External Finance for the Chemical Industry, 1962–67," *Indian Economic Review*, October, 1971.
22. J.R. Meyer & E. Kuh, *op. cit.*, pp. 67–68.
23. The distribution of correlation coefficients between different sales change lags is given in Table 4.1.
24. J.R. Meyer & E. Kuh, *op. cit.*, pp. 93–94.

5

CAPITAL SURROGATES AND PRODUCTION FUNCTION

D.U. SASTRY

Introduction

The Cobb-Douglas and Constant Elasticity Production Functions have been estimated for the period 1949-70. The elasticity of substitution between capital and labour, and elasticity of output with respect to capital and labour have been estimated and comparisons made for Maharashtra, Tamil Nadu and for all India. Although the regional contrast will continue as before, the focus will be on the usefulness of capital surrogates in production analysis.

The complexities of capital measurement, conceptual as well as empirical, have been discussed elsewhere. Broadly, they are heterogeneity, aggregation, vintage, capital consumption and price changes. These get compounded in the Indian context due to lack of data on age distribution of capital assets and appropriate price deflators. The conventional measure of capital would also require correction for capacity utilization. We have seen that the problems of capacity measurement are equally complex if not more than those of capital measurement. These complexities have led scholars to think in terms of surrogates to capital.[1] A number of surrogates have been suggested in the literature such as horsepower rating of electric motors, electricity consumption and machine hours. These have certain inherent advantages over the conventional measure of capital. We shall examine them presently .But before we do that, let us look at the existing studies on production functions.

There have been a number of studies on production functions for the industry.[2] Some are cross-section studies and some are time series studies. Time series studies are somewhat more than cross-section studies. Most of them are based on the CMI and ASI data, some have used company balance-sheet data. All of them, with the exception of the NPC study, use conventional measure of capital. The NPC study uses machine hours in place of capital and a physical measure of output in terms of metres of cloth and kilograms of yarn. These studies are for all-India and none of them examines the regional dimension.

In these studies, the estimates of elasticity of output with respect to capital are generally unsatisfactory. They are either negative or very low and statistically not significant. The estimates of elasticity of output with respect to labour are very high and in most studies about unity and in some more than unity. The elasticity of substitution between capital and labour is either close to unity or not significantly different from unity. Most of the studies generally suggest constant returns to scale. Their results are tabulated in D.U. Sastry (1980).

The unsatisfactory nature of existing results on the elasticity of output with respect to capital provides a strong motivation for further work in this area. Our efforts in this chapter are mainly directed towards this end.

Arguments for Capital Surrogates

Among the capital surrogates we shall consider two alternatives—electricity consumption and a composite measure of total energy consumption. These have certain advantages over the conventional measure of real gross fixed capital. Power consumption being a physical measure problems of price deflation are not present. It is also relatively more homogeneous and hence free from aggregation problem. One could however argue that high voltage power is different from low voltage power, industrial power is different from domestic power, and power used in running electric motors is different from power used in a blast furnace for heat treatment. What is claimed is not absolute homogeneity. It is homogeneous in a relative sense as compared to conventional measure of capital. Power consumption being a flow concept is consistent with other flow variables like output and man-hours which is the appropriate concept needed in production analysis. It takes care of capacity utilization as it relates to actual consumption, and in this respect it is superior to horsepower which is a capacity concept. Quality changes in capital stock get reflected in greater use of power consumption. Modernization and mechanization imply increased capital intensity which in turn may mean greater use of power. However, greater use of power does not necessarily imply more capital intensity. It may be due to old equipment and machinery. But in so far as power consumption is largely related to output, the problem is taken care of. That is to say, power consumption per unit of output is greater for old capital equipment as compared to new equipment.

Despite these advantages, we may not find one to one correspondence between capital used and electricity consumption. In the case of mill industry the elasticity of capital with respect to energy consumption is nearly unity, and with respect to electricity consumption it is about 0.7. Even after adjusting capital for underutilization of capacity these elasticities continue to be high. Experience suggests that power consumption increases much faster than capital stock. This is also borne out by our data for cotton textiles. While electricity consumption increased at the compound rate of about 6 per cent per annum in Maharashtra and 8 per cent per annum in Tamil Nadu over the period 1949-70, capital stock increased at the rate of 3.2 and 4.2 per cent respectively. Furthermore, technical change may often take the form of saving energy rather than using more of it as at present. Economies of scale associated with energy consumption may be more than those associated with capital. If we were to use a single energy input like electricity consumption as a proxy, we might ignore substitution possibilities of one fuel for another. This problem can be solved by considering a composite measure of total energy consumption.

Despite these limitations, it would appear on balance that electricity consumption and total energy consumption are useful surrogates to capital stock. It may be worthwhile to try these surrogates in order to get round some of the problems of capital measurement. To the best of our knowledge, the composite measure of total energy consumption has not been tried so far in production analysis.

Construction of Capital Surrogates

We shall describe here how the two capital surrogates, electricity consumption and the composite measure of total energy consumption, have been constructed. Other variables that enter production function like value added, man-hours and capital have been described in elsewhere.

The basic sources of statistical data used in the construction of capital surrogates are: (1) *Census of Manufacturing Industries and*

Annual Survey of Industries; (2) *Public Electricity Supply Statistics—All India*.

The CMI and ASI volumes present detailed data on fuels consumed industrywise both in value and quantity terms. These data relate to purchased inputs only. In the case of electricity, for instance, there is some self-generation of power within the establishment which is not included in the census data. The data on self-generation of power in the mill industry has been obtained from Annual Reports of the Central Water and Power Commission. Thus, total electricity consumption includes electricity generated within the establishments plus electricity bought from outside minus electricity sold to others. At all-India level for cotton textiles it is possible to construct this series as data on self-generation of electricity are available. However, at the State level we run into difficulties due to lack of data on self-generation. We have tried to estimate this in the following manner. The proportion of self-generation of power in cotton textiles to total self-generation of power in all-industry is known for all-India. We have data on self-generation of power for all-industry at the State-level for the period 1956-70. These State level aggregate of self-generation of power have been split by assuming the same proportion of self-generation of power in cotton textiles to total self-generation of power in all-industry for all-India level. For earlier period 1949-56, no State level aggregate data on self-generation of power are available. We had to rely only on all-India total. We have tried to allocate from this all-India total self-generation of power in cotton textiles to Maharashtra and Tamil Nadu on the basis of percentage distribution of self-generation of power in cotton textiles at the State level. The average of two years, 1956-58, has been used for this purpose. It is apparent that our estimates of self-generation of power in cotton textiles at the State level are much less firm as compared to all-India.

For the construction of composite index of total energy consumption, all fuels for which detailed quantity data are available in the CMI and ASI have been included except for two items—'other fuels' and 'water'. 'Water' is not a fuel item: for 'other fuels' only value data are given which is a negligible proportion in total fuel consumption. Each fuel is expressed in a different unit in the basic source such as coal in tonnes, electricity in kilowatt hours, gas in cubic foot, and so on. These have been converted into a common denominator in terms of coal replacement. The coal conversion coefficients which have been used for this purpose are presented in Table 5.1. For coal gas and lubricating oils no conversion coefficients are available. Therefore, the conversion coefficient of manufactured gas has been used for coal gas. In the case of lubricants, the conversion coefficient of fuel oil has been used as the range of specific gravity is the same between fuel oil and lubricants. Self-generation of power is not included in the construction of composite index of total energy consumption as it is already covered in coal and diesel oil consumption.

TABLE 5.1: Fuel Composition and Conversion Factors in the Cotton Mill Industry

Fuel components	Conversion factors in terms of coal replacement	
	Million tonnes	Million tonnes of coal replacement
1. Coal	1.0	1.00
2. Coke	1.0	1.50
3. Coal gas	1 cub. mtr of mfd. gas	0.00083 tonnes
4. Fire wood	1.0	0.95
5. Charcoal	1.0	1.00
6. Fuel oils	1.0	2.00
7. Electricity	10^9KWH	1.00
8. Motor spirit	1.0	7.50
9. Diesel oil	1.0	9.01
10. High speed diesel oil	1.0	9.00
11. Light diesel oil	1.0	9.00
12. Furnace oil	1.0	2.01
13. Kerosene oil	1.0	8.31
14. Liquified petroleum	1.0	8.31
15. Natural gas	$10^9 m^3$	3.60
16. Lubricating oil	1.0	2.01

Source : (1) Petroleum Information Service, *A Glossary of Terms and Conversion Factors used in the Petroleum Industry*, 1961.
(2) U.N., *World Energy Supplies*, 1970-73, 1975.
(3) P.D. Henderson, *India : The Energy Sector*, World Bank, 1975.

Note : (1) No conversion coefficient was available for coal gas. The coefficient of manufactured gas has been used in its place.
(2) For lubricating oils the coefficient of fuel oil was used because the range of specific gravity between the two is roughly the same. Fuel oil : 0.920-0.990. Lubricating oil : 0.850-0.950.

Approach of Production Function

The production function approach typically involves the estimation of parameters by regression techniques. Production function is essentially an engineering concept and defines underlying technology. It gives maximum output obtainable for a given combination of inputs. At least three aspects of production function are of interest to the economist: elasticity of substitution between capital and labour, returns to scale and marginal products of factors.

Among the family of production functions, the most famous is the Cobb-Douglas:

$$V = AL^{\alpha} \; K^{\beta} \tag{1}$$

Where V, L and K are output, labour and capital respectively. A is efficiency parameter, α and β are elasticities of output with respect to labour and capital, and their sum determines the degree of homogeneity of the function. Other properties are : (1) marginal products are positive and (2) they decline if $0 < \sigma, \beta < 1$.

The most restrictive assumption of the Cobb-Douglas production is that of unitary elasticity of substitution. This assumption is relaxed in the Constant Elasticity Production Function, CES for short. The CES function is :

$$V = \gamma \left(\delta L^{\rho} + (1-\delta) K^{\rho}\right)^{-\upsilon/\rho} \tag{2}$$

Where V, L, K are as defined before. The four parameters of the function are :

γ = efficiency parameter
δ = capital intensity parameter defined in the interval $0 \leqslant \delta \leqslant 1$
υ = degree of homogeneity of the function
$\sigma = \dfrac{1}{1+\rho}$ elasticity of substitution between labour and capital with limits, $\partial \geqslant 0$ or $\rho \geqslant -1$.

The function satisfies properties of the neo-classical production function described earlier. The CES is a more general function in that it reduces to Cobb-Douglas if $\sigma = 1$, reduces to Leontief production function, if $\sigma = 0$, and for $\sigma = \infty$ it becomes linear production function underlying the Kendrick Index. One of the most important properties of the CES function is that elasticity of substitution is independent of the capital labour ratio[3].

The CES function is intrinsically non-linear. Alternative methods of estimation exist .But the most extensively used is the Arrow, Chenery, Minhas and Solow (1961) method (ACMS). We shall use this method to estimate elasticity of substitution.

Elasticity of Substitution

The estimation of elasticity of substitution between capital and labour is based on a side relation of the marginal productivity condition for labour.[4] Simplicity and direct estimation are its merits. Capital data are not required. Alternative forms are not tried, as our objective is modest in the sense that we are primarily interested in the substitution parameter. The Ordinary Least Squares method of estimation is used. The specification of the function is as follows :

$$\log (V/M) = \alpha + \sigma \log W + e \tag{3}$$

Where,

(V/M) = output per man-hour

W = real wage rate per man-hour

σ = elasticity of substitution

e = error term

The equation assumes constant returns to scale and perfect competition, which are hard to sustain. The assumption of constant returns to scale can be relaxed by the inclusion of *log M* (man-hours) in the above equation . If the coefficient of *log M* is zero, the equation reduces to the case of constant returns to scale. A time trend is also included to capture technical progress.[5] The results for all-India, Maharashtra and Tamil Nadu are presented for the period 1949-70 in Table 5.2. Equations 1 and 2 assume constant returns, while equation 3 allows for non-constant returns to scale. It can be seen from the table that non-constant returns to scale formulation is not borne out by the data. The coefficient of *log M* is not significant. It has perverse sign in Maharashtra.

The introduction of time trend in the equation has altered the sign, magnitude and statistical significance of the coefficient of elasticity of substitution in all-India and Maharashtra. The coefficient has become negative and non-significant in Maharashtra. In all-India, its magnitude has considerably reduced and has also become non-significant. The coefficient of time trend is positive and significant in

TABLE 5.2: Estimates of Elasticity of Substitution for the Cotton Mill Industry, 1949-70

CES Function : ACMS Method					Dependent Variable : *(Log V/M)*		
		Constant	*Log W*	*Log M*	*T*	R^2	*DW*
All India							
	1.	0.21*	1.22*			0.42	1.07††
		(5.15)	(4.04)				
	2.	0.03	0.34		0.01*	0.64	1.41††
		(0.52)	(0.01)		(3.65)		
	3.	-1.25	0.85	0.33		0.42	1.05††
		(0.82)	(1.73)	(0.96)			
Maharashtra							
	1	0.17*	0.96*			0.26	0.86†††
		(5.65)	(2.91)				
	2	–0.005	-0.09		0.01*	0.60	1.32††
		(0.11)	(0.26)		(4.23)		
	3	1.46	1.07**	–0.32		0.24	0.91†††
		(0.70)	(2.81)	(0.62)			
Tamil Nadu							
	1	0.27*	1.06*			0.85	2.39†
		(13.78)	(11.06)				
	2	0.21*	0.91*		0.002	0.85	2.37†
		(4.07)	(5.49)		(1.09)		
	3	0.06	1.05*	0.06		0.84	2.32†
		(0.07)	(9.58)	(0.23)			

(V/M) = Real value added per man-hour.
W = Real wage rate per man-hour.
M = Man-hours.
* = Significant at 1% level.
** = Significant at 5% level.
††† = Serial correlation.
†† = Serial correlation inconclusive.
† = No serial correlation.
T = Time trend.

all-India and Maharashtra, and in Tamil Nadu it is positive but not significant. The results suggest technical progress at the rate of about 1 per cent per annum in all-India and a little more than 0.5 per cent per annum in Maharashtra and about 2 per cent per annum in Tamil Nadu. These results are in broad agreement with the results of the Domar Index of total factor productivity.

Our choice is obviously for equation 1 for all-India as well as for Maharashtra and Tamil Nadu. The fit as revealed by R^2 corrected for degrees of freedom is very good for Tamil Nadu, reasonable for all-India and somewhat poor for Maharashtra. No evidence of serial correlation is observed for Tamil Nadu, the test is inconclusive for all India but serial correlation seems to be present in the case of Maharashtra. The coefficient of *log W* is significant at 1 per cent level and has the right sign. The estimates of elasticity of substitution between capital and labour are 1.21 for all-India 0.96 for Maharashtra and 1.06 for Tamil-Nadu. These estimates are not statistically different from unity as revealed by *t* test. The substantive conclusion that emerges from our analysis is that there is no evidence to reject the hypothesis of unitary elasticity of substitution. Thus, factor prices are important in influencing factor proportions. Some corroborative evidence exists to confirm out finding.[6]

Cobb-Douglas Estimates

Our finding that the elasticity of substitution between capital and labour is unity provides some justification for using Cobb-Douglas production function as the maintained hypothesis. Three different formulations of Cobb-Douglas production function have been tried. (1) In the first, output, capital and labour variables enter in levels. (2) In the second, variables enter in terms of per establishment. Since the number of establishments has been changing from year to year, homoscedasticity assumption of error variance is violated. The variance of the error term will be $\sigma \sqrt{n}$. This is corrected by dividing the equation by $\sqrt{n}$. (3) In the third, which may be called the ratio form, variables enter in intensive magnitudes. No meaningful results could be obtained in the first two formulations. In the first, high correlations are found between labour and capital or its proxies of the order of .9 for all-India, and about .6 for Maharashtra and Tamil Nadu. In the per establishment formulation capital coefficients turn out to be zero and labour coefficients are too high. By a process of experimentation and elimination, we settle to the ratio form .[7]

The specification of the basic ratio form is the following :

$$log\ (V/M) = \alpha + \beta \log (K/M) + \epsilon \quad (4)$$
$$log\ (V/M) = \alpha + \beta \log (TECR/M) + e \quad (5)$$
$$log\ (V/M) = \alpha + \beta \log (EP/M) + u \quad (6)$$

Where,

(V/M) = Output per man-hour
(K/M) = Capital per man-hour
(TECR/M) = Total energy consumption in terms of coal replacement
(EP/M) = electricity consumption per man-hour
ϵ, *e* and *u* = error terms

The essential difference in these equations is in the use of alternative capital measure. Time trend is also tried in order to capture technical progress. This formulation assumes constant returns to scale. To allow for non-constant returns to scale *log M* is added to the above equations. In all, there are three sets, each set contains three equations. Each set is different in terms of its use of capital measure. In each set the first two equations assume constant returns to scale, while the third relaxes this assumption. The equations are estimated by the method of Ordinary Least Squares for the period 1949-70 separately for all-India, Maharashtra and Tamil Nadu. The results are presented in Tables 5.3 to 5.5

TABLE 5.3: All-India : Estimates of Cobb-Douglas Production Function for the Cotton Mill Industry, 1949-70

Dependent Variable : *Log (V/M)*

Constant	*Log (K/M)*	*Log (TECR/M)*	*Log (EP/M)*	*Log M*	*T*	$\bar{R}^2$	*DW*
1. −0.33*	0.60*					0.64	1.43††
(5.40)	(6.25)						
2. −0.19	0.32				0.003	0.65	1.42†
(1.35)	(1.16)				(1.07)		
3. −1.26	0.52*			0.23		0.65	1.42††
(1.44)	(4.15)			(1.06)			
4. −1.24*		0.56*				0.70	1.79†
(6.82)		(7.09)					

TABLE 5.3 *(Contd.)*

Constant	*Log (K/M)*	*Log (TECR/M)*	*Log (EP/M)*	*Log M*	*T*	$\bar{R}^2$	*DW*
5. –2.15**		0.98**			–0.005	0.70	2.16†
(2.26)		(2.22)			(0.97)		
6. –0.49		0.65*		–0.23		0.70	1.94†
(0.55)		(4.82)		(0.87)			
7. 0.03*			0.33*			0.67	1.26††
(4.71)			(6.53)				
8. 0.12			0.80		–0.01	0.66	1.16††
(1.18)			(1.47)		(0.86)		
9. 2.32			0.48*	–0.53		0.69	1.41††
(1.69)			(4.75)	(1.67)			

(V/M) = Real value added per man-hour.
(K/M) = Real fixed capital per man-hour
(TECR/M) = Total energy consumption per man-hour.
(EP/M) = Electricity consumption per man-hour.
M = Man-hours.
T = Time trend
* = Significant at 1% level.
** = Significant at 5% level.
† = No serial correlation.
†† = Serial correlation inconclusive.

TABLE 5.4: Maharashtra : Estimates of Cobb-Douglas Production Function for the Cotton Mill Industry, 1949-70

Dependent Variable : *Log (V/M)*

Constant	*Log (K/M)*	*Log (TECR/M)*	*Log (EP/M)*	*Log M*	*T*	$\bar{R}^2$	*DW*
1. –0.27*	0.57*					0.70	1.66†
(5.32)	(7.07)						
2. –0.29**	0.61**				–0.001	0.68	1.68†
(2.22)	(2.28)				(0.16)		
3. –0.72	0.56*			0.11		0.69	1.62†
(0.62)	(6.80)			(0.39)			
4. –1.07*		0.49*				0.66	1.74†

TABLE 5.4 *(Contd.)*

Constant	*Log (K/M)*	*Log (TECR/M)*	*Log (EP/M)*	*Log M*	*T*	$\bar{R}^2$	*DW*
(5.99)		(6.48)					
5. –1.12		0.51			–0.0004	0.64	1.76†
(1.53)		(1.54)			(0.08)		
6. 0.72		0.53*		–0.47		0.68	2.03†
(0.59)		(6.70)		(1.48)			
7. 0.36*			0.29*			0.59	1.18††
(7.30)			(5.64)				
8. –0.43			–0.36		–0.02	0.61	1.49††
(0.73)			(0.74)		(1.34)		
9. 2.48			0.32*	–0.51		0.62	1.34††
(1.70)			(5.85)	(1.45)			

Note : Variables and signs are as defined in Table 5.3.

TABLE 5.5: Tamil Nadu : Estimates of Cobb-Douglas Production Function for the Cotton Mill Industry, 1949-70

Dependent Variable : *Log (V/M)*

Constant	*Log (K/M)*	*Log (TECR/M)*	*Log (EP/M)*	*Log M*	*T*	$\bar{R}^2$	*DW*
1. –0.44*	0.72*					0.62	1.22††
(5.05)	(5.90)						
2. –0.18	0.22				0.01	0.63	1.10††
(0.78)	(0.51)				(1.26)		
3. –1.91	0.67*			0.44		0.62	1.11††
(1.50)	(5.15)			(1.15)			
4. –1.07*		0.53*				0.68	0.90†††
(6.31)		(6.73)					
5. –0.79		0.38			0.003	0.67	0.96†††
(1.79)		(1.65)			(0.68)		
6. –1.84		0.50*		0.24		0.67	0.90†††
(1.53)		(5.73)		(0.65)			
7. 0.45*			0.39*			0.77	1.17††
(9.86)			(8.51)				

TABLE 5.5 *(Contd.)*

	Constant	*Log (K/M)*	*Log (TECR/M)*	*Log (EP/M)*	*Log M*	*T*	$\bar{R}^2$	*DW*
8.	0.93*			0.75*		–0.01	0.80	1.55††
	(3.94)			(4.21)		(2.06)		
9.	0.34			0.39*	0.03		0.76	1.17††
	(0.30)			(7.27)	(0.09)			

††† = Serial correlation.

Note : Other variables and signs are as defined in Table 5.3.

TABLE 5.6: Elasticity of Output with respect to Capital in the Cotton Mill Industry, 1949–70

		Elasticity	$\bar{R}^2$
All–India			
	Log (K/M)	0.60	0.64
	Log (TECR/M)	0.56	0.70
	Log (EP/M)	0.33	0.67
	Share of non-wage income	0.44	
Maharashtra			
	Log (K/M)	0.57	0.70
	Log (TECR/M)	0.49	0.66
	Log (EP/M)	0.29	0.59
	Share of non-wage income	0.32	
Tamil Nadu			
	Log (K/M)	0.72	0.62
	Log (TECR/M)	0.53	0.68
	Log (EP/M)	0.39	0.77
	Share of non-wage income	0.45	

Note: All coefficients are significant at 1 per cent level. Share of non-wage income is the average of 1949-70.

An examination of the results reveals that non-constant returns to scale formulation of the Cobb-Douglas production function is not supported by the data as the coefficient of *log M* is not significant in any equation for all-India as well as for Maharashtra and Tamil Nadu. The influence of time trend is also not observed. These reasons dictated our choice in favour of equation 1 in all sets and for all regions. The results based on equation 1 are tabulated in Table 5.3. The elasticity of output with respect to capital is given by β coefficient and 1– β gives the implied elasticity of output with respect to labour. The relative share of non-wage income is also presented for purposes of comparison.

It is evident from the table that the fit, as given by R^2 corrected for degrees of freedom, is generally good in all equations. All capital coefficients including those of capital surrogates are highly significant at 1 per cent level. All of them are positive and fall in the range of plausible magnitude. Serial correlation is by and large absent. In short, the results are generally good.

The magnitude of capital coefficients vary according to capital measure. The lack of proportionality between capital and its surrogates could lead to such differences. When capital is defined in the conventional sense of real gross fixed capital, the estimates are somewhat higher than those of capital surrogates. It may be noted that capital is not adjusted for possible underutilization of capacity, whereas this is automatically taken care of in capital surrogates. As between the two capital surrogates, the elasticity of output with respect to electric power consumption is somewhat lower as compared to the elasticity of output with respect to total energy consumption for all-India as well as for the two regions. Total energy consumption is a larger aggregate consisting of all fuels including electricity used in the production process, which may possibly account for differences in magnitudes between the two surrogates.

We may compare capital coefficients with the relative share of capital in value added. Under conditions of competitive equilibrium, the two will be the same. However, the results indicate divergence between the two. Market imperfections may exist specially in labour and credit markets. Such imperfections may cause divergence between capital coefficients and the relative share of capital in value added.

If we look at the regional level, we will find that Tamil Nadu capital coefficients are generally higher as compared to Maharashtra capital coefficients. The nature of industry being different, Tamil Nadu with heavy concentration of spinning and Maharashtra with heavy concentration of both weaving and spinning, production function may be different for the two regions. It may be recalled that Tamil Nadu capital stock is of recent vintage as compared to Maharashtra's which is relatively old. The implied labour coefficients are also higher for

Maharashtra. These results seem to tally with higher wage rate and higher wage share in value added in Maharashtra as compared to Tamil Nadu.

In order to capture technical progress, a time trend variable is included in the equations. The inclusion of time trend has robbed the significance of capital coefficients in most of the equations. Further, time trend coefficient has turned out to be negative, especially in equations with capital surrogates. However, in other equations with capital stock time trend coefficients is positive but not statistically significant in all-India and Tamil Nadu. These results seem to suggest a rate of technical progress of 0.3 per cent per year in all-India and 1 per cent per year in Tamil Nadu. A comparison of these results with those obtained earlier from the CES production function indicates broad agreement in terms of direction and ordering for all-India and Tamil Nadu. These results are also in general agreement with the growth of total factor productivity as revealed by Domar Index.

Between the two capital surrogates, our preference is obviously for total energy consumption in terms of coal replacement. Both theoretical and statistical consideration have guided our choice. First, total energy consumption is a composite measure consisting of all fuels used in the production process. This inclusiveness makes it conceptually a more meaningful capital surrogate. Second, the elasticity of capital stock with respect to total energy consumption is closer to unity (0.95) as compared to the elasticity of capital stock with respect to electricity consumption (0.73). Third, the magnitudes of total energy consumption as capital surrogate are in the range of 0.49 to 0.56 which appear to be quite plausible. Finally, equations with total energy consumption have higher total explanation and no serial correlation as compared to equations with electricity consumption in all-India and Maharashtra. Thus, it would appear both from conceptual and statistical considerations that total energy consumption in terms of coal replacement is a more meaningful surrogate to capital in production analysis.

Conclusions

The estimates of elasticity of substitution between capital and labour are 1.22 for all-India, 0.95 for Maharashtra and 1.05 for Tamil Nadu which are not statistically different from unity. Thus, there is no evidence to reject the hypothesis of unitary elasticity of substitution in the mill industry.

The above finding provides some justification for estimating the Cobb-Douglas production function. The ratio form of the Cobb-Douglas production function gives the best results. Three alternative variants of capital measure have been used in this formulation. One is the conventional measure of capital defined as real gross fixed capital. The other two are surrogates to capital, namely, electricity consumption and total energy consumption in terms of coal replacement. The results indicate that the elasticity of output with respect to capital is positive and statistically significant in all-India as well as in Maharashtra and Tamil Nadu. This result is invariant to the capital measure.

Estimates of elasticity output with respect to capital vary according to capital measure. Elasticity of output with respect to capital is somewhat higher as compared to elasticity of output with respect to capital surrogates. As between capital surrogates, elasticity of output with respect to total energy consumption is somewhat higher as compared to elasticity of output with respect to electricity consumption.

Estimates of elasticity of output with respect to capital are different for Tamil Nadu and Maharashtra. They are higher for Tamil Nadu as compared to Maharashtra irrespective of capital measure because the Tamil Nadu industry is comparatively new and its capital stock is of more recent vintage. This would mean production functions are different for Tamil Nadu and Maharashtra. In fact, the product mix of Tamil Nadu is heavily weighted in favour of yarn whereas cloth has a dominant weight in Maharashtra.

The implied elasticity of output with respect to labour is high in Maharashtra as compared to Tamil Nadu. It could be due to difference in the quality of labour. The higher wage rate and higher wage share in Maharashtra is consistent with higher elasticity of output with respect to labour. Given the differences in product mix between the two regions, it would appear that efficiency of labour is higher in Maharashtra whereas efficiency of capital is higher in Tamil Nadu.

Our analysis leads to the conclusion that capital surrogates such as electricity consumption and total energy consumption have definite advantages as they help in overcoming some of the difficult problems of capital measurement. As between the two capital surrogates our analysis suggests obvious preference to total energy consumption. Estimates of elasticity of output with total energy consumption appear to be in the plausible range. Elasticity of capital with respect to total energy consumption is closer to unity. Equations with total energy consumption generally show higher total explanation and no serial correlation. Total energy consumption is a comprehensive measure including all fuels and hence conceptually more satisfying. Thus, it would appear from conceptual and statistical points of view that the composite measure of total energy consumption seems to be a more meaningful surrogate to capital in production analysis.

NOTES

1. Maddala (1965), Jorgenson and Griliches (1967), Taylor (1967), Heathfield (1972), Mody (1974), Dhar and Sastry (1969).
2. Murti and Sastri (1957), Sankar (1970), Rama Rao and Anjaneyulu (undated), Venkataswamy (1975), Banerji (1975), National Productivity Council (1976), Umar Kazi (1978).
3. Murray Brown (1966).
4. Elasticity of substitution is sensitive to specification, method of estimation, data and time period. It has been generally found that time series estimates are lower than unity, while cross-section estimates are higher and close to unity, Nerlove (1967).
5. The coefficient of time trend does not give a direct estimate of technical progress in the CES function. It is obtained by the coefficient of time trend divided by $1-\sigma$ where σ is elasticity of substitution.
6. Banerji (1975), Venkataswami (1975), Umar Kazi (1978), All estimates for Indian cotton textiles reject the hypothesis of zero elasticity of substitution. Some estimates are in the neighbourhood of 0.8.
7. Griliches has extensively used this form in estimating production functions. Griliches and Ringstad (1971).

REFERENCES

Arrow, K.J., H.B. Chenery, B.S. Minhas and R.M. Solow, 'Capital Labour Substitution and Economic Efficiency,' *Review of Economics and Statistics*, August 1961.

Banerji, Asit, *Capital Intensity and Productivity in Indian Industry*, Macmillan, India, 1975.

Brown, Murray, *On the Theory and Measurement of Technological Change*, Cambridge, UK 1966.

Dhar, P.N. and D.U. Sastry, 'Inter-State Variations in Indian Industry,' *Economic and Political Weekly*, 22 March 1969.

Griliches, Z. and V. Ringstad, *Economies of Scale and the Form of the Production Function*, North Holland, 1971.

Heathfield, D.F., 'The Measurement of Capital Usage Using Electricity Consumption Data for the U.K.', *Journal of the Royal Statistical Society*, 135, 1972.

Henderson, P.D., *India : The Energy Sector*, World Bank 1975.

Jorgenson, D.W. and Z. Griliches, 'The Explanation of Productivity Change', *The Review of Economic Studies*, July 1967.

Kazi, Umar, 'Productivity Functions with a Variable Elasticity of Substitution: Analysis and Some Empirical Results', *Artha Vijnana*, June 1978.

Maddala, G.S., 'Productivity and Technical Change in the Bituminous Coal Industry 1919-54', *The Journal of Political Econonry*, August 1965.

Moody, Carlisle E. Jr., 'The Measurement of Capital Services by Electrical Energy', *Oxford Bulletin of Economics and Statistics*, February 1974.

Murti, V.N. and V.K. Sastry, 'Production Functions for Indian Industry', *Econometrica*, April 1957.

National Productivity Council, *Productivity Trends in Cotton Textile Industry in India*, Delhi 1976.

Nerlove, Marc, Recent Empirical Studies of the CES and Related Production Functions' in Murry Brown (ed), *The Theory and Empirical Analysis of Production*, NBER, 1967.

Petroleum Information Service, *A Glossary of Terms and Conversion Factors Used in the Petroleum Industry*, India 1961.

Rama Rao, T. and D. Anjaneyulu, *An Econometric Model of the Indian Cotton Textile Industry*, undated (mimeo).

Sankar, U., 'Elasticity of Substitution and Returns of Scale in Indian Manufacturing Industries,' *International Economic Review*, October 1970.

Sastry, D.U., *Productivity in the Indian Cotton Mill Industry*, Institute of Economic Growth, Delhi, February 1981 (mimeo).

Taylor, J., 'A Surrogate for Regional Estimates of Capital Stock', Bulletin of the *Oxford Institute of Economics and Statistics*, August 1967.

United Nations, *World Energy Supplies*, 1970-73, 1975.

Venkataswami, Thurai, 'Production Functions and Technical Change in Indian Manufacturing Industries', *Indian Journal of Economics*, April 1975.

6

THEORIES OF AGRICULTURAL DEVELOPMENT: Trends and Perspectives

S.K. THORAT

I

Theory is, in the ultimate analysis, a logical file of our factual knowledge pertaining to a certain phenomenological domain, and to each theory, therefore, must correspond a specific domain of reality. A theory of agricultural development is only a part of a more general theory of economic development. But it would be erroneous to conclude that this implies that the domain of reality that corresponds to a theory of agricultural development can be really cut off from the rest of economic activity. On the contrary, from a purist point of view, the phenomenological domain that corresponds to a theory of agricultural development is the whole gamut of economic activity, not agricultural activity alone. But then these are too extreme positions that can produce no good results. For a theory that attempts to grapple with as diverse and as varying a phenomenon as agricultural activity must of necessity face insuperable problems of generalizations.The only way out is to strike a balance between extreme particularism and generalization, for, whereas only strong assumptions can give rise to strong theorems, sweeping generalizations can only produce prescriptions that are operationally sterile. Ultimately it is the kind of policy implications that one wants to derive from theory which determines the extent of generalization and delimits the domain of reality that seems relevant. But some degree of ambiguity seems unavoidable.

"Since any sector is part of an interdependent system represented by the country's economy what a sector does is not fully attributable to it but is contingent upon what happens in the other sectors".[1]

Considerations such as these suggest that a meaningful economic theory of agricultural development must incorporate the following interrelated parts :

(a) an analysis of the role of agriculture in economic development,
(b) an analysis of the economic nature of traditional agriculture, and
(c) an analysis of the economic process of modernization of agriculture.

Since our task is to attempt a systematic analysis and criticism of the various theories of agricultural development it seems useful to classify the various contributions to theory in the following manner:

1. Dual economy models that are predominantly concerned with the process of transfer of rural surplus labour to the urban industrial sector and the consequent "commercialization" of agriculture. In this category we shall examine the contributions of Arthur Lewis and its later refinements by Ranis and Fei, and D.W. Jorgenson.
2. Growth stage theories that emphasize agriculture. Here we shall concern ourselves with Mellor's contributions.
3. Agriculture-in-itself theories. These theories somewhat abstract from the role of agriculture in the total development process and concentrate on understanding agricultural development in itself. Professor Schultz's contribution and its extension by Y. Hayami and V.W. Ruttan have been included in this category.

Admittedly, to call these theories as above is somewhat misleading if not erroneous. However, even at that risk we shall stick to that name if only to stress the shifts of emphasis that are implied in these theories.

II

The classical paradigm of economic development envisages it as a process of transforming a predominantly agricultural economy to one containing a large and growing industrial economy, to one containing a large and growing industrial sector. Once we adopt this perspective the intersectoral relationships in a dual economy assume a crucial importance. The several points of interaction between the agricultural and the industrial sector[2] are briefly mentioned below:

(a) a substantial amount of labour force from the agricultural sector is transferred to the industrial sector;
(b) the creation of non-farm jobs in the urban sector requires capital, and agriculture being the dominant sector "is in historical evidence and in economic logic an important source of such capital";[3]
(c) the agricultural sector is a potential market for the industrial output of consumer goods;
(d) transformation of traditional agriculture depends to a large extent on the introduction of high-pay-off inputs which must of necessity be produced in the industrial sector.

The dual economy models concentrate on the first two of the above interactions. Thus, the shift of the labour force and the attendant problems of sectoral terms of trade that threaten to arrest the process of capital formation are their major concern. Increasing agricultural productivity is let into the discussion only in so far as it affects the process mentioned above.

Lewis analyzes the process of economic expansion in a dual economy composed of a "capitalist" sector and a "subsistence" sector. The former is defined as that part of the economy which uses reproducible capital, pays capitals for the use thereof, and employs wage labour for profit-making purposes. The subsistence sector does not produce reproducible capital. Here output per head is much lower than in the capitalist sector. Given the available techniques, the marginal productivity of labour (MP_L) is zero as a limiting case, constituting a case of disguised unemployment. However, as a result of institutional arrangements such as family farms, members of the farm labour force consume essentially the average product of the farm's output even though the marginal productivity of some of the farm labourers may be well below the average product. A fundamental relationship between the two sectors is that when the capitalist sector expands it draws labour from the subsistence sector. It is assumed that the supply of unskilled labour is "unlimited" in the sense that when the capitalist sector offers additional employment opportunities at the existing wage rate the numbers willing to work at that wage will be greater than the demand. A large component of this "unlimited" supply is of course composed of the disguisedly unemployed in the subsistence sector.

The wage in the capitalist sector is determined in Lewis's model by what labour earns in the other sector. In the capitalist sector labour is employed up to the point where MP_L=W. The driving force in the system is generated by the reinvestment on the capitalist surplus in creating new capital. As the capitalist sector expands absorbing more and more labour from the subsistence sector into wage employment the capitalist surplus becomes ever larger; still more profits are reinvested and the process continues until the absorption of surplus labour is complete. Capital accumulation has then caught up with the excess supply of labour. Beyond this turning point real wages no longer remain constant but rise with increasing capital formation so that the share of profits in the national income will not necessarily rise and so will not investment. We need not be skeptical about Lewis's reliance on the concept of disguised unemployment because its existence is not strictly necessary for the expansionary process that Lewis describes. All that is required is that labour productivity be relatively low in the subsistence sector and that the supply of labour to the capitalist sector be greater than the demand for labour. However, skilled labour is never in "unlimited" supply. Lewis recognizes this problem but discounts its importance by considering it to be only a temporary bottleneck. A more serious limitation of Lewis's model is that it simply takes for granted the demand side of the investment process. First, he assumes the prior existence of a capitalist class, and secondly, it is assumed that whatever the capitalist sector produces it can sell. Despite these limitations the model retains high analytical value for its insights into the role of capital accumulation in the development process.

Renis and Fei subject the whole process of transfer of labour to closer scrutiny, skill within Lewis's framework, adding a bit of rigour and a shift of emphasis to the analysis of the role of the neglected agricultural sector.

The process of development is divided into three stages. In the first stage the redundant (MP_L=0) labour force is transferred with no fall in farm output or rise in industrial wages. In the next stage, when labour with marginal productivity positive but less than farm wages is shifted out, farm output falls causing the terms of trade to alter in favour of the subsistence sector and consequently nominal wages in the industrial sector rise. A point is soon reached when marginal productivity in the subsistence sector equals the wage rate. This ends the take-off stage of the economy and self-sustained growth begins. "The industrial supply curve of labour finally rises as we enter a world in which the agricultural sector is no longer dominated by non-market institutional forces but assumes the characteristics of a commercialised capitalistic system."[4] Increasing productivity in the subsistence sector is then introduced into the analysis in the form of innovations which are neutral in the Hicksian sense, i.e. they raise the MP_L curve everywhere by the same constant multiple. Thus, they are able to show the difficult take-off stage. This is due to the fact that for each amount of labour allocated to the industrial sector the average surplus per migrant increases with the increase in total physical productivity, the total amount of food consumed by the agricultural labour remaining unchanged.The increase in the average surplus will depress the terms of trade for the agricultural sector and will cause the industrial wage (in terms of industrial goods) to fall. As Oshima[5] points out, the tilt in the terms of trade against the agricultural sector could be avoided if the model included foreign trade. Then, industrial goods could be exchanged for agricultural goods produced in a foreign country. The suggested technological change the type of shift in the MP_L curve seems unrealistic in the case of the bio-chemical technologies. Such technologies will require additional labour as it necessitates more fertilizer, more weeding, etc. This implies that "the flat portion of the new productivity curves will disappear, and there is not likely to be proportional shifts in other parts of the new curve.[6] Finally, the assumption that with the rise in farm productivity farm wages in the first two phases remain constant is hard to defend in view of the fact that the tax structure in most of developing countries is incapable of taxing away even a small part of the increases.

One major concern for Ranis and Fei was perhaps to analyze the dynamics of the take-off stage. More specifically, they have concentrated on the effects of a rise in productivity in the agricultural sector on the length of the take-off stage. But productivity rise in a catch-all term that summarizes various changes. Thus, productivity can rise among other reasons due to improvements in techniques or fall in the man-land ratio. It follows that the same problem can be studied as a race between technology and population growth. D.W. Jorgenson seems to have this perspective in mind.[7] Population growth is endogenous to his system, its rate being a linear function of agricultural output per man up to some physiological maxima. Technical progress is assumed to be taking place in both sectors. The entire agricultural surplus is being made available to the nascent industrial sector while agricultural consumption is being maintained at a certain level. Given this, the economy achieves balanced growth with capital and output growing at the same rate and with the real wage raising at a rate equal to the increase in output per man. However, what makes the model particularly sterile for economic policy making is the fact that the crucial shift factor in the Cobb-Douglas production function is exogenous.[8] Thus, technical progress is separated from the rate of investment ; " in the agricultural sector we are asked to conceive of constant rate of technological change which somehow can be influenced by social policy and yet is totally devoid of embodiment in capital formation".[9]

In sum, the analysis in dual economy models reveals that the process of economic transformation is signalled by a change in the terms of the trade in favour of agriculture. As labour is drawn out of agriculture, output of this sector falls, and in the absence of a technological change in agriculture, food prices rise. This twist in the terms of trade redistributes income to a sector which saves little. This and other deleterious effects can be avoided only by taxing agricultural income and using the proceeds to develop the industrial sector or by an increase in the productivity of the agricultural sector.

III

In J.W. Mellor's scheme the continuum of development is broken up into three specific phases:

Phase I : Providing for agricultural development precondition.

Phase II : Rising agricultural production—low capital, labour intensive technology

Phase III : Rising agricultural production—high capital, labour saving technology.

The motive is to study the changes in the level and technique of production of agricultural commodities. The basis of this linear conception of phases is formed by marked differences in the key factors influencing output; "differences (which) sharply limit the extent to which observation in one phase can be generalized to another and require that development policies be modified as an agricultural economy makes the transition from one phase to another".[10] All this is well taken but to maintain that "for contemporary low-income countries the optimal path for growth will normally involve taking these phases roughly in the form and order suggested here",[11] seems to overschematize the complex force of development and to give the sequence of phases a generality that is unwarranted. However, Mellor's pattern is suggestive and useful in isolating the strategic factors which make for change. We do get an analytical, and not merely a descriptive set of phases.

The factors that influence output are divided into the two categories of : (a) traditional inputs, and (b) new production processes resulting from new technology that alters input-output relationships. The level of use of inputs is a function of : (a) the total stock available, and (b) the percentage utilization of the stock. Development of new production processes is viewed as a consequence of the introduction and increased application of unconventional inputs. He has in mind research, training, and other institutions as the new categories of inputs.

In phase I output changes are traceable to changes in the quantity of traditional inputs within the confines of the traditional production process. Despite the significant stock of idle rural labour, MP_L is positive and close to the wage rate. This somewhat startling anomaly is explained by a "substantial discontinuity in the schedule of marginal utility of income.[12] Thus, beyond subsistence income a substantially higher return is required to stimulate them to work. He also assumes that in most areas of the world rural wage levels are above the subsistence level. Given these, and some other plausible assumptions, it follows that population growth can be matched by a nearly proportional increase in agricultural production. Increased capital input in the form of large-scale irrigation, land reclamation, and inorganic fertilizers do not have a significant impact on output because of their low marginal productivity which, in turn, is due to a lack of complementary factors. These complementary factors are achievable only in Phase II. Thus, the MP of investments in inorganic fertilizers tend to be low in Phase I when the level of application is small—the striking effect from fertilizers comes only when its level of use is raised substantially. Further, it is only with the introduction of HYV that one reaps the full benefits of increased fertiliser application. But these inputs as HYV are possible only in the second phase which ushers in technological advances.

Mellor maintains that the traditional farmer is responsive to price variations. But the aggregate production response to price changes is not strong because in Phase I output changes largely through changes in the labour input which is hard to effect in view of the discontinuity in the utility schedule.

It is interesting to compare at this stage Schultz's characterization of traditional agriculture as a long-run stationary equilibrium, where the existing stock of reproducible means of production remain constant at zero net savings and investments, with Mellor's Phase I, where output increases as a result of population growth and a tightening up of the slack in the utilization of the existing stock of inputs. For Mellor, this stock is influenced by factors outside the economic control of farmers in traditional agriculture. The population growth rate is then determined by forces exogenous to his system. Thus, an increase in output in Phase I comes about as a result of both increases in stock and increases in the percentage of utilisation. In Schultz's scheme stationary equilibrium implies to net addition to stock and hence to output. Significantly enough, consequences of population growth are never brought into his analysis. As we are running ahead of our story we shall keep for later consideration the consequences of population growth in Schultz's model. Suffice it to say that, while a steady growth of population in Mellor's analysis yields more output, it destroys the stationary equilibrium in Schultz's framework, and ushers in a state of constant deterioration with negative saving and investment and a steady reduction in the stock of capital.

Coming back to Mellor's thesis after our brief digression let us recollect: Phase I is characterized by low MP of land, labour and capital due to a lack of complementary inputs of a technical, educational, and institutional nature. In Phase II these complementary inputs are identified, decisions are made concerning the proportions in which they should be combined, priorities are set for programmes to increase them, and the programmes are put forward. Thus, it is the substantial changes in technological and institutional factors that make for growth through increasing MP of the old inputs which in turn provides incentives for further employment of the inputs of Phase I.

As we shall see later, Mellor is anticipating Schultz's more detailed analysis of the process of modernization of traditional agriculture, Mellor emphasized certain institutional and technological changes as well as changes in facilities, as the sources of development. These are changes in institutions like land-tenure, promotion of research to improve production possibilities, facilities to produce the new material inputs which now must be supplied to agricultural sector from outside, education for farmers, and a host of others in the same vein. This whole sweep of changes has been summarized and classified by Schultz with a slightly different pattern of emphasis into the three categories of : (a) high pay-off inputs, (b) supply of such inputs, (c) adoption of these by farmers. Regarding institutional changes in land-tenure, e.g. a shift from lease to owner cultivation, Mellor regards them as essential preconditions that must be brought about in Phase I itself. He does not subject these and other changes to any economic reasoning. The induced institutional innovation hypothesis proposed by A. Hayami and V.W. Ruttan views institutional changes as being induced by the human endeavour to internalize the benefits from technological change, and hence necessarily succeeds the latter in time. In Mellor's analysis, causality apart, even the temporal sequence seems to have been reversed.

IV

Prof. Schultz's problem is to explain the production behaviour of farmers who are bound by traditional agriculture (hereafter TA), and then to find a way of transforming this type of agriculture. To this end he first addresses himself to the task of finding the critical attributes of TA. He contends that an economic conception of TA cannot be formulated rigorously in terms of cultural attributes, institutional arrangements of technical properties of factors of production.[13] Instead he treats TA as a particular type of economic equilibrium which is arrived at over a long period provided the following conditions prevail:

(a) the state of arts underlying the supply of reproducible means of production remain constant,

(b) the state of preferences and motives for holding and acquiring income streams remain constant,

(c) both these states remain constant long enough for marginal preferences and motives for acquiring agricultural factors and income to arrive at an equilibrium with the MP of these sources.

Analytically speaking these conditions merely state that the supply and demand for the reproducible means of production remain constant over a long enough period. This gradual approach to an equilibrium ensures perfect knowledge about marginal rates of return to investment in agriculture, eliminates risk and ensures that the demand and supply of agricultural factors as a source of income are equalized. Equivalently, it also ensures the equilibrium of saving and investment. We have zero net saving and a stationary stock of reproducible means of production which includes, apart from material factors, the skills and capabilities of man that are augmented by investment in him. From this conception of TA Schultz derives two hypotheses: (a) there are comparatively few significant inefficiencies in the allocation of the factors of production in TA, (b) the prices of the sources of income streams from agricultural production is relatively high in TA. We shall take them up one by one.

(a) The poor-but-efficient hypothesis. It seems reasonable to maintain that an economy characterized for a long period by a stationary stock of the reproducible means of production will reach a state of equilibrium in the sense that productive services are being combined in the right proportions to produce the right amount of goods. Thus, no appreciable increment of output is possible by reallocating the traditional factors. But Prof. Schultz in not content with this, for he maintains that the poor-but-efficient hypothesis also implies that "an outside expert however skilled he may be in farm management will not discover any major inefficiency in the allocation of factors."[14] This does not necassarily follow from the hypothesis because he includes the "knowledge of how to employ each of the productive agents including himself"[15], among the factors of production. All that this can mean, taken in conjunction with the hypothesis, is that "the allocation of factors of production in TA is as efficient as the managerial capacity in it is capable of".[16]

Another implication that he is particularly eager to spell out is that no productive factors remain unemployed. In particular, he wants to explode the myth of the doctrine of zero value.

In TA a clear distinction between employment and

unemployment is not always possible. In case of societies where agricultural labourers are non-existent and cultivation is carried out by family farms (and this seems to be true for a large part of TA) the very concept of wage is under a cloud of doubt.[17] But in Schultz's TA approach the farm is conceived of as a commercialized enterprise. But this is certainly not the dominant form of economic organization in underdeveloped agriculture where the overwhelming majority approach the subsistence peasant form of organization. The peasant form of organization partakes of some of the characteristic of the commercial enterprise but nevertheless displays aspects peculiar to itself. It is a household, both a production and a consumption unit, which uses its own labour to produce primarily for its own consumption; engages only in limited exchange; participates only marginally in any widespread monetized market network. It is an economic unit which can be typified by a paucity of resources which must be allocated to a number of ends including those laying outside a strictly economic field. The peasant endeavours to produce enough to meet his requirements. The constraints are his time, energy, and material resources he possesses. The form of strategy employed is one of fulfilling various commitments to at least some minimum level. This is illustrated by the difficulty encountered by D.W. Hopper[18] himself in eliciting precise answers regarding production allocations: "This confusion between production expenses and household outlays made the job of building a realistic matrix picture of village interaction a practical impossibility".[19] It is suggested that the "confusion" demonstrated by the peasants in their inability to separate household outlays from production expenditure indicates an organizational pattern which is different from that of commercialized agriculture."The confusion is in the mind of the observer who is applying different categories and perspectives to the peasant than the peasant applies to himself".[20] Notwithstanding all this, Schultz still feels that "the data that Hopper collected have permitted him to make a rigorous test of the allocative hypothesis under consideration".[21]

Quite apart from philosophical disputes over the economic organisation of TA some have expressed doubt about the logical consistency of the analytical tools used to arrive at the results confirming the allocative efficiency in TA, as well as the logical soundness of the interpretation of these results.[22] They argue that the methodological drawbacks are so serious that nothing whatsoever has been proved or disproved so far about the allocative behaviour of farmers in TA.

Schultz's "critical test" concerning the existence of surplus labour in TA consists of demonstrating a fall in the agricultural production due to the deaths in agricultural labour force caused by the influenza epidemic of 1918-19 in India. As N.Georgescue-Roegen[23] has pointed out, illustrations of a fall in agricultural output following labour transfer is not sufficient to disprove the existence of surplus labour. Before one accepts that the observed consequences of labour transfer are not those that are expected of the doctrine of zero MP_L, one has to ascertain also whether the relevant economies were really in a state of overpopulation when the observation was made. Evidently, whether MP is or not equal to zero depends on the size of the labour force in relation to the stock of reproducible capital in TA. Thus, "If, in particular case, it is in fact zero it is not inconsistent either with the long-run stationary equilibrium that TA is postulated to be, or with the derived hypothesis regarding the efficient allocation".[24] However, to the extent that a growing population is contradictory to the hypothesis of a stable equilibrium with constant stock of capital, Prof. Schultz is right in being so concerned about disproving the doctrine of surplus labour.

Before we embark upon the final part of Schultz's analysis we shall briefly consider the consequences of an exozenous population growth in his model.[25] With the stock of capital being constant, output or flow of income will not, in general, grow in proportion to the growth of population. This will mean a decline in the per capita income and saving. Consequently, the "equilibrium price of the stock of capital, at which the stock was maintained stationary with zero net saving and investment, will no longer be an equilibrium price because at that price net dissaving will occur and the stock of capital will be reduced".[26] The equilibrium is disturbed and a state of continuous deterioration ensues. There is net negative savings and investment, and the characteristic conditions of TA is that it soon begins to live on capital consumption.

Within TA, however, we have a sector which produced a surplus and another which does not. This is because the former bears a lesser population pressure on land than the other. The surplus sector comes close to Schultz's concept of TA for, in spite of its savings potential, little saving and investment takes place because adding to the existing stock of capital is not worth making. Prof. Dandekar maintains that it is labour which is the limiting factor in the surplus in spite of its being in the midst of another sector overburdened with population. This anomalous situation is due to the fact that farmers in the surplus sector do not find it worthwhile to hire labour from the other sector even at subsistence wages because of the low productivity of hired labour as compared to family labour. "The shortage of family labour of the farmer in relation to the size of his holding explain the condition of zero net investment in this sector inspite of its saving potential". In the other sector man works on land with a continually declining stock of reproducible means of production and "move inexorably towards the ultimate equilibrium where both (land and man) are reduced to the irreducible minimum".[27] The surplus sector also experiences the pressure of a growing population. It will also acquire additional land resources from the other sector. At the margin of this sector there are firms where the growth of population overtakes the organization of additional land and consequently these farms are pushed down to the below-subsistence sector. Thus, the surplus sector continually shrinks in size. The relationship between these two sectors is "based on exploitation callous disregard resentment and latent hostility". By failing to include population growth in his model Prof. Schultz seems to have missed these things.

An exogenous increase in population will disturb the equilibrium by shifting[28] both the demand and supply of capital goods, and how the final equilibrium is reached (if it is reached at all) depends crucially on: (i) how the demand for capital shifts, (ii) how the supply of capital shifts, (iii) whether these shifts are in opposite directions or otherwise, and whether the extent of the shift are or are not equal. Conceivably, only when the schedules move in opposite directions and to the same extent do we have an equilibrium situation at the original price level. Even this would be denied if we include the possibility of lags in the shifts. The concepts of demand and supply are simply convenient devices for organizing empirical material and facilitating our understanding of the phenomenon of prices. But such devices are useful only to the extent that an enumeration of the forces affecting demand in any problem and of the forces affecting supply will yield two lists that contain few item in common".[29] The approach to capital theory which Prof. Schultz adopts, and which his critics pursue, namely that in terms of buying and selling capital goods, does not seem to be of much use in the context of a traditional agricultural economy where decisions about buying and selling are taken by the same persons. Under such a situation growth of population is a force which will affect both the demand and supply curves. As Prof.Dandekar points out, (since) "we are studying one single decision making process of an individual may be more convenient to treat it as such than put in the demand supply approach apparatus".[30]

(b) We now return to the mainstream of Prof. Schultz's argument. Having described the equilibrium in TA he next erects a "theoretical scaffold" for determining the price of agricultural factors (as sources of income streams), and proceeds to examine its implications for economic growth from TA. Basically, he is searching for a logical basis for a low ratio of savings to income. Since this could be provided by a low rate of return on investment in factors of production, his task is to explain a low rate of net investment in TA. His approach to the capital theory as mentioned before is in terms of the supply and demand of capital goods, viewed as sources of income streams. Since he assumes that the state of preferences and motives of demanders for acquiring and holding sources of permanent income streams remains constant over time, and further because his concept of capital is all-inclusive (i.e. includes both human as well as non-human capital), he arrives at a horizontal demand curve[31] for permanent income streams. Then, he assumes a positively sloping supply curve.[32] The intersection would determine the price consistent with long-run motives, regarding acquisition of income sources.This brings us to his second hypothesis, namely that the price of the sources of income streams from agricultural production is relatively high in TA, or alternatively, that the rate of return to capital is low. This hypothesis is then used to explain why so little of domestic capital is invested per year to increase the existing stock of reproducible agricultural factors used traditionally, and also why the inducement to save for this purpose is exceedingly weak. The most important implication, however, is that factors in TA are expensive sources of growth.

This whole exercise in economic analysis is rather curious.The price of income stream which prevails in TA is the stationary equilibrium price at which the existing stock of reproducible means of production remains constant with zero net savings and investment. Thus, (1) to talk of this price as being high or low is meaningless; (2) it is unnecessary to hypothesize a high price in order to prove that inducement to saving and investment is low or non-existent because the very fact that a long-term stationary equilibrium has been reached implies that net savings and investment is zero.

This completes Prof. Schultz's analysis of TA. From the analysis the prescriptions follow for affecting a transformation. It is interesting to note how his rejection of "technological change" as a suitable explanatory variable of economic growth leads him to a supply-demand approach.

Since a technology is always embodied in particular factors of production he argues that it is logically impossible to separate a technique of production from the factors of which it is a part. This necessitates an all-inclusive concept of factors of production "including not only material forms of capital (which contains whatever inclusive knowledge is part of such capital) but also human agents (which in turn contains the know-how that man acquires,i.e. skills and useful knowledge that are a part of the capabilities of labour)".[33] Granted this, the notion of technological change becomes essentially "a consequence of either adding or dropping or changing at least one factor of production".[34] Accordingly, when all the factors of production are completely specified the technology is also specified. The limitations of the notion of "technological change" in explaining economic growth leads him to reject the concept which he replaces with "new factors of production". "Technological change is an unexplained residual which conceals most of the important sources of the relatively low priced permanent income streams that induce the savings and investment related to growth. What is concealed under technological change then are particular (new) factors of production that are adopted and employed because it is profitable to do so".[35] The stage is thus set for a supply-demand approach to economic growth. Once the economic basis of the slow growth associated with TA is explained by the dependency upon a particular set of factors of production for profitability of which has been exhausted, a way to break this stagnation is that farmers must somehow "acquire, adopt, learn how to use effectively a profitable net set of factors of production".[36] The concept of demand and supply and are then applied to analyse the process of attaining this end; the demanders are the farmers in TA; the suppliers are the persons who discover, develop, produce, and distribute the new set of factors of production. Apparently, Prof. Schultz seems to imply that growth via an upward shift of the demand curve is not of much consequence. Consequently, it is the downward shift in the supply curve which is his focus of attention. The state of long-run equilibrium had arisen on the one hand out of an unchanging preference pattern, and on the other, from an unchanging "state of arts". The escape from stagnation is by changing the "state of arts". In sum, the key to a transformation of TA is investment to make modern high-pay-off inputs available to farmers. This implies three types of relatively high productivity investments for agricultural development : (a) in the capacity of agricultural research stations to produce new technological knowledge ; (b) in the capacity of the industrial sector to develop, produce, and market new technical inputs; and (c) in the capacity of farmers to use modern agricultural factors effectively. A high private and social return to investment in education and research is indicated. "The only substantial point gained through this rather long-winded argument is that technological progress is not something which simply occurs over time but something which can be attempted and achieved by well conceived investments, and further that this is not something which can be done only once and for all, for then we reach another state of stagnation though with a larger stock of capital than before. Continued progress along this direction requires continued technological progress and this need basic long-term investment which will promote knowledge, science and skills".[37]

Prof. Schultz's high-pay-off input model remains incomplete as a theory agricultural development. A meaningful theory must incorporate the economic behaviour of public and private sector suppliers of knowledge and technology, and the response of institutions to new economic opportunities. In Prof. Schultz's model both technical and institutional changes are treated as exogenous, as unresponsive to economic forces. Typically, the market, the education, and research are public goods not traded through the market. The mechanism through which resources are allocated among education, research and other alternate public and private sector activities is not fully incorporated into his model. He does speak of investment in research as the source of new high-pay-off techniques, but he does not explain how economic conditions induce the development and adoption of an efficient set of technologies for a particular society.

This is the point of departure for Ruttan and Hayami[38], who have attempted to develop a model in which technological change is treated as an endogenous variable rather than an exogenous factor that operates independently. They identify the capacity to develop a technology consistent with environmental and economic conditions as the single most important variable that explains the growth of agricultural productivity of nations.

Their induced innovation model is basically a theory of

technological change based on the division of technological processes into two classes, mechanical processes, and biological-chemical processes. They hypothesize an agricultural production function in which mechanical equipment is viewed primarily as a substitute for labour. Evolution of mechanical equipment is designed to bring about larger output per worker by increasing land area which can be operated per worker. Bio-chemical technologies embodied in new husbandry techniques or new seeds is viewed primarily as facilitating the substitution of land by artificial sources of plant nutrients.

A country at a given point of time is characterized by constraints imposed by inelastic supplies of some factors of production. These constraints may be overcome by advanced in mechanical and bio-chemical technologies. The induced innovation model offers an economic explanation of the mechanism by which a society chooses an optimum path of technological change in agriculture. The multiple paths to technological change which these alternative processes make possible provide the basis for a theory of induced technological change. It hypothesizes that technological change is guided along an efficient path by price signals in the market provided that : (i) the prices efficiency reflect changes in the demand and supply of products and factors, (ii) that there exists effective interaction among public research institutions and private agricultural supply firms.

If the demand for agricultural products increases due to growth of population and income, prices of the inputs for which the supply is inelastic will rise relative to the prices of inputs for which the supply is elastic. In consequence, technological innovations that save the factors characterised by an inelastic supply become relatively more profitable for agricultural producers. Farmers are induced by shifts in relative prices to search for technological alternatives which save the increasingly scare factor of production. They press the public research organisation to develop the new technology, and also demand that agricultural supply firms supply the modern inputs which substitute for the more scarce factor. Scientists and science administrators respond by making available the new technical possibilities and inputs that enable the farmers to profitably substitute the factor, which is increasingly abundant for increasingly scarce factors thereby guiding the demand of farmers in a socially optimal direction. This dialectical interaction among farmers, researchers, and administrators is likely to be more effective if the farmers are politically organized and the response of the agricultural research system is likely to be greatest when it is decentralised.

Ruttan and Hayami's model is structurally similar to the Hicksian theory of induced innovation. Essentially, what they have done is to leave the borrow confines of the framework of the theory of firm and extend the idea of induced innovation to include the process by which the public sector investment in agricultural research, in the adaptation and diffusion of agricultural technology and in the institutional infrastructure that is supportive of agricultural development, is directed towards releasing the constraints on agricultural production imposed by factors characterized by a relatively inelastic supply. Thus, the model involves the following mechanism : (a) induced innovation[39] in the private sector; (b) induced innovation in the public sector; (c) interaction between technological change and institutional development, and, (d) the dynamic sequences of technological change and economic growth.

It is important to note that advanced in mechanical and bio-chemical technologies are in response to change in relative factor prices, and also in response to changes in the prices of factors relative to product, and further, that the process is not confined to the agricultural sector.

Their investigation into the process by which public sector research responds to economic and social forces leads them to a consideration of the process by which institutions more generally evolve in response to economic and technical opportunities. Thus, they further hypothesize that the institutions that govern the use of technology or the mode of production can also be induced to change in order to enable individual and society to take further advantage of new technological opportunities. They share the Marxist perspective on the relationship between technological change and institutional development but do not accept the monolithic sequences of evolution based on clear-cut class conflicts as envisaged by Marx. According to them, the major source of institutional development has been an effort by society to internalize the benefits of innovative activity. In some cases, the institutional innovations have involved the re-organization of property rights. The modernization of land-tenure relationship involving a shift from share tenure to lease tenure and owner cultivator systems of cultivation can be explained in part as a shift in property rights to internalise the gains from entrepreneurial innovation by individual farmers. Similarly, the socialization of much of agricultural research, particularly the research leading to advances in biotechnology is an example of a Public Sector Institutional innovation designed to realize for society the potential gains from advanced in agricultural technology. Institutional transformations are, however, not smooth because, typically, the gains are merely distributed so that the group which stands to lose will oppose the changes and social and political stress and disruptions seem inevitable. They, however, seem to ignore these costs of institutional innovation.

Finally, they highlight critical role of imbalance in inducing technological change and economic growth. "The cumulative sequences resulting from technological change in agriculture also induce changes in other sectors of the economy. Imbalances within agriculture and between agriculture and other sectors of the economy are an important source of backward and forward linkages in transmitting technological progress in agriculture to overall economic development".[40]

The theory provides a basis for understanding how the technological state of the world is determined and throws much light on the inter-country differences in productivity. But as a theory of induced technological innovation, the model is incomplete. "It emphasized factor prices and resource endowments and as a result is quite useful in explaining the direction which innovation takes in the resource-resource dimension. However, it says little about either the rate or the extent to which technological change is adapted, and both (rate and extent of adoption) are important if technology is in fact to become an endogenous variable within the system".[41] Further they are concerned about land and labour as constraints to agricultural development but leave out capital completely. In India, for instance, land and labour are not serious constraints as compared to the constraints imposed by the scarcity of capital. The model would, in this case, fail to identify any basis for technological change since land and labour are both in relatively good supply. But this is absurd. A logical extension of the model would indicate a direction of technological change which economizes on the use of capital; and this is equally absurd as we seldom conceive of technological change as economizing on the use of capital. Thus, the Hayami-Ruttan model, by its assymetric treatment of land and labour, seriously limits its applicability to situation of capital scarcity that characterizes most developing countries today. Another limitation of the model arises from the possible existence of a lag in the rational adjustment process of scientific research and public policies to the factor endowment of the country. This lag arises due to the existence of some dichotomy between the factor endowments of developed pockets and large farmers on the one hand, and the rest of the farm economy on the other. To add to this,the scientific infrastructure of many developing countries is conditioned by a factor use bias of developed economies from whence they originated. These factors often cause the lag. "It is necessary to focus on these lags and on the possible mechanism for speeding up adjustment. To this extent the induced-innovation hypothesis by Hayami and Ruttan may need elaboration in the light of the recent experience".[42]

An over-view of the theories of agricultural development reveals certain broad trends. The paradigm of economic development that theorists had in mind was one of rapid industrialisation, and the agricultural sector was introduced into the analysis when it was realized that industry and agriculture were not activities that were mutually exclusive but complementary in nature. This led to a lot of theorizing on the role of agriculture in the development process as a whole. Subsequently, the attention shifted to agricultural development as such. This was the core of the analysis. It is important to note that it is logically impossible to discuss agricultural development without considering what was going on in the rest of the economy. Significantly enough, it was realized that modernization of agricultural development was crucially dependent on the supply of inputs that must of necessity be manufactured in the industrial sector. Thus, it seems that we are back at square one—but with a greater understanding of the nature of interdependence among the sectors, and what is more important is the realization that even agriculture development in itself is inextricably tied up with industrial development.

Another tendency seems to be to abstract from institutional or "non-economic" factors, and to try to formulate the theories vigorously in terms of economic categories. This is excellent as far as pure theory is concerned, but it makes the transition from the general to the particular even more difficult for it violates the proposition that, at a fundamental level, an economy is characterized by its institutions and not by the type of economic equilibrium or disequilibrium it has. Since institutions and economic forces act and react upon each other, it seems that a theory must incorporate elements of both and analyse the nature and direction of causation. Once this is done the neglected question of the distribution of gains would find a place in development theory.

NOTES

1. S. Kuznets: Economic Growth and the Contribution of Agriculture: Notes on Measurement, in : C.K. Eicher and I.W. Witt, (eds.): *Agriculture in Economic Development*, New York, McGraw Hill,1964, p. 104.
2. Somewhat incorrectly we shall use the terms "traditional", "agricultural", "subsistence", "rural", etc. interchangeably. The same applies for "modern", "industrial", "capitalist", "urban", etc.
3. J.W. Mellor: Towards a Theory of Agricultural Development in : H.M. Southworth and B.F. Johnston (eds.): *Agricultural Development and Economic Growth*, Cornell University Press, New York 1967, p. 24.
4. G. Ranis and J.C.H. Fei: Theory of..., in: H.M. Southworth and B.F. Johnston (eds.) : *Agricultural Development..., op. cit.*, p. 192.
5. H.T. Oshima: The Ranis-Fei Model: A Comment. AER, June 1963, reprinted in: C.K. Eicher and I.W. Witt (eds.): *Agriculture in Economic..., op. cit.*, p. 194.
6. *Ibid.*, p. 198.
7. J.W. Mellor, Toward a Theory of Agricultural Development, *op.cit.* however seems to think that the basic difference between the models of Jorgenson and Ranis-Fei is that any withdrawal of labour from traditional agricultural will cause a fall in agricultural output so that right from the start the process of capital formation cannot proceed smoothly without technological change in the agricultural sector.
8. D.W. Jorgenson assumes a Cobb-Douglas production function for agriculture with an exogenous shift factor that comes pending to neutral technological progress which is not embodied in any capital investment in land and causes a continuous increase in output.
9. A.L. Marty: Prof. Jorgenson's Model of a Dual Economy, in: *Indian Economic Journal*, June 1965, p. 439.
10. J.W. Mellor, in: T. Shukla (ed.): *Economics of Underdeveloped Agriculture*, 1969, p. 24.
11. *Ibid.*, p. 25.
12. On account of a discontinuity in the income-utility schedule there must be a substantial increase in labour productivity in order to ensure an increased level of labour inputs in Phase II. This evidently is a major concern for Mellow because technological advance in Phase II increases income and reduced the incentive for more work.
13. As we shall see later Schultz's concept of technological changes is that it is not something which simply happens outside the production process. In that case one must raise and answer within the realm of economic analysis, the question as to why no technological change occurs in traditional agriculture. If the question is not answered, then "we must agree that an appeal to certain cultural and institutional attributes of the community concerned is necessary" to have a full explanation of traditional agriculture the line is quoted from V.M. Dandekar: Transforming Traditional Agriculture: A Critique of Prof. Schultz,

EPW, 20 August 1966.

14. T.W. Schultz : *Transforming Traditional Agriculture*, New Haven: Yale University Press, 1964, p. 39.
15. *Ibid.*, p. 134.
16. V.N. Dandekar, *op. cit.*, p. 25.
17. D. Thorner's first essay in : D. Thorner *et al.* (eds.): *Chayanov and the Theory of the Peasant Economy*.
18. D.W. Hopper's unpublished thesis is approvingly quoted by Schultz as empirical evidence for his efficiency hypothesis.
19. D.W. Hopper: The Economic Organization of a village in North-Central India", quoted by B.H. Michie : Variations in Economic Behaviour and the Green Revolution: An Anthropological Perspective", *EPW*, Review of Agriculture, June 1973.
20. B.H. Michie, *op. cit.*
21. T.W. Schultz : *Transforming Traditional..., op. cit.*, p. 46.
22. For example A.Rudra: Allocative Efficiency of Indian Farmers: Some Methodological Doubts, in : *EPQ*, 20 Jan. 1973.
23. N.Georgescue-Roegen : Economic Theory and Agrarian Economics, Oxford Economic Papers, February 1960, reprinted in : T. Shukla (ed.), *op. cit.*
24. V.M. Dandekar, *op. cit.*, p. 27.
25. This aspect of Schultz's model was analyzed by Dandekar in : Transforming Traditional, *op. cit.*, and in : Reply to Commentaries, *EPW*, 24 December 1966, and we shall heavily rely on his analysis and on its criticism by T. Shuki in: *EPQ*, 24 December 1966.
26. V.M. Dandekar, *op. cit.*, p. 31.
27. *Ibid.*, p. 35.
28. The demand for capital will shift because it depends not only upon price but also upon the income of the buyers: and the income per capita will fall as population grows with a constant stock of capital.
29. M. Friedman : *Essays in Positive Economics*, University of Chicago Press, 1970, p. 8.
30. V.M. Dandekar, *op. cit.*, p. 809
31. The capitalized value W of an infinite income stream $Y_1, Y_2, \ldots, Y_1$ is $W = Y_1 / / 1 + /^1$ where r is the rate of interest. This infinite income stream is equivalent to an income or rW indefinitely because $W / / 1 + /^1 = W$. Since all wealth has been capitalized, permanent income is $Y = rW$. Thus $\frac{1}{r} / = \frac{W}{Y} /$, the price of a source of a permanent income stream is the ratio of wealth to income. If the community wishes to maintain a fixed ratio of wealth to income regardless of the absolute value of income, then it implies a horizontal demand curve. See Friedman, *op. cit.*, pp. 247-248.
32. This seems strange for if one assumes an all-inclusive concept of capital, as Prof. Schultz does, one arrives at a horizontal supply curve. In that case, a long-run stationary equilibrium is not obtained immediately. Under the conditions such an equilibrium can be reached only if income from land and capital is taken as fixed.
33. T.W. Schultz, Transforming Traditional.., *op. cit.*, p. 133. Further, since the

productive agents include the human agent, the knowledge of how to use each of the productive agents including himself is also an integral part of the factors of production.

34. *Ibid.*, p.133.
35. *Ibid.*, p.139.
36. *Ibid.*, p. 144
37. V. M. Dandekar, *op. cit.*, p. 29.
38. Y. Hayami and V.W. Ruttan: *Agricultural Development. An International Perspective*, John Hopkins Press, 1971,
39. Contrary to Schumpeter who identified innovation as the activities of the entrepreneurs, Hayami and Ruttan extend the term to include "the entire range of processes resulting in the emergence of novelty in science, technology, industrial management and economic organization", see: Y. Hayami and V.W. Ruttan, *op. cit.*, p. 32.
40. *Ibid.*, p. 32.
41. G.E. Schuh in : *American Journal of Agricultural Economics*, February 1973, vol. 55, pp. 124-126.
42. C.H.H. Rao : Factor Endowment, Technology and Farm Employment: Comparison of Eastern UP with Western UP and Punjab. *EPW*, 25 September 1976.

REFERENCES

Dandekar, V.M., Transforming Traditional, Agriculture : A Critique of Prof. Schultz, *EPW*, 20 August 1966.

Dandekar, V.M., Reply to Commentaries, *EPW*, 24 December 1966.

Eicher, C.K. and I.W.Witt (eds.), *Agriculture in Economic Development*, New York, McGraw Hill, 1964.

Friedman, M., *Essays in Positive Economics*, University of Chicago Press. 1970.

Friedman, M., *Price Theory: Four Provisional Text*, 1970.

Georgescue-Roeger, N., *Economic Theory and Agrarian Economics*, Oxford Economic Papers, February 1960.

Hayami, Y. and V.W. Ruttan, *Agricultural Development, An International Perspective*, John Hopkins Press, 1971.

Johnston, B.F. and J.W. Mellor, The Role of Agriculture in Economic Development. *American Economic Review*, September 1961.

Jorgenson, D.W., Development of a Dual Economy, *Economic Journal*, 1961.

Kuznets, S., *Economic Growth and Contribution of Agriculture : Notes and Measurements*, 1961.

Lewis, W.A., Economic Development with Unlimited Supplies of Labour, The Manchester School, May 1954, reprinted in Aggarwal & Singh (ed.) : *Economics of Underdevelopment*.

Lipton, M., The Theory of the Optimising Peasant, *Journal of Development Studies*, June 1968.

Marty, A.L., Prof. Jorgenson's Model of Dual Economy, *Indian Economic Journal*, June 1965.

Mellor, J.W., Toward a Theory of Agricultural Development.

Mellor, J.W., *Increasing Agricultural Production in Early Stages of Economic Growth: Relationships*, Problems and Prospects, 1962.

Mellor, J.W., *The Economic of Agricultural Development*. Ithaca, Cornell University Press, 1966.

Michie, B.H., Variations in Economic Behaviour and the Green Revolution: An Anthropological Perspective, *EPW*, Review of Agriculture, June 1973.

Oshima, H.T., *The Ranis-Fei Model: A Comme, AER*, June 1963.

Ranis, G. and I.C.H. Fei, *A Theory of Economic Development, AER*, September 1961.

Rao, C.H.H., Factor Endowment, Technology and Farm Employment: Comparison of Eastern UP with Western UP and Punjab, *EPW*, 25 September 1976.

Schultz, T.W., Economic Growth From Traditional Agriculture.

Schultz, T.W., *Transforming Traditional Agriculture*, New Haven, Yale University Press, 1964.

Schun, G.E., Review of (10) in *American Journal of Agricultural Economics*, February 1973, Vol. 55, pp. 124-126.

Shukla, T., (ed.), *Economics of Underdeveloped Agriculture*, 1969.

Southworth, H.M. and B.F. Johnston (eds.), *Agricultural Development and Economic Growth*. Cornell University Press, New York 1967.

Thorner's, D., first essay in: D.Thorner *et al.* (eds.), Chayanov on the Theory of the Peasant Economy.

7

EXPENDITURE ON REPAIRS IN SELECTED INDIAN INDUSTRIES: An Exploratory Study

D. U. SASTRY

Introduction

In this chapter an attempt has been made to analyse the expenditure on repairs in selected Indian industries. The importance of this study lies in the fact that repairs and maintenance are related directly to capital assets and, therefore, has implications for productivity and profitability. Maintenance and repairs is a routine item of current expenditure. It is undertaken by firms to keep their capital assets in good working condition. While maintenance relates to cleaning, greesing and oiling of machines, repairs arise mostly due to breakdown of machinery. Neglect of proper maintenance can lead to frequent breakdowns of machinery. But breakdown can also arise due to other reasons as well such as sabotage, power failure, improper handling of machinery and use of inferior inputs not compatible with capital equipment. Repairs would also include replacement of worn out parts and components.

It is important to distinguish repairs and maintenance from depreciation. Depreciation refers to wear and tear of capital. Accumulated depreciation over the life of the capital assets is intended to help replacement of capital assets, No such meaning is implied in the case of expenditure incurred on maintenance and repairs. It is incurred solely with the object of maintaining physical assets in proper working order. It is the servicing aspect of physical assets which distinguishes maintenance and repairs.

Analytical Framework

A number of factors influence the expenditure on maintenance and repairs. Maintenance and repairs expenditure are directly related to fixed capital assets like plant and machinery, buildings and structures. That is to say, this component of expenditure will increase with the increase in capital stock. It is not merely the growth of capital stock but also the level of activity which has a direct bearing on the expenditure of repairs and maintenance. It is the intensity with which capital assets are put to use in the production activity which influences the expenditure on repairs and maintenance. In other words, capacity utilization is an important determinant of the expenditure on repairs and maintenance.

Another important factor influencing the expenditure on repairs and maintenance is the age of capital assets. When capital assets are new, repairs and maintenance expenditure would be low. Conversely, when capital assets are old, expenditure on repairs and maintenance would be more. In economies like ours, there is an additional factor, namely, that capital assets continue to be in use in production activity even beyond their useful life. In such situations, expenditure on repairs and maintenance would be all the more greater. Assets are discarded only when firms are not able to recover the expenditure on repairs and maintenance. In other words, the net realisation has to be positive after meeting all the costs, including costs of repairs and maintenance.

Apart from these two important determinants, profits may also influence the expenditure on repairs and maintenance. Profits, especially retained, earnings will be an enabling factor for firms to undertake repairs and maintenance. Major repairs are undertaken by firms when there are no constraints on the availability of funds. Of all the sources of funds available to the firm, the generation of funds through internal sources would provide a more secure basis for meeting the expenditure on repairs and maintenance, We would expect therefore a positive association between profits retained and the expenditure on repairs and maintenance.

Many other factors affect the expenditure on repairs and maintenance. A firm with higher capital intensity may have to spend more on repairs and maintenance than a firm with lower capital intensity. The nature of production activity and the structure of organisation might influence the amount spent on repairs and maintenance. Industries with sophisticated technologies might have to spend more on repairs and maintenance than industries with simple technology. In this study we propose to analyse some of the important determinants of repairs in selected Indian industries.

The Data Base

The Reserve Bank of India has been publishing company financial data for the Indian corporate sector for a number of years. These are consolidated balance sheet data of a number of companies, The sample changes from period tc period. It is not a probability sample. In our data set 1970-71 is a common year between the two samples and wc have taken the average of two years for our purpose. The accounting year is from April to March. We have covered 14 industries and most of them relate to manufacturing. Some industries have to be excluded due to data gaps and others for want of suitable price indices.

The period covered in the analysis is from 1965-80. Before 1965 data on repairs are not given separately and they have been combined with other expenditure. After 1980, only group-wise data are available. The RBI gives data on expenditure of repairs only. Repairs on plant and equipment is separately given from repairs on buildings and construction. For our purpose we have combined both these items. Bulk of the expenditure on repairs relate to plant and machinery and only about 20 per cent is incurred on repairs to buildings. The major limitation of the data is that it relates to expenditure on repairs only. Expenditure on maintenance is not given. Our data relate to medium and large public limited companies.

Problems of Deflation

The most difficult problems are related to deflation and price changes. Repairs and maintenance expenditure is an item of current expenditure whereas gross fixed assets are accumulated investment expenditure. The latter is a stock concept and the former is a flow concept. This current-constant relationship poses a difficult problem. First of all, whether expenditure on repairs and maintenance requires any price adjustment at all. If so, what is the price index one should use. There is no clear cut answer to this. We argue below that expenditure on repairs is incurred on fixed assets like buildings, plant and machinery, perhaps it is reasonable to use the same deflator to adjust for price changes in both. That is to say, we have used the same price index both for the expenditure on repairs and gross fixed assets.

In the case of fixed assets, perpetual inventory methods is followed.

Investment series are derived from gross fixed assets, and price adjustment is done for investment. These are cumulatively added to the base year capital stock. We have used different machinery price index numbers for different industries. Three price series are used, namely, price index of Non-Electrical Machinery, price index of Electrical Machinery and price index of Transport Equipment. The industries we have covered in the analysis have been grouped under the three broad groups and the relevant machinery price index has been used. The question of how to treat base year capital stock still remains. The base year capital stock is inherited from the past and we do not know the age distribution of these assets. In this study, we have adopted the following procedure. We have grouped the industries into old and new. Most of the industries in our set are new.

In the case of new industries we have not adjusted base year capital stock for price changes for the following reasons. First of all, base year capital stock has been very small because they are new industries. Most of these industries have grown fast especially after the Second Five Year Plan, with the implication that initial capital stock in relation to the growth of capital stock would also be small. Furthermore the period 1950-65 was a period of relative price stability in the Indian economy and capital goods price index must have followed the general pattern. On the basis of these arguments we are inclined to think that no great damage is done if initial stock of capital is left unadjusted for price changes. In the case of four industries: Chemicals, Basic Industrial Chemicals, Cement, Paper and Paper Products which are somewhat older than other industries we have adjusted the base year capital stock for price changes. For Chemicals, we have used the machinery price index of Chemicals and Allied plant of U. K. compiled by the London Economist with base 1937=100. For Cement, Paper and Paper Products, we have used the wholesale price index of Machinery and Machine Tools with 1970-71 as base, which is available from 1947. No separate index was used for buildings and construction. We have used machinery price index to all the fixed assets, including buildings and construction.

The RBI consolidated accounts give data on the value of production. These are gross output figures in current prices. The wholesale price index of output of the relevant industry has been used to adjust for price changes. The gross output figures are net of excise duty, but the wholesale price index of output is inclusive of this duty.

Financial variables like profits, bank loans and other borrowings are difficult to adjust for price variations. For one thing, it is not clear what deflators one should use. Second, the concept of profits in real terms is an abstract thing for the industrialist. But the real side of the economy is of interest to the economist. We have used in this study the price index of machinery for deflating retained profits.

All price indices used for purpose of deflation are in 1970-71 prices. It is necessary to emphasise that all deflation procedures are approximations to capture the real side of the picture.

Specification

Keeping in mind the broad analytical framework that was discussed earlier, we now specify the relationship between expenditure on repairs and some of the important factors which influence such expenditure in the following equation :

RG2 = f (O2G2, N2G2, PRG2)

Where,

RG2 = Repairs to gross fixed assets
O2G2 = Output to gross fixed assets
N2G2 = Net fixed assets to gross fixed assets
PRG2 = Retained Profits to gross fixed assets

All variables are in constant prices, 1970-71 = 100. As the number of companies change from period to period, all variables have been normalised with respect to gross fixed assets. In this process some variables acquire special meaning. For example O2G2 could be interpreted as a proxy for capacity utilization. Similarly, repairs are taken as a ratio of gross fixed assets because repairs are directly related to fixed assets. We expect capacity utilization to be positively related to the expenditure on repairs. The ratio of net fixed assets to gross fixed assets is used as a proxy for age and is expected to be inversely related to the expenditure on repairs. That is to say, if N2 > G2 fresh investment will be taking place and consequently, the expenditure on repairs would be much less. In addition, we have also tried the growth of capital stock as an alternative proxy for age. Alternative definitions of profits have been tried. Finally, we have confined to profits retained inclusive of expenditure on repairs.

Some Basic Ratios

We have presented in Tables 7.1 and 7.2 two key ratios namely, repairs to output and repairs to gross fixed assets for 14 industries in current and constant prices. The means, coefficient of variation and

TABLE 7. 1: Mean and Coefficient of Variation of Repairs to Output and Gross Fixed Assets for Selected Industries, 1965-66 to 1980-81

(in percentage)

Industry	RO1	RO2	RG1	RG2
1. Silk & Rayon	1.95 (0.21)	1.86 (0.14)	2.03 (0.29)	0.03 (0.26)
2. Aluminium	2.52 (0.13)	2.53 (0.22)	1.50 (0.22)	0.03 (0.23)
3. Basic Non-Ferrous Metals (other than Aluminium)	1.65 (0.15)	1.77 (0.23)	3.50 (0.30)	0.05 (0.24)
4. Transport Equipment	1.11 (0.05)	1.16 (0.05)	1.69 (0.16)	0.03 (0.23)
5. Motor Vehicles	0.92 (0.16)	0.98 (0.17)	1.40 (0.28)	0.03 (0.32)
6. Electrical Machinery, Apparatus and Appliances	1.00 (0.16)	1.02 (0.16)	2.55 (0.27)	0.06 (0.45)
7. Chemicals	1.67 (0.20)	1.65 (0.18)	2.59 (0.36)	0.02 (0.53)
8. Basic Industrial Chemicals	2.54 (0.18)	2.80 (0.28)	2.57 (0.42)	0.01 (0.46)
9. Medicines and Pharmaceuticals	0.98 (0.14)	0.81 (0.11)	2.57 (0.25)	0.01 (0.31)
10. Paper and Paper Products	2.74 (0.10)	2.93 (0.09)	2.16 (0.19)	0.02 (0.31)
11. Glass and Glassware	2.48 (0.24)	2.83 (0.26)	2.72 (0.29)	0.04 (0.29)
12. Electricity	3.61 (0.10)	3.75 (0.11)	2.48 (0.39)	0.03 (0.40)
13. Cement	4.39 (0.15)	4.45 (0.13)	4.07 (0.27)	0.03 (0.22)
14. Rubber & Rubber Products	0.92 (0.22)	0.92 (0.23)	2.20 (0.27)	0.05 (0.39)

RO1 = Repairs to output ratio in current prices.
RO2 = Repairs to output ratio in constant prices.
RG1 = Repairs to gross fixed assets ratio in current prices.
RG2 = Repairs to gross fixed assets ratio in constant prices.

Note : Figures in parentheses are coefficient of variation

TABLE 7.2: Growth Rates of Repairs to Output and Gross Fixed Assets for Selected Industries, 1965-66 to 1980-81

(in percentage)

Industry	RO1	RO2	RG1	RG2
1. Silk & Rayon	3.93	1.32	5.66	4.78
2. Aluminium	0.59	– 1.88	4.46	4.53
3. Basic Non-Ferrous Metals (other than Aluminium)	2.56	4.74	6.06	4.15
4. Transport Equipment	0.45	0.23	3.11	4.58
5. Motor Vehicles	3.25	3.41	6.12	8.84
6. Electrical Machinery, Apparatus and Appliances	3.47	3.40	5.62	10.53
7. Chemicals	4.30	3.80	6.63	13.25
8. Basic Industrial Chemicals	3.55	5.61	8.62	4.60
9. Medicines and Pharmaceuticals	2.76	– 0.96	5.26	7.06
10. Paper and Paper Products	– 0.49	– 0.58	2.36	4.07
11. Glass and Glassware	– 1.83	– 0.05	3.25	3.07
12. Electricity	0.91	1.66	8.88	9.10
13. Cement	2.90	2.30	5.85	4.75
14. Rubber & Rubber Products	4.61	3.68	5.00	9.21

RO1 = Ratio of Repairs to output in current prices.
RO2 = Ratio of Repairs to output in constant prices.
RG1 = Ratio of Repairs to gross fixed assets in current prices.
RG2 = Ratio of Repairs to gross fixed assets in constant prices.

trend growth rates of these ratios relate to the period 1965-80. Some differences are observed in current and constant prices. Such differences are somewhat more pronounced in the ratio of repairs to gross fixed assets. We shall restrict our analysis of ratios and growth rates which are in constant prices.

The means of the ratio of repairs to output varies from a low of 0.81 per cent in Medicines and Pharmaceuticals to 4.45 per cent in Cement which is the highest. A large number of industries have ratios less than 2 per cent. Variability as given by coefficient variation of this ratio ranges from 0.05 in Transport Equipment to 0.28 in Basic Industrial Chemicals.

The means of repairs to gross fixed assets is the lowest 0.01 per cent in the two Chemical Industries and it is the highest 0.06 per cent in

Electrical Machinery. In as many as 6 industries it is 0.03 per cent. Variability in this ratio is somewhat more pronounced as compared to the variability in the ratio of repairs to gross output. It is the lowest (0.21) in Paper and Paper Products and the highest in Chemicals (0.53).

An examination of the trend growth rates in the two basic ratios also reveals differences between current and constant prices. The highest growth rate in the repairs to gross output ratio of 5.61 per cent is recorded in Basic Industrial Chemicals. In four industries i.e, Aluminium, Medicine and Pharmaceuticals, Paper and Paper Products and Glass and Glassware, the trend growth rates of repairs to output are negative.

The growth rate of repairs to gross fixed assets is the highest 13.5 per cent in Chemicals and it is the lowest 3 per cent in Glass and Glassware. In four industries it is 8-9 per cent, but in a large number of industries it is 4-5 per cent.

Analysis of Regression Results

In this section, we shall examine the regression results. The ratio of repairs to gross fixed assets has been explained by the ratio of output to gross fixed assets, which we call as capacity utilization, the ratio of net fixed assets to gross fixed assets is used as a proxy for age variable, and retained profits inclusive of repairs expenditure to gross fixed assets is used as an enabling factor in undertaking expenditure on repairs. However, our basic variable will be capacity utilisation. We have estimated alternative sets of equations by the method of Ordinary Least Squares. Among the alternative sets, our preferred set of equations contain all the three variables. We shall focus our attention on this final set given in Table 7.3.

We reject the results of Basic Non-Ferrous Metals because the results are poor and the equation explains nothing. Of the remaining industries, total explanation is uniformly high in all the industries except in Aluminium and Glass and Glassware. Capacity utilization has the right sign and statistically significant in all but two industries, Aluminium, Glass and Glassware. Glass and Glassware has a perverse negative sign and statistically significant coefficient. The age variable seems to take away the effect of capacity utilization. On the whole, the results clearly indicate the influence of capacity utilization on the expenditure on repairs. There is a strong positive relationship between

TABLE 7.3: Determinants of Repairs in Selected Indian Industries

Dependent Variable : RG2

Time Period : 1965-66 to 1980-81

Industry	Intercept	O2G2	N2G2	PRG2	$\bar{R}^2$	DW
1. Silk & Râyon	0.5623 (0.915)	2.3358* (5.766)	–1.0683 (–0.922)	–2.3929 (–0.878)	0.67	0.7158
2. Aluminiun	1.6554* (3.122)	–0.0969 (–0.284)	–2.0886* (–3.087)	4.4933** (1.896)	0.53	0.8016
3. Basic Non–Ferrous Metals (other than Aluminium)	0.0206 (0.581)	1.3696 (1.163)	–0.0178 (–0.595)	0.3010 (0.045)	–0.055	0.6822
4. Transport Equipment	–0.8503*** (–1.590)	1.8735* (4.463)	1.3844*** (1.587)	–3.9026 (–1.311)	0.95	2.2963
5. Motor Vehicles	–0.0776 (–0.155)	1.6699* (4.379)	0.0997 (0.124)	–1.2830 (–0.429)	0.98	1.7978
6. Electrical Machinery, Apparatus and Appliances	0.7491 (1.194)	1.2910* (6.573)	–1.0973 (–1.230)	0.7747 (0.403)	0.99	1.7268
7. Chemicals	–0.0078* (–5.585)	2.1903* (13.523)	0.0031*** (1.6577)	3.0257 (1.1220)	0.99	1.4899
8. Basic Industrial Chemicals	2.7401* (6.076)	2.4519* (6.066)	–3.8656* (–6.070)	–0.6928 (–0.218)	0.96	0.8503
9. Medicines and Pharmaceuticals	3.1340* (2.889)	0.2667* (2.268)	–4.8843* (–2.889)	8.2130* (3.120)	0.95	1.6621

(Contd.)

TABLE 7.3 *(Contd.)*

10.	Paper and Paper Products	−0.4769 (−0.581)	2.8360* (3.545)	0.7234 (0.583)	1.9868 (0.897)	0.80	1.4232
11.	Glass and Glassware	6.4660* (2.978)	−3.9640*** (−1.757)	−9.8619* (−2.971)	6.4227*** (1.529)	0.38	2.4711
12.	Electricity	−0.4920 (−0.241)	3.7729* (4.328)	0.6592 (0.238)	12.8912 (1.192)	0.95	1.2569
13.	Cement	3.3436* (2.220)	4.2755* (3.639)	−5.3672* (−2.226)	−4.5329 (−0.672)	0.84	1.1586
14.	Rubber & Rubber Products	2.5619* (2.4108)	0.5767*** (1.703)	−4.0071* (−2.436)	5.2711*** (1.710)	0.85	0.7493

* Indicates significance at one per cent level.
** Indicates significance at five per cent level.
*** Indicates significance at ten per cent level.
RG2 = Repairs/Gross fixed assets in constant prices.
O2G2 = Output/Gross fixed assets in constant prices.
PRG2 = Profits Retained/Gross fixed assets in constant prices.
N2G2 = Net fixed assets/Gross fixed assets in constant prices.

Note : Figures in parentheses are t - values.

the two. Expenditure on repairs will increase with the increase in capacity utilization.

The impact of age on expenditure on repairs is observed in six industries: Aluminium, Basic Industrial Chemicals, Medicines and Pharmaceuticals, Glass and Glassware, Cement and Rubber and Rubber Products. Age is inversely related to the expenditure on repairs in these industries. Expenditure on repairs will increase with the increase in age. On the other hand, if new investment increases faster, capital assets would be younger and correspondingly expenditure on repairs would be smaller. In two industries, Transport Equipment and Chemicals, age shows a perverse sign with statistically significant coefficient. In all other industries, the impact of age is not present. High intercorrelation between age and capacity utilization is observed in Transport Equipment, Motor Vehicles, Electrical Machinery and Paper and Paper Products.

The influence of retained profits on expenditure on repairs is observed in four industries i.e. Aluminium, Medicines and Pharmaceuticals, Glass and Glassware and Rubber and Rubber Products. In these industries retained profits will serve as an enabling factor to undertake repairs. In all other industries it has no impact. High intercorrelation is observed between retained profits and capacity utilization in six industries : Transport Equipment, Motor Vehicles, Electrical Machinery, Chemicals, Basic Industrial Chemicals and Electricity. Similarly, profits retained and age are highly correlated in Transport Equipment, Motor Vehicles and Electrical Machinery. Intercorrelation is low in all other industries between age and retained profits.

We have also tried with alternative definitions of profits, such as gross profits, retained profits and total borrowing, retained profits and borrowing from banks. All these versions were tried both in current and constant prices. Comparatively better results were obtained when retained profits in constant prices was used.

In two industries, namely, Medicine and Pharmaceuticals and Rubber and Rubber Products all the three determinants show their impact on the expenditure on repairs.

From the point of statistical estimation, collinearity among capacity utilization, age and profits appears to be a problem. The severity of serial correlation is much less. In six industries it is not present. In others it is inconclusive. There may be some simultaneity between expenditure on repairs and profits and capacity utilization. Higher expenditure on repairs may help better utilization and bring in greater profits.

Conclusions

The main conclusions of the study are the following :

(1) There is a clear and unmistakable evidence of positive role of capacity utilization on the expenditure on repairs.
(2) The influence of age of the capital stock on repairs expenditure is observed in a large number of industries.
(3) The impact of retained profits on the expenditure on repairs is somewhat limited.

8

GOVERNMENT ROLE AND THE EFFICIENCY OF POLICY INSTRUMENTS

K.N. REDDY

Government role and the efficiency of policy instruments relates to the gap that often exists between Government goals and the availability of fiscal instruments necessary to pursue those goals and how governments react to that gap. Because, the policy instruments are the vehicles that must implement or are supposed to implement the intentions of the policy makers, when these gaps exist, there are two possibilities, either the policy makers give up in pursuing some of their objectives or, at least they modify their objectives to make them consistent with the available instruments, or they continue to pursue the same objectives but they do so through reliance on less efficient instruments. Unfortunately, the second possibility seems to be common, thus resulting in poor economic policy and in a more confused role of the State. The final results from governmental action are thus often different from the intended results.

Economists and political scientists have generally associated the scope and the importance of the public sector (or, putting it differently, the role of government) with the share of public spending or tax revenue in national income. The implicit assumption is that the objectives can only be pursued through tax and public expenditure instruments. The higher the level of taxation or of public spending, the greater the role of the government in the economy is assumed to be. On this assumption, the government plays a much larger role in Sweden than in Japan and the industrial countries than in developing countries.

While the evidence available points to a greater need for government action in developing countries as compared with industrial countries, it is the latter that exhibit a much larger role for the government when that role is measured by levels of taxation and public spending. On the average, the level of taxation and of public spending, measured as a share of GDP, is at least twice as large in industrial countries as in developing countries. This difference cannot be explained by a lower need for public sector intervention in developing countries. It is rather explained by these countries' difficulties in raising tax revenue. For a variety of reasons, the developing countries are far less successful at collecting taxes than the industrial countries.

Does this mean that the developing countries scale down their policy objectives to reflect this reality? No. They rather attempt to pursue that role through non-fiscal instruments. The typical examples of such instruments are "quasi-fiscal regulations", such as rent controls and "quasi-fiscal activities" such as borrowing from commercial banks (raising statutory liquidity ratios) at a concessional rate, and appreciated foreign exchange rates for imports and exports. These do not result in explicit tax revenue or public spending.

The use of quasi-fiscal instruments is common among countries, but it is more so in developing countries and transition economies. Fiscal experts feel the use of fiscal instruments is more efficient than the use of non-fiscal instruments. But that feeling has no empirical base. Thus, *a priori*, one cannot be sure that taxation is always preferable to inflationary finance.

The conclusion is that the choice of instruments must be based on the efficiency of a measure—Efficiency in Tinbergen's sense (that is an instrument is efficient when a modest change in it brings about a significant change in the policy objective pursued through the use of that instrument) and not the usual allocative definition of efficiency.

9

FIFTY YEARS OF THE INDIAN ECONOMY AFTER INDEPENDENCE

P.R. BRAHMANANDA

Fifty years ago I was a research student at the Bombay School of Economics. I cannot forget the delirious joy we felt on the midnight of 14 and the early hours of 15, when India became free. We went around the city of Bombay, dancing with abandon, all throughout the night. We had only hopes then. None of us were worried about our personal anxieties about our future. We all thought that our country would emerge in course of time as the greatest nation in the world with the highest ideals put into actual practice. We thought India's future would be untrammelled by internal dissensions and divisions on the grounds of religion, caste and language. I need not tell you that the actual experiences have been otherwise. The growing up of free India has been a very very painful process. Apart from this being very slow, it seems that all the ghosts of problems that kept us in bondage have all come back to us. For all practical purposes, Mahatma Gandhi, Balgangadar Tilak, Jawaharlal Nehru, Subhas Bose, Vivekananda, Aurobindo and the whole galaxy of dedicated leaders, seem to have been all forgotten currently. The big question that is being asked is to whether the Indian polity will survive in the next 50 years as an integrated entity. A nation torn by ethnic, religious and caste divisions and feuds and bereft of ideals cannot last long on the past momentum. We have yet to learn the lessons of history. Economics can only work over the long run. It cannot provide healing touches if the political leaders do not allow the economic process to work with long-term goals.

I hope and pray that the things will be better.

I propose to briefly survey different aspects of the growth and development process in the Indian economy during the last 50 years.

We first take up the issue of the race between population growth and food supplies. Between 1950-51 and 1960-61 the average growth rate of food production was 4.8 per cent. Between 1960-61 and 1970-71 the growth rate was 2.8 per cent. Between 1970-71 and 1980-81 the growth rate was 1.8 per cent. Between 1980-81 and 1990-91 the growth rate was 3.1 per cent. Between 1990-91 and 1996-97 the growth rate would be about 1.24 per cent. Between 1950-51 and 1978-79 the growth rate of food production was 3.41 per cent per annum. But between 1978-79 and 1996-97 the growth rate was 1.32 per cent per annum. Thus there seems to have been a substantial reduction in the annual growth rate of production of foodgrains in the recent period. Malthus's important hypothesis of the propensity of growth of food supplies to lag behind population growth is getting vindicated. As we have already used up most of river water potential, ground water resources have also been fully exploited, fertilizer inputs are getting diminishing yields, the green revolution potential is also getting exhausted, further yield growth is going to become more and more input-intensive. This means that the capital-output ratio in food and agricultural production will go on moving up both on an average and on an incremental basis.

I give below some extracts from the articles in process in *The Hindu-Business Line* on Saturdays.

Population Growth *Versus* Foodgrowth

This leads us to the population growth issue. According to the late Jaipal Ambannaver's population growth projections made in 1974, which have been substantially confirmed by the result of the 1991 Census and the projections made therefrom, the Indian population may stabilize at around 162.4 crores by 2081. This is subject to the qualifications mentioned below. Assuming Ambannaver's projections, by 2081, the population would be about twice the current population. We would have added another India in terms of population to the existing India. What an achievement to be proud of ! In the late 70's the goal of reaching NRR=1 by 2001 was put forth. But no step to achieve the above goal was taken. The NRR may turn out to be above 1.3 by 2001. However the World Bank projections expect population size to be stabilised by about 2051 or so. What the World Bank misses is the desire of Indian women to have the ideal size of fertility at about 2.9. The two children norm is, therefore, difficult to be achieved unless strong opinion is built in the economy on the need for the same. More on this later.

That free India has abolished famines is our boast. In 1950-51 we were living from ship to mouth. Had it not been for the imports of 4.1 million tonnes in 1950-51 and 3.9 million tonnes in 1951-52, thanks to the U.S. which could spare the supplies, India would have faced a big famine. The rationing system then was very tight and austere. Further cuts in consumption were out of question. Food imports were close to 10 per cent of net production.

During 1965-67 we imported 26 million tonnes, an amount more than 15 per cent of net production. Had the supplies from the U.S. not come, obviously huge famine deaths would have taken place. These imports took place because of the compassion of Nehru in accepting the PL480 agreement much against the opinion of extreme ideologues. Nehru had probably realised within himself that the Mahalanobis strategy would involve serious slowdowns and stagnations in food production and its growth. Somebody must have told him that the Feldman model which was the main basis of Mahalanobis strategy had frozen aggregate consumption output, specially of agricultural commodities in his model. Had Nehru not accepted the PL480 assistance, India would have had a succession of famines in the late 50's and 60's. The crisis of mid 60's was only a tip of the iceberg Even in 1974-75, thanks to I.M.F. loan, we imported 7.5 million tonnes close to 10 per cent of net production. We should not deceive ourselves as regards history. We are a mature nation.

On all these occasions, we survived thanks to Divinity. Will we be able to do so in the future if the weather gods become unkind? This make the population issue very very crucial.

Tamil Nadu (1.13%), Kerala (1.14%) and Andhra Pradesh (1.57%) have the lowest rates of natural increase of population per year during 1980-90, India's average being 1.94%. In terms of the lowest birth rates, the order is Kerala (17.4), Tamil Nadu (19.5) and Andhra Pradesh (24.3), India's average being 28.7. The highest natural rates of increase are in Rajasthan (2.49%), UP (2.46%), MP (2.23%) and Bihar (2.14%). In terms of highest birth rates, UP (36.2), MP (34.9), Rajasthan (34), Haryana (30.9) and Assam (29.5) take the dubious distinction. In terms of death rates, Kerala (6), Maharashtra (7.3) West Bengal (7.4), Haryana (7.9), Punjab (7.9), Karnataka (8), Gujarat (8.2) and Tamil Nadu (8.2), have the lowest death rates. India's average is 9.3. The highest death rates are in MP (12.6), Orissa (12.2), UP (11.6), Bihar (10.6) and Assam (10.2). In infant mortality rates, as against the Indian average of 74, the lowest are in Kerala (13), and with a great distance, Maharashtra (50), Punjab (55), Tamil Nadu (56), West Bengal (58) and Gujarat (58). The highest rates are in Orissa (110), MP (106), UP (94), Rajasthan (82), Karnataka (67), Haryana (66) and Assam (64). The total fertility rate, which is 3.39 for India, is lowest in Kerala (2), followed by Tamil Nadu (2.48), Andhra Pradesh (2.59), Karnataka (2.85), Maharashtra (2.86), Punjab (2.92), West Bengal (2.92) and Gujarat (2.99). The total fertility rate is highest in UP (4.82), Bihar (4), Haryana (3.99), MP (3.9), Assam (3.53) and Rajasthan (3.36). The female sex ratio, (the ratio of females to males), which for India is 927, is the highest in Kerala (1036), Himachal Pradesh (976), Tamil Nadu (974), Andhra Pradesh (972) and Orissa (971). The lowest is in UP (879), Punjab (882), Rajasthan (910), Bihar (911), and Marxists may note, West Bengal (917) and Assam (923). The female literacy rate, which for India is 39.3% is the highest in Kerala (86.2%), Maharashtra (52.3%) (by a large distance), Himachal Pradesh (52.1%) and Tamil Nadu (51.3%). The lowest rates are in Rajasthan (20.4%), Bihar (22.9%), UP (25.3%), MP (28.8%) and Andhra Pradesh (32.7%). In terms of mean age of marriage of females, 18.3 for India, the highest is in Kerala (21.8), Punjab (21.1), Tamil Nadu (20.3), Gujarat (19.5), Karnataka (19.2), West Bengal (19.2) and Orissa (19.1). The lowest are in Rajasthan (16.1), Bihar (16.6), MP (16.6), UP (16.7), Andhra Pradesh (17.3) and Haryana (17.8).

In terms of proportion of couples using contraceptives, 40.6% for India, the highest proportions are in Kerala (63.3%), Punjab (58.7%), Himachal Pradesh (58.4%), West Bengal (57.4%), Orissa (57.4%) and Maharashtra (53.7%). The lowest are in UP (9.8%), Bihar (23.1%), Rajasthan (31.8%) and MP (36.5%). The proportion of couples who would benefit from family planning facilities but are not able to get the same, which is 19.5% for India, is the lowest in Andhra Pradesh (10.4%), Kerala (11.7%), Punjab (13%), Gujarat (13.1%) and Maharashtra (14.1%). The largest proportion of unmet need is in UP (13.1%), Bihar (25.1%), Assam (21.7%), MP (20.5%), Rajasthan (19.8%), Marxists may again note, West Bengal (17.4%) and Orissa (17.4%).

In the above indicators, from the point of view of population control, Kerala, Tamil Nadu, Andhra Pradesh and by some distance Maharashtra seem to be in an advanced state, followed by Karnataka, Punjab and Gujarat. But from the point of view of the absence of such control, Bihar, Madhya Pradesh, Rajasthan and UP dominate the country. (The acronym for these States is BIMARU, meaning 'sick').

With high female literacy, very low infant mortality rates, more than unity female sex ratio, a high mean age of marriage and a high proportion of contraceptive users, and a high level of hygiene and sanitation, no wonder, Kerala's population growth rate has already reached below replacement levels. Its success is due to the policy of its pre-independence rulers and the practical wisdom of its people. Tamil Nadu which is both conservative and progressive, and which has long tradition in social uplift movements, will also reach the above state within a decade. By and large Southern and Western States in India may reach the rubicon of NRR=1 before 2020. But the Northern and Eastern States have miles to go. If the Western and Southern States stabilise their populations and also start growing at a high rate and the Northern and Eastern States continue to have exponential growth in population and there emerge pressures of migrations from the latter to the former national integration will be under heavy strain. *Here is a warning. If the Authorities are complacent on the population issue, they will be planting seeds of disintegration.* The fertility rate among Sikhs, Jains, Parsies, is lower than among Hindus, Christians and Muslims.

A most interesting information supplied by the National Family Health Survey is that for the country as a whole, the optimum number of children desired by couples is around 2.9, whereas the total fertility rate for the country is around 3.4. Thus, the proportion of excess births would be about 17 per cent. Though in the Southern States the optimum is close to 2, in many of the Northern and Eastern States it is above 3. To repeat, this points to the long way ahead of us if we have to reach a population stationary state, a situation already being reached by Western developed countries and by Japan. China, it is expected, would reach the above state long before India is able to do it.

Probably independent of, and despite the Government, people in the Southern and Western States in India in the post-independence period have become conscious of the need for controlling the family size. This is because of the hard reality of a gap between the desired standard of living prospect for children as against what can be afforded by parents in the context of the high and rising cost of rearing of children. We should remember here the contributions of missionaries like R.D. Karve, Shakuntala Paranjape, Mrs Wadia, J.R.D.Tata, and others. The late B.T. Ranadive, the firebrand communist, in his seminal thesis on "The Population problem of India" published in the 30s was a strong proponent of preventive checks including the then modern devices for family planning. He was ably supported by his teacher late

Prof. C.N. Vakil. Later Ranadive seems to have lost his interest on the population issue. Harold Laski was strongly for population control. But unfortunately neither Nehru nor Krishna Menon followed Laski in this respect.

We give below the optimum number of children desired in each of the above States. The current number is given in the brackets : UP 3.82 (4.82), Bihar 3.18 (4.00), Rajasthan 2.78 (3.63), MP 3.21 (3.90), Assam 2.52 (3.53), Orissa 2.32 (2.92), Gujarat 2.33 (2.99), West Bengal 2.20 (2.92), Karnataka 2.18 (2.85), Andhra Pradesh 2.09 (2.59), Kerala 1.82 (2.00), Tamil Nadu 1.76 (2.48). It may be noted that West Bengal, Orissa, Gujarat, Karnataka and Andhra Pradesh are ripe for a two-children norm; Kerala and Tamil Nadu may, in course of time, go for a one-child norm. But UP, Bihar and MP as also Rajasthan have to be induced to accept a three-children norm.

There are three components of a new population policy. The first and the immediate is to aggressively expand family planning services of all types specially to States like UP, Bihar, MP and Rajasthan. A little less aggressively to West Bengal, Orissa, Gujarat, Karnataka and Andhra. Kerala and Tamil Nadu on their own steam will reach and stabilise populations at an early date. This component of the new population policy has to speedily obtain a 60% couple protection rate in the first two categories above.

It must be pointed out that a second component is also necessary. This refers to expansion of female literacy rate, female schooling rate raising the age of marriage, extension measures regarding education and awareness in family planning, reductions in infant and child mortality rates, facilities for MTP etc. These measures will reduce the optimum number of children desired in the two categories of the different States. The first component will have immediate results over the near future.

The new population policy in the future will have to be two-tiered as above. The Indian economy has now reached an explosive state of regional dualism. The BIMARU States have a heavy concentration of below the poverty line people. At the same time, the demographic indicators point to a heavy explosion of population in them. The level of social development is rather low in these States. It is however, fortunate that people in these States also desire a reduction in the number of children. They are aware of the excess burden of population.There is a large unmet need for family planning and related facilities. It is the bounden duty of the State to treat the supply of these services as part of basic needs. As was pointed out earlier, if we do not take quick and active steps in the above respect, the dualism may lead to the break up of the country. It is necessary that the rest of the States must put pressure on the leaders of the BIMARU States to control their populations by active policies.

The third component is to create those economic and social conditions under which the Male Issue Preference on the part of the couples as parents gets diminished. In most of the States irrespective of educational status or religion households expressed a distinct preference for sons against daughters. This is the major reason why the Female Sex Ratio is less than 1000. This is so even in States like West Bengal, where the Sex Ratio has been even falling. Active policies to make parents neutral in regard to the sex of their offsprings are necessary. Equality of gender status in socio-economic planning matters is necessary. The main opposition to the 30% reservation of seats in Parliament for women has come from the so called leaders in the BIMARU States. If at all for anything else this reservation is necessary to reduce the desired children norms and in the BIMARU States. Cheap populism on the population issue would be sealing India's future prospects, let alone that of the helpless people in the BIMARU States.

The Ninth Plan approach document is not aware of the population bomb exploding in the Northern and Eastern States. The paper is very goody goody on the population issue. Its attitude is no different from the attitudes of the existing leaders of political parties in the Parliament and in the above States. This is the tragedy of India. The leaders who run this country are hardly aware of the gigantic economic problems and the new insights that are getting provided through research. There is a huge gap between knowledge at the level of experts and at the level of political leaders. The heaviest price is being paid by the BIMARU States for the innumeracy and relative economic illiteracy of the leaders thrown up in these States. Jayaprakash Narayan was very positive on the need of population control. But his so called followers have thrown his ideals for India to the winds.

The High Capital-Output Ratio

Let me now turn to the capital-output ratio, a crucial determinant in the growth rate of the economy. About the time of India's Independence, in 1950-51 the annual flow of output was on an average about 42 per cent of the value of capitals or of productive capacities. The bulk of India's capital then consisted of agricultural tools, seeds, live stocks, inventories of food and other articles of consumption, transport specially Railway stock, factories with machinery and plant, irrigation, dams and canals, power stations, mining establishments, Government and Private buildings, etc. The bulk of the capital was in agriculture. The Gross Capital-Output Ratio was about 2.4 in 1950-51. By the end of the First Five Year Plan it had risen to 2.69. With the induction of the Mahalanobis model in the structure of the plan from the Second Five Year Plan onwards, the capital-output ratio went on rising. By 1965-66 it had gone up to 3.65; the rise in 1965-66 also due to a sharp drop in agricultural output. In 1967-68 a very good year from the point of view of rainfall the capital-output ratio was 3.77. By 1973-74, the end of the Fourth Pan, the capital-output ratio was 4.32. By the close of the Fifth Plan, the ratio rose further to 4.45. By the end of the Sixth Plan (1984-85) the Ratio had further moved up to 4.87. But by the end of the Seventh Plan (1990-91) the ratio had gone down to 4.83. It was from 1983-84 onwards that the policy of reduction of import duties on capital goods and other materials, liberalization of domestic economy, and the induction of a large number of low-capital intensive industries began in right earnest, thanks to the initiative of Rajiv Gandhi, and others. The Mahalanobis strategy was slowly getting discarded. That is why from middle 80s onwards the capital-output ratio was getting stabilised at about 4.8. The continuous rising trend in the ratio was halted. By 1995-96 it was about 4.85.

Thus, over a period of 45 years the capital-output ratio had doubled in the Indian economy. A unit flow of output was costing double the amount of capital than at the beginning of Independence.

We give below the incremental capital output ratios for successive quinquenniums. For 1950-51 to 1955-56 = 4.17; for 1955-56 to 1960-61 = 4.70; for 1960-61 to 1965-66 = 7.64; 1965-66 to 1970-71 = 4.69; 1970-71 to 1975-76 = 7.26; 1975-76 to 1980-81 = 8.11; 1980-81 to 1985-86 = 5.22; 1985-86 to 1990-91 = 4.5; 1990-91 to 1995-96 = 4.9. Except during the 4th quinquennium when the ratio came down because of the high base in 1965-66 and the advent of the Green Revolution in 1967-68, the incremental capital output ratio has been more or less going up till the commencement of 80's. Two factors have been responsible for the declining drift thereafter. The advent of liberalisation and liberal imports of machineries etc. and the higher growth rate of services as against goods in the post-80's.

There are many reasons why the Indian economy and its industrial structure became a high cost economy. A most important reason lies in our contempt for evolving a system with low capital goods costs, low capitalization of outputs and with incentives for maximum economy for use of capital. We behaved as if we were the most capital abundant country in the world!

It is time that we now rethink our priorities and policies for the period of the second 50 years of independence. We should introduce the objective in our plans of bringing down the capital-output ratio in our future developments. Our macro policies should also have the above objective.

The following would be the components of a policy-frame to bring down the capital-output ratio.

1. Choice of investment projects specially in the public sector as would be economising on the unit capital per unit of output. Also choice of projects of production as would involve high turnovers.
2. Choice of the most update and cheapest types of capital goods for production processes in different products.
3. Reduction of gestation lags in the commissioning of projects.
4. Removal of excise and sales taxes on all capital goods and accessories.
5. Substantial reduction in import duties on capital goods and accessories.
6. A gradual upward movement of the exchange rate.
7. Interest rates on the longer term as would be reflective of capital scarcity.
8. Modernization of the technologies of production in different industries.
9. Encouragement of choice of those products as would be cheaper in respect of capital per unit of output.
10. Pricing policies as would enable firms, industries including public enterprises as would enable them to accumulate depreciation and replacement reserves in sufficient measures and as quickly as possible.
11. Special attention to maintenance of capital through appropriate repairs etc.
12. Reductions in the required levels of inventories in relation to flows of production in firms, industries and enterprises.

Improvements in communication, transport, exchange reserves, etc., can help in this respect.

These 12 components for a policy to reduce the capital-output ratio over a period of next five to ten years should be treated as a chief instrumentality for obtaining high growth rates in the years to come. The Union and State budgets and policies at Central and State Governments, as also monetary policies, should always keep in focus the effects of policies on the capital-output ratios at micro and macro levels. The Central Statistical Organisation can monitor the effects of policies on the capital-output ratios in its annual national income accounts or supplementary publications to the above. The Industrial costs and prices commission as well as the proposed tariff commission should be given the above 12 objectives. The Economic Surveys each year should have a section on whether the above policies are getting implemented. In negotiating with foreign companies on infrastructure investments, the implicit capital-output ratios should be estimated.

The Savings Ratio

At the time prior to the commencement of the First Five Year Plan, our net domestic savings to net domestic product was about 6.8 per cent. It reached a figure of 9.1 per cent by the end of the First Five Year Plan. The Second Plan period saw a decline in the above ratio which came down to 7.4 per cent in 1960-61. The Third Five Year Plan also witnessed a decline in drift in the net savings ratio. But because of the sharp drop in income in 1965-66, the net savings ratio was about 9.3 per cent in that year. Again the low levels of savings to income continued and by 1970-71 the ratio had become 9.6 per cent. It was only after 1973-74 (12.4 per cent) that the ratio started rising and reached a figure of 16.4 per cent in 1978-79. This is the highest ratio reached in India till then, remarkable also despite the bumper increase of an average of 6.5 per cent in NDP for the two years 1977-78 and 1978-79. Thereafter, the ratio went on falling till 1986-87, when it reached a low of 9.6 per cent. From that year onwards, though there have been ups and downs in the ratio some rising drift has been witnessed. In 1994-95 and 1995-96 the ratios were 16.7 per cent and 17.3 per cent, higher than the levels reached in 1978-79. Over 45 years, the net savings to income ratio seems to have nearly doubled. From 1955-56 to 1973-74 the net savings to income ratio was stagnant by and large. The Mahalanobis strategy period witnessed low levels of net savings to income ratio. The acceleration in the above witnessed during the First Plan was reversed thereafter. It is the period from 1987-88 that has been witnessing some upward drift. A similar upward drift was witnessed from 1975-76 to 1980-81.

In a developing economy the proportion of financial savings to total savings should be going up. The overall savings ratio also should be going up. There should be diversifications in the channels through which financial savings are mobilised. However, the financial savings ratio has been witnessing up and down changes. In many of the categories the ratios were higher in some earlier years than in later years. Financial savings depend upon interest rates offered by banks and financial institutions. It is only after mid-seventies that nominal interest rates started moving up. Even then for quite some years the inflation rate was higher than the nominal interest rates. Consequently, the real rates were negative. It is only after mid-eighties and specially from the nineties that interest rates to savers started exceeding by a good margin—the inflation rates. But this process has received a setback during the last year. Financial savings were down heavily in 1995-96. The high cost of the working of banks as reflected in a margin of 4 percentage points is a big handicap in the mobilization of savings through banks. Institutions like the UTI were able to mobilise high savings primarily because of their low margin. But the interference in the working of UTI by the Government and its use for indirect purposes like stabilization of stock prices has weakened that institution. Today the net interest offered by the UTI is very close to the deposit rates of some banks. The UT, let alone the mutual funds, have been adversely affected by the heavy fluctuations in the stock market and the sharp reduction in the trend growth rate of the stock indices. The Life Insurance Corporation, despite the recent advantages it obtained by the rising trend in interest rates specially on Government bonds, has not been able to make much headway. Its contribution to savings is well below 1 per cent of GDP which is very poor compared to the other developing countries, let alone countries like Japan. Here also the high costs of working and intermediation have kept down its potential growth. The very size of the organisation is a big handicap to its efficient working. The contributions through pension and provident funds should atleast be 4 per cent of GDP. But they are yet less than 2-1/2 per cent. The Government should have permitted higher contributions from employees with suitable fiscal incentives. This has not been done except in the present budget.. We have a long way to go here. The contribution from banks to savings has been witnessing ebb and flows. In India, banks can be a great success in the mobilization of savings through increases in deposits. But unless interest rates are high, the bank margins are low and the efficiency of banking increases a great deal, it is difficult to raise contributions in the form of net savings in the form of increases in bank deposits to 6 to 7 per cent of GDP. The contribution of households to savings in the form of addition to their purchases of Government claims has been falling. This is primarily due to the stagnation in the interest rates and small savings and the erosion of fiscal concessions for investments in them. The Ranina committee's suggestion to exempt from tax Rs. 1 lakh invested in specific savings is timed. This suggestion is a forward step towards a disguised expenditure tax. We have to give premium to savers and savings in view of our low savings in relation to that in South, North and East Asian countries.

Poor Maintenance of Capital

In the Indian economy a significant portion of capital stock is owned by Government and Government-owned and operated enterprises. From 1980-81 onwards the Central Statistical organisation has started making book provision in their National Accounts for the depreciations and amortisations of capital stocks on the basis of perpetually revalued inventory approach. The theoretically required depreciation provisions have been shown in the accounts of the enterprises. These provisions are substantially larger than the actual provisions made in the accounts of these enterprises. The new national accounts concerning these enterprises naturally shows low or negative profits against these concerns. The profits of these enterprises as shown in the Economic Surveys do not take the above into account. Since the accumulated book provisions are very much larger than the actual provisions, the implication is that the fixed capitals in these enterprises have been heavily worn out and the firms do not have reserves to actually replace the equipments and at current values. If we hypothetically assume that somehow these equipments are replaced by modern equipments, the capital stocks would go up in value and probably efficiency. The CSO accounts are naturally underestimating the growth of net capital stock as would have taken place had actual replacements paralleled the new book provisions. Therefore, an illusion is created that the net capital-output ratio has not been rising in India. Great care has to be taken in interpreting the CSO figures and drawing conclusions therefrom.

Neither the Planning Commission nor the Government encouraged these enterprises to build internal resources to meet the replacement needs as and when they would arise. We transferred their potential surpluses and used them for other purposes. The current predicament of public enterprises is mostly due to gross mismanagement at the fiscal levels. It would be wrong to blame only the workers in these enterprises for the present sorry state of affairs. Had internal resources been allowed to be built up, the firms would have modernised their plants and would have been ready to face the new challenges. Their markets would have been preserved and expanded.

For populist reasons we also did not want these enterprises to stand on their own bottoms. We did not even allow them to charge prices equal to costs of production and supply. The present oil case is only one such example.

The national accounts show that negative savings of public administration were about 1 per cent of GDP in 1980-81. Currently they amount 3 per cent of GDP.

If we achieve zero revenue deficits and wipe out the negative profits through improvements in efficiency of public enterprises, reductions in non-functional expenditures in their operation, reductions, albeit temporarily, in wage and salary bills and introduction of viable pricing policies, our savings ratio for the economy can go up by more than 3 per cent of GDP. Our gross savings ratio is currently about 24-25 per cent. If we add 3 percentage points to the above, our gross savings can go up to 28-29 per cent.

Beyond the above, firms have to reduce their luxury consumption. Governments draft on the economy has to be further reduced and households have to reduce their luxury consumption. All this involves from the fiscal end, maximum incentives for savings. From the monetary end, inflation has to be completely eschewed and real rates of interest must be such as to slightly above the growth rate. If the growth rate is 6-7 per cent, the real rate will have to be atleast 8 per cent. If there is a zero rate of inflation, at the above interest rate, foreign inflows will also be substantially larger. It is in the above manner that we can reach a gross savings to income ratio of atleast 35-40 per cent. This must be the aim of the economy. With even a gross investment ratio of 35 per cent and a capital-output ratio of 4, we can easily obtain an annual growth rate of 9 per cent. We can then proudly match our performance against that of China. By raising the growth rate we also further boost the savings to income ratio. The cumulative upward process of sustained growth rate of 9 per cent plus for a democratic country will place India in three decades at the top levels in the world in economic performance.

The Widening Gap between Per-capitå Products in Agriculture and in the Rest of the Sectors

At the time of Independence around 1951, 72 per cent of our work-force were dependent upon agriculture and related activities, the latter consisting of livestock, forestry, fishing, hunting, plantations, horticulture etc. In 1961 and 1971, the proportion remain more or less the same. In 1981, the proportion slightly declined to 69 per cent. In 1991 the proportion was about 67 per cent. The proportion of cultivators in 1951 was 50 per cent. In 1961 it went up to 53 per cent. And from 1971 onwards, it has been declining (in 1971, 43 per cent; in 1981, 42 per cent; and in 1991, 38 per cent). But the proportion of agricultural labour which was 20 per cent and 17 per cent in 1951 and 1961, however rose sharply in 1961. In 1971 it was 26 per cent; in 1981, 25 per cent; and in 1991, it was again 26 per cent. There may be partly statistical reasons for the sharp rise in 1961. But there is no doubt that whereas the proportion of cultivators has been going down, the proportion of agricultural labour has moved up. Even in regard to the latter, the proportion of casual labour has moved up in relation to regular, contractual labour. It is interesting that the land reforms which were ostensibly aimed at improving the lot of labour in agriculture have tended to actually worsen their lot. Passionate ideology can get its objectives defeated if it is not imbibed with practical economics. If at all there is one group which has consistently suffered the worst in our development process, it is the class of agricultural labourers, which in 1991 amounted to 74 millions about 4 times the number of organised, urbanised labour, so assiduously cultivated by trade unions and the leftist parties. We have excluded small and marginal farmers, who have also fared ill in the development process. Their numbers also constitute millions.

At the time of Independence, say in 1950-51, the relative share of agricultural and allied activities in net national product at 1980-81` prices was 49 per cent. In 1960-61 it came down to 46 per cent, in

1970-71 it further went down to 40 per cent and in 1980-81 it had slided to 35 per cent. In 1990-91 it had further declined to 29 per cent. In 1996-97 it was about 28 per cent. Over nearly 50 years the relative share of agriculture and allied activities has dropped by 44 per cent, whereas the relative share of work-force in them has declined only by less than 6 per cent. Further the relative share of agriculture etc., in net product has been declining more or less continuously, whereas the modest decline in the relative share in work-force is only in the recent periods. Consequently the ratio of per worker net product in agriculture to that in the rest of the economy has been going down. In 1950-51, it was 68 per cent; in 1960-61 it was 64 per cent; in 1970-71 it was 56 per cent; in 1980-81 it was 51 per cent and in 1990-91 it was 43 per cent. Probably in 1996-97 it would have been about 40 per cent. The ratio has thus come down by about 42 per cent in the post-Independence period. The rate of growth of per worker product in agriculture has been going up at a lower rate than that in non-agriculture over the post-Independence and post-Plan era. The real wages in agriculture have been going up at a lower rate than in non-agriculture. In fact, there has been stagnation in the nineties so far in the real wage. The minimum wages in rural areas has been only on paper. The real wage in agriculture has probably been going up at a lower rate than the growth rate of yields, at least in recent years. Probably the income distribution pattern in agriculture has been getting skewed particularly in prosperous areas. This does not mean that the green revolution has not benefited agriculture labour and small and marginal farmers. Their conditions would have been more severely and absolutely adversely affected had the green revolution had not taken place. In fact, in areas where the green revolution's effects have been sparse, the conditions of the above categories of workers have improved relatively very little as compared to the conditions of the above categories of workers in the green revolution benefited areas. The bulk of India's poor are in the above two categories of workers. If we add workers in the handloom textile sector to the above category, we would probably find most of the poor and most of the illiterate among them and their families. The conditions of women in these categories would be still worse than those of men.

It may be worthwhile outlining the probable causes for the growing gap eluded to earlier.

1. The growth rate of agricultural production in the post-

Independence period has been lower than that in non-agriculture.

2. Whereas physical and human capital are important sources for value-added in industry etc. and services, land is the important source of value-added in agriculture. Land area has not been increasing whereas capital stock has been increasing.
3. Capital and infrastructure for agriculture have grown at a lower rate than those required for industry etc. The human capital application in agriculture has been limited. Even primary education is not universal in rural areas.
4. The burden of disguised unemployment has been borne mostly by agriculture. There has been some migration from rural to urban areas but the barriers to movement of surplus labour in agriculture to activities outside agriculture and across regions are quite strong. These barriers have been growing more and more unpierceable.
5. Production systems in agriculture continue to be characterised by small and marginal farms in most of India. Instead of planning for removal of surplus labour through planned capital formation programmes, we pursued the policy of encouraging smaller and smaller-sized farms, thus discouraging labour mobility. Even employment guarantee and such schemes also made labour immobile.
6. The growth of crop productivity has occurred in a few portions of India. A small portion of farms produce the bulk of the marketable surplus.
7. Crop productivity and its growth in dry areas has been heavily neglected.
8. The terms of trade have not been always in favour of agriculture. Not all crops get the full benefit of public purchases at convenient prices. Farms are still exposed to incidence of fluctuations in prices due to fluctuations in production.
9. The sources of non-farm employment in rural areas have also not expanded in a big way. The pressure on agriculture continues.
10. There is a significant growth of casual employment in agriculture. This is due to mechanisation, hidden evasions of ceilings, substitution of family labour against outside

labour, the unreality of minimum wages etc.

11. Inflation has adversely affected workers in agriculture more than workers in other sectors. Agricultural prices in recent years have risen at a lower rate than general prices.

Poverty in Rural Area—A Direct Consequence of Wrong Strategy

Nehru was influenced largely by the Soviet model of industrialisation with emphasis on heavy industries. In the famous Feldman model which lay at the back of the Stalinist economic model, the output of wage-goods and of agricultural commodities was kept constant and all savings, even in a gross sense, were ploughed back for heavy industry development. This pattern emphasised the network of activities consisting of machine building, heavy transport, mining and related infrastructure like electricity. The forward expansion of production of final consumer goods which would have consisted mostly of agricultural commodities was not the goal of planning. At the same time following the thesis of Probrianzski, industrial goods were to be sold to agriculturists at high prices thus turning the terms of trade against them.

Mahalanobis produced a model similar to that of Feldman. This appealed to Nehru and the strategy of development visualised in the second plan was forced on the economy. Even our leftist economists treated Marx in a naive manner. They interpreted the Stalinist model as tantamount to Marxist theory in practice. We added two other components; these were Deficit Financing and an over-valued exchange-rate. Agricultural development and infrastructure for the same got naturally neglected. The massive PL480 food inflow also made us neglect the need for domestic agricultural growth. The two drought years of 1965 and 1966 made us partly recover our lost sights. The Green Revolution came along with the devaluation of the rupee and the establishment of the Agricultural Prices Commission. The devaluation made food imports excessively prohibitive. We had to change our strategy of development. It was at this time we suddenly became aware of the huge measure of poverty of our people who had barely enough access to food to meet even marginal requirements of subsistence. It was shown that poverty eradication had to place cardinal emphasis on food and agricultural production. The heavy industries strategy could not have led to increased supplies of food and agricultural commodities.

By middle Sixties we had exhausted the scope for bringing new area under cultivation. Further development require massive investments in irrigation, heavy consumption of fertilisers and adoption of high yielding seeds. The growth of agricultural production from 1967-68 has been largely obtained through sustained rising trend in yields. The three inputs: water, fertilisers and high quality seeds transform have helped to avoid famines and without resort to food imports. Between 1949-50 and 1995-96 the growth rate of food production has been about 2.5 per cent per annum; the growth rate of area has been half a per cent per annum and the growth rate of yields has been 2 per cent per annum. Since no more growth of areas is possible in the future, we have to depend primarily upon sustaining a high trend in yields. The growth rate of non-food-grains production over the last 46 years has been about 2.9 per cent per annum. The growth rate of area here has been 1.3 per cent per annum and the growth rate of yields has been slightly more than 1 per cent per annum. The growth rate of agricultural production in the post-Independence period has been about 2.6 per cent per annum. Whereas, the growth in area has been 0.7 per cent per annum and that in yield has been 1.9 per cent. It may be noted that the growth in yields has been lower than that in population. This is so in regard to both food and non-food commodities. In the post-Green Revolution period yield growth has been our saviour. Can this be maintained and how long ?

The Low Growth Rate of Agricultural Production

Taking the long period from 1950-51 to 1996-97, the growth rate of agricultural production at 2.8 per cent would be above the population growth rate of 2.1 per cent. But during the period 1990-91 to 1996-97, at 2.4 per cent it would be only very slightly above the population growth rate of 1.9 per cent. The growth rate of food production at 2.9 per cent would have been very slightly above the population growth rate but during the period 1990-91 to 1996-97, at 1.3 per cent, it would be substantially less than the population growth rate.

The following table 9.1 gives the long period, the decadal and the recent 6 year period semi-logarithmic growth rates of major crops and of inputs.

In most crops there seems to be a deceleration in the growth rates

TABLE 9.1: Crops and Inputs · Growth Rates (Per cent)

Commodities	1950-51 to 1996-97	1950-51 to 1960-61	1960-61 to 1970-71	1970-71 to 1980-81	1980-81 to 1990-91	1990-91 to 1996-97
Rice	2.94	5.19	1.99	2.39	3.26	1.15
Wheat	5.00	5.32	7.73	4.21	4.18	2.64
Coarse Cereals	1.88	4.34	2.52	-0.51	1.19	1.75
Total Pulses	1.11	4.12	-0.72	-1.06	2.94	-0.30
Total Foodgrains	2.88	4.79	2.79	1.78	3.08	1.34
Sugarcane	3.41	8.57	1.39	1.99	4.46	2.11
Oilseeds	3.35	3.02	3.22	-0.27	6.86	4.32
Cotton	3.37	8.11	-1.63	4.01	3.25	6.23
Jute & Mesta	2.22	4.63	1.63	2.77	1.23	-0.07
Tobacco	1.70*	1.75	1.50	2.88	1.54	0.00*
Potato	5.44*	4.94	5.70	6.98	4.52	4.70
Coconut	3.03*	2.59	2.69	-0.60	5.31	7.23*
Tea	2.18*	NEG	2.88	0.38	6.45	3.72*
Coffee	N.A	N.A	N.A	3.07	2.64	0.54
Rubber	N.A	N.A	N.A	6.93	4.05	10.22*
Non-foodgrains	3.13*	3.86	1.50	2.19	4.73	3.65*
All Crop Production	2.82*	3.98	2.22	1.73	3.74	2.03*
Fertilizer Consumption	12.17**	16.39	20.61	8.22	7.26	1.06**
Fixed Capital Stock	2.44***	2.18	2.60	2.87	2.22	1.62***
Irrigated Gross Area	2.81*	2.15	3.11	3.53	2.69	2.42*

* Period taken for calculation 1950-51 to 1995-96.
** Period taken for calculation 1951-52 to 1995-96.
*** Period taken for calculation 1951-52 to 1994-95.

for the period 1990-91 onwards. The position in regard to cereals (rice and coarse) and pulses is truly alarming, as also in respect of total foodgrains. Pulses are the primary source of proteins for the majority population. There are widespread reports that soil fertility in regard to sugarcane is declining. Jute is almost dying. Tobacco is stationary. Improvements are noticed in oilseeds, potato, cotton and coconut. Non-foodgrains as a whole are growing at a higher rate than population. Taking all crops, the growth rate of 2 per cent in the most recent period is a sure sign of overall declining growth rate in agriculture. Particularly so because of the excellent state of the monsoons during this period.

The successive Five-Year plans barring the Fifth Plan have been showing a wide gap between actual growth and target growth in respect of foodgrains and most of other crops. During the Sixth Plan as against the goal of 154 million tonnes, the terminal production was 146 million tonnes. During the Seventh Plan, as against a target of 183 million tonnes, the achievement was 171 million tonnes. During the Eighth Plan, the goal was of 210 million tonnes. What we have reached is 191 million tonnes. There are similar shortfalls in cotton, jute and oilseeds. The planners, God bless them, are targeting for the Ninth Plan, a growth rate of agriculture crops of above 4 per cent and of food crops of above 3 per cent and in the face of a less than half of the above rate of achievement during the Eighth Plan. None of the Chief Ministers, let alone the then humble farmer Prime Minister, seem ever to have concerned themselves about the nitty-gritty of the targeted growth rates in the face of such poor achievement.

Growth Rate in Industry

The post-Independence period has witnessed during 1950-51 and 1996-97 a semi-log growth rate of 7.81 per cent per annum. During the decade of the Fifties, the growth rate was 6.82 per cent per annum. During the decade of the Sixties it came down to 5.9 per cent per annum and during the decade of the Seventies it came further down to 4.26 per cent per annum. The declining growth rates were the effects of the adoption of the Mahalanobis strategy. But during the decade of the Eighties, thanks particularly to the policy initiatives of Rajiv Gandhi towards liberalization of imports and reduction of import duties specially in capital goods, the growth rate moved up to 7.54 per cent per annum. But owing to the severe exchange crisis of 1991, and its immediate impact the growth rate came down to 5.97 per cent per annum, during 1990-91 and 1996-97. (We assume a growth rate of 7 per cent during 1996-97). If we take the period from 1991-92 to 1996-97 the growth rate would work out to 7.04 per cent per annum. The growth rate per annum between 1983-84 to 1996-97 works out to 7.13 per cent as compared to a growth rate of 5.71 per cent per annum during the period from 1950-51 to 1983-84. This could be the best testimony for the relative success of the path of liberalization in the organised industrial sphere.

The levels of growth rates in the post-Independence have been high from international standards from mid Eighties onwards. A sustained growth rate of 7 to 8 per cent per annum, which is fifty per cent higher than the general growth rate is something to be proud of. We have achieved this without any serious upset to the growth of small scale industries. Both registered factories and un-registered factories have shared in the general expansion. Around late Seventies it was feared that because of the exhaustion of the import-substitution stimulus, the growth rate of industry would come down in the Eighties and thereafter. The rapid phase of industrial growth rate from the mid Eighties witnessed despite continuous reductions in import duties on capital goods and process materials, despite local interest rates higher than abroad, and despite growing opportunities for inflow of foreign capital and technology through multinationals, etc., points to the inherent strength and resilience of our organised industry. The small scale industrial sector consisting of unregistered factories has also been growing at a commendable rate. During 1950-51 and 1994-95 it has grown at a rate of 4.64 per cent per annum as compared to the growth rate of registered factories during the same period at 5.93 per cent per annum. It seems that the organised industry's growth rate as represented in the industrial index is higher by above 1 percentage point even as compared to the growth rate of output of registered factories.

It is interesting to note that most of the recently expanding industrial lines are connected with the products associated with the new industrial revolution and the technology associated with the same. Though India lagged behind other countries in the earlier industrial revolutions, this lag has been narrowed in the recent phase. What is most significant is also the revival of the textile industry specially in the sphere of exports. It was the textile and food processing, leather, jewellery and such industries which got the worst treatment during the stage of domination of heavy industries and of import substitution in our planning phase. For nearly two decades their growth impulses were put down. It is these industries that are now in the vantage points in the current phase. They are also involved in exports.

Around independence the capital output ratio was rather low in industry. But by about Seventies it had gone up. The high ratio continued to remain so till mid Eighties but thereafter the ratio started coming down. Just as the mid Fifties marks a turning point in the pattern of industrial development because of the shift to heavy industry thanks to the Mahalanobis strategy, from mid Eighties there was a new turning point because of the Rajiv Gandhi—initiated path of liberalisation. The industrial growth rate also jumped up thereafter. The employment elasticity of industry also increased both directly and indirectly thereafter. This is more particularly reflected in the period after 1991-92. From all angles industry started performing much better and the social effects seemed to have been more beneficial in the post-mid-eighties space than earlier. The post-Eighties also witnessed a remarkable boom in the stock market. The capital issues market has breathed new life. Foreign funds also started flowing in. In fact, it is from the mid-Eighties that we seem to be noticing a long Kondratief boom in industrial development. If this is sustained over the next one and a half decades or so, the Indian economy would have transformed itself not only in industry but in other related sectors. A Kondratief boom can have an upward phase of even 20 to 25 years. Such a long boom will witness several recessions but yet the slope of the underlying upward trend will still be quite high. These are termed as recessions on a high growth path. India has not yet witnessed an upward phase of a long waive. Probably the best achievement in the industrial sphere would have been the beginning of the liberalization and related era from the mid-Eighties. Critics should not be too hasty in condemning the above era.

There are a number of broad tendencies which may be noted : 1. By and large the proportion of value added to value of output has slightly gone down from about 20 to 21 per cent in mid 70's to about 18 to 19 per cent in early 90's. 2. The proportion of wages in value added has gone down from 30 per cent in mid 70's to 24 per cent in early 90's. 3. The ratio of higher level workers to wage earners has been constant at about 30 per cent. 4. The proportion of interest plus profits in value added has been going up. It was 42 per cent in late 70's and 0.50 per cent in early 90's. 5. The proportion of interest payments in value added has gone up from 22 per cent in late 70's to 30 per cent in early 90's. 6. The proportion of current depreciation to value added has gone up from 14 per cent in mid 70's to about 20 per cent in early 90's. 7. The ratio of capital to output has gone up from 2.2 per cent in mid 70's to 2.7 per cent in early 90's. 8. The ratio of outstanding loan to invested capital has been about constant at about 60 per cent i.e. the debt-equity ratio is about 1.6 to 1.7. 9. There has been a rise in the proportion of charges for fuels consumed to gross output from about 7 per cent in mid 70's to about 8 per cent in early 90's. 10. The proportion of gross capital formation to gross value added has been fluctuating with a low of 47 per cent in mid 80's to a high of 65 per cent in early 90's.

Industrial Growth in Different States: The Serious Decline in West Bengal's Status

There have been some important changes during the last three decades in the relative share in the value added in manufacturing among the different States. Maharashtra (28%), West Bengal (22%), Gujarat (10%), Tamil Nadu (7%), Bihar (7%), Uttar Pradesh (6.5%), Karnataka (3.1%), Assam (3%), Andhra Pradesh (2.7%), Kerala (2.5%), Madhya Pradesh (2.4%), Punjab & Haryana (1.9%), Rajasthan (1.1%) and Orissa (1%) in that order, were the leading industrial States in 1960. This order has changed very rapidly over the last three decades. Around 1992-93, the relative shares of value added of different States was as follows: Maharashtra (22.7%), Gujarat (11.3%), Tamil Nadu (10.3%), Uttar Pradesh (9.1%), Punjab & Haryana (6.4%), Andhra Pradesh (6%), West Bengal (5.9%), Karnataka (5.8%), Madhya Pradesh (5.5%), Bihar (4.8%), Rajasthan (3.3%), Kerala (2.55%), Orissa (2%), Assam (1.2%), Maharashtra has suffered a decline by its relative share by more than 5 percentage of points. Andhra Pradesh has gained in its relative share by 3.3 percentage points. Karnataka has gained in relative share by 2.7 percentage of points. Gujarat has gained by 1.3 percentage of points. Tamil Nadu has gained by 3.3 percentage of points. Maharashtra seems to have lost potentially to all these four States. Punjab & Haryana together have gained by 4.5 percentage points. Madhya Pradesh has gained by 3.1 percentage points. Uttar Pradesh has also gained in its relative share by 2.6 percentage points. Rajasthan had gained by 2.2. percentage points. Orissa has also gained by 1 percentage point. Assam has lost its relative share by 1.8 percentage points. But the most radical decline in the relative share has been that of West Bengal. It was only next to Maharashtra in its industrial status throughout the Fifties and Sixties. But it lost heavily from the Seventies. It has lost in relative share by nearly 16 percentage points. West Bengal was next only to Maharashtra in industrial leadership around the time of Independence and till about the end of the Sixties. To what extent ideological factors are responsible for this big decline in West Bengal's industrial status has to be examined carefully specially by the Leftists themselves. Indian economic leftism may not have had much effect at the national level atleast in recent years. But it has certainly harmed West Bengal where it is the predominant ideology. Over the long run workers will themselves lose in this process. Some rethinking is absolutely necessary in this State if the situation is not to worsen. It is in the Seventies and Eighties that West Bengal lost its relative share and in a big way. It is during these two decades that we witnessed a tremendous boost in West Bengal to the power of leftist ideology. Industrial relationships became highly strained. The atmosphere seems to have become hostile to existing enterprises and budding entrepreneurs. The regime of Jyoti Basu has tried valiantly to repair the damage done by ideology to West Bengal's prosperity. Despite his pragmatism, he has not been successful so far. Probably the industrial outlook for the future has improved but enterprise and capital have yet to flow and flow back in a large and sustained measure to West Bengal.

Though Kerala's relative share which was absolutely small has remained constant over the years, it seems in this State as well considerable damage has been potentially caused by the force of ideology specially in the matter of industrial relations. From the middle Seventies Kerala has been witnessing, more or less continuously, large inflows of net remittances from abroad. The overall potential of investible funds in Kerala has been quite large. But very little of this potential has gone towards industrial and related development within Kerala. Both labour and capital have been migrating from the State to the other States in India, and of course, to outside India. The level of real wages in Kerala is probably higher than what can be sustained under potential conditions of high industrial investment in the State. This is a pity because Kerala has advantages in natural resources, trained manpower, and now in investible funds. The system of industrial relations may also have to be restructured in this State.

Limits to Future Growth

The knowledge of our ultimate irrigation potential has not expanded much since the time of Independence. Currently the ultimate irrigation potential has been placed at about 114 million hectares. By the end of 1994-95, according to the Report of the Ministry of Water Resources for 1996-97, we had used up 87 million hectares out of the ultimate. This means that the unutilised irrigation potential is only 27 million hectares. And this would be mostly in major and medium irrigation. Here further progress would be blocked by inter-State water disputes.

By the end of 1995-96, Tamil Nadu had used up all the ultimate potential in major and medium projects for irrigation, Punjab had used up about 81 per cent of its potential, Rajasthan had already exploited 75 per cent of its potential, Andhra Pradesh had exploited 62 per cent of its potential, Haryana had exploited 62 per cent of its potential, Karnataka had used up by now nearly 62 per cent of our irrigation potential has been actualised, West Bengal had used about 59 per cent of its potential, Jammu and Kashmir had used about 53 per cent of its potential and Kerala had used about 52 per cent of its potential.

As regards minor irrigation, by 1995-96, the country would have used up 96 per cent of its ultimate potential, Gujarat and Haryana would have used up 100 per cent, Uttar Pradesh also 100 per cent, Punjab would have used up 95 per cent, Tamil Nadu 90 per cent, Bihar 87 per cent, Maharashtra 74 per cent, Karnataka 71 per cent, West Bengal 70 per cent, Andhra 66 per cent, Orissa 56 per cent and Kerala 50 per cent. One must note that our ground water resources are getting very highly exploited. The scope for expansion of production through more and more of tube wells will only mean in course of time the sharing of a given potential of water.

Further growth in agricultural production based on extension of irrigation cannot be more than 30 per cent, allowing for a margin of higher yields from irrigated crops. The further increases have to come from applications with greater intensity of fertilizers and better seeds. Even taking into account the yields on demonstration farms, it would be rash to postulate more than a doubling of our agricultural production in prospective time. Specially in respect of foodgrains my own judgement is that even with full utilisation of all technical and irrigation possibilities, further increases are going to be more and more difficult.

At the current levels of production, our Coking Coal resources will not last more than 56 years. But if we assume a modest growth rate of 6 per cent they will not last more than 3 decades. Non-Coking Coal resources at the current level may last for 150 years. But at a growth rate of 6 per cent they will not last for more than 100 years. Iron-Ore resources at the current level may last for 135 years. But at 6 per cent growth rate they will not last for more than 80 years. Crude oil resources may last for 16 years at the current level of production. But at the growth rate of 6 per cent they may not last for more than a decade. So also Natural Gas resources which, at the current level may last for 23 years, but at a modest growth rate they will not last for more than 15 years. We have already exhausted the Kolar Gold Mines and the further discoveries of gold are not very large. Taking Lead, Manganese Ore, Zinc, Kyanite, Copper, Manganese etc., at a growth of 6 per cent they may not last together beyond 3 to 4 decades.

There is a third important conclusion. We have been all along mortgaging the future. The future generations will surely condenm our casualness in the matter of exploitation of our very limited physical and natural resources.

Shall we now atleast start rethinking about our resource endowment in relation to population and comparative advantage ? Shall we wake up the Planning Commission to think in terms of reducing the burdens we are throwing on posterity?

Relative State Domestic Products

We have now information on State domestic products at current and constant prices for the periods 1960-61 to 1980-81 at 1970-71 prices and 1980-81 to 1994-95 at 1980-81 prices. By inter-linking the two, we get a measure of change over 34 years in net State domestic products of most of the States. This is sufficiently a long span of time over which we should expect some notable improvements in real income. We can also find out which of the States have performed better in both the periods and over the long period. We can also compare the national measure of growth and see which of the States have bettered the national measure. It is only after we get an idea of the overall growth of States products that we can go into the question of per capita growth in different States.

Around 1960-61, Maharashtra had 12.39 per cent of all India product. By 1994-95, its share had gone up to 17.12 per cent. Between 1960-61 and 1980-81, Maharashtra's compound growth rate was 3.65 per cent per annum, But between 1980-81 and 1994-95, its growth rate was 6.20 per cent per annum. For the entire period of 34 years its growth rate was 4.85 per cent per annum.

Gujarat in 1960-61, had a share of 5.99 per cent of all India product. By 1994-95, its share had risen to 6.89 per cent. Between 1960-61 and 1980-81, its compound growth rate was 3.96 per cent per annum. But during 1980-81 to 1994-95, its growth rate had risen to 5.66 per cent per annum. For the entire period its growth rate was 4.66 per cent per annum.

Haryana had a share of 2.08 per cent in all-India product in 1960-

61. By 1994-95 its share had gone up to 3.19 per cent. Its growth rate during 1960-61 to 1980-81 was 5.24 per cent per annum. During 1980-81 to 1994-95, its growth rate was still higher at 5.66 per cent per annum, the same as that of Gujarat. For the entire period of 34 years, Haryana's growth rate was 5.42 per cent per annum, the highest among all the States other than the Delhi area.

Punjab had a relative share of 3.71 per cent in all-India product in 1960-61. By 1994-95 its share had risen to 4.40 per cent. Its growth rate during 1960-61, to 1980-81 was 4.87 per cent per annum. During 1980-81 to 1994-95, its growth roused to 5.20 per cent per annum. For the entire period, its growth rate was about 5 per cent per annum. Together Punjab and Haryana improved their share in national product from about 5.79 per cent to 7.59 per cent.

Orissa had a relative share of 1.73 per cent in all-India product in 1960-61. By 1994-95 its share went up to 2.60 per cent. Its growth rate during 1960-61 to 1980-81 was 5.77 per cent per annum, the highest among all States for that period. During 1980-81 to 1994-95, its growth rate came down to 3.19 per cent per annum. For the period of 34 years its growth rate was relatively still high at 4.7 per cent per annum.

Karnataka's relative share in national product was 5.23 per cent in 1960-61. This went up modestly to 5.78 per cent in 1994-95. Its growth rate during 1960-61 to 1980-81 was 3.66 per cent per annum. But during 1980-81 to 1994-95, it steeply went up to 5.54 per cent per annum. For the period of 34 years, its growth rate was relatively higher 4.43 per cent per annum.

The small State of Tripura, had a growth rate of 3.88 per cent during 1960-61 to 1980-81. Its growth rate went up to 5.32 per cent per annum during 1980-81 to 1994-95. For the entire period, its growth rate was 4.42 per cent.

Rajasthan had a relative share of 4.34 per cent in national product in 1960-61. This went up to just 4.66 per cent by 1994-95. Its growth rate during 1960-61 to 1980-81 was low at 2.91 per cent per annum. But during 1980-81 to 1994-95, its growth rate leaped to 6.20 per cent per annum, equalling that of Maharashtra. For the entire period its growth rate was 4.25 per cent per annum.

Delhi Metropolitan region had a share of 1.17 per cent in national product in 1960-61. It more than doubled to 2.82 per cent in 1994-95. Its growth rate during 1960-61 to 1980-81 was 6.02 per cent per annum. But in the second period of 1980-81 to 1994-95, its growth rate went up further to 7.30 per cent per annum. For the entire period its growth rate was as high as 6.53 per cent per annum.

The above are the States which had a growth rate for the entire period of 34 years, above that of the economy which was 3.99 per cent. We now turn to the States which performed less than the national economy.

Bihar's relative share in national product was 7.65 per cent in 1960-61. It slumped to 5.21 per cent by 1994-95. Its growth rate during the first period was just 2.69 per cent per annum. During the second period Bihar performed better with a growth rate of 3.81 per cent per annum. But for the whole period its growth rate was just 3.15 per cent per annum, the lowest among all the States.

Uttar Pradesh had a relative share of 14.5 per cent in national product in 1960-61. It had slumped to 11.99 per cent by 1994-95. Its growth rates during the two periods were respectively 2.73 per cent and 4.12 per cent. For the entire period, its growth rate was just 3.30 per cent per annum.

Tamil Nadu had a relative share of 7.88 per cent in national product in 1960-61. It had come down slightly to 7.48 per cent by 1994-95. During the two periods, its growth rates were respectively 2.11 per cent and 5.55 per cent. The growth rate for the entire period being 3.51 per cent per annum. The redeeming feature is the high growth rate during the period 1980-81 to 1994-95. Its slow during the earlier period has to be accounted.

Kerala's relative share in national product in 1960-61 was 3.62 per cent. In 1994-95 it had gone down to 3.14 per cent. Its growth rates during the two periods were respectively 3.12 per cent and 3.82 per cent. For the entire period, its growth rate was just 3.41 per cent per annum. But Kerala's income in 1994-95 would have substantially higher because of the large inflows of remittances from Gulf countries.

West Bengal the cynosure of left economists had a high share of 10.87 per cent in national product in 1960-61. By 1994-95, it had slumped to 8.57 per cent. The growth rates during the periods were 2.66 per cent and 4.44 per cent per annum. In both the periods, West Bengal's growth rate was well below that of the nation. Though it had improved during the second period, for the entire period of 34 years, the growth rate was just 3.39 per cent.

Assam, the problem State of the economy, had a relative share of 2.27 per cent in national product in 1960-61. It came down to 2.03 per cent by 1994-95. Its growth rates during the two periods were 3.67 per cent and 4.16 per cent respectively. For the entire period of 34 years its growth rate was 3.87 per cent, below the national average.

Himachal Pradesh had a growth rate of 1.99 per cent and 3.63 per cent in the two periods respectively. For the entire period its growth rate was just 2.62 per cent.

Madhya Pradesh had a share of 6.92 per cent in national product in 1960-61. It came down to 6.01 per cent by 1994-95. Its growth rates during the two periods were 1.03 per cent and 3.82 per cent. For the entire period its growth rate was 3.16 per cent.

Jammu & Kashmir had a growth rate of 4.06 per cent during 1960-61 to 1980-81. But during the period 1980-81 to 1994-95, it slumped to 2.78 per cent. For the entire period the growth rate was 3.55 per cent, below the national average. Part of the troubles in this area may be due to the slump in the growth rate during the second period as compared to the first period. It is necessary to keep the growth rates of this area at a higher rate than the national average and than in Pakistan. The forces of economic improvement over the long run are very important in sensitive areas.

It is interesting to observe that by and large most of the States have performed better during the period 1980-81 to 1994-95, than during the earlier periods of 1960-61 to 1980-81. Again by and large the States which were above the national average in growth rates during the first period were also above the national average during the second period also. If we take the growth rates of States above the average, they would bave relative share of more than 50 per cent in national product, in 1994-95.

Relative Improvements in Per-Capita Income in Different States

We have worked out information on an interlinked basis for the period from 1960-61 to 1994-95 in respect of almost all the States. The highest per capita real income growth during the period 1960-61 to 1980-81 was in respect of Orissa. Its per capita real product was doubled during this period. A major reason has been the relatively low population growth rate in the State because of high death rates. The compound growth rate for the above period was as high as 3.58 per cent per annum. But during the period from 1980-81 to 1994-95 the per capita real income grew in Orissa at just 1.31 per cent per annum. For the whole period of 34 years, the per capita real income growth rate in Orissa was 2.64 per cent per annum. Orissa seems to have seen more prosperous years in the past than currently.

Punjab had a growth rate of per capita real income of 2.73 per cent per annum during the 1960-61 to 1980-81, but during the period 1980-81 to 1994-95 per capita real income grew at a high rate of 3.37 per cent per annum higher than in most developed Western countries. For the whole period of 34 years the per capita real income growth rate was close to 3 per cent, the actual rate being 2.98 per cent per annum. Punjab enjoys the enviable privilege of having the highest per capita real income growth in post-Independence India. Haryana had a per capita real income growth rate 2.48 per cent in 1960-61 to 1980-81. During 1980-81 to 1994-95 its growth rate went up to 3.23 per cent per annum. It could have been probably higher but for the uprise of terrorism which must have adversely affected non-agricultural growth. For the whole period of 34 years the growth rate was 2.78 per cent per annum. In overall growth Haryana led Punjab, but in per capita growth Punjab led Haryana. This is due to the higher population growth in Haryana as compared to Punjab. Both these States owe their high growth rates sustained over more than three decades to the remarkable agricultural prosperity, both prior to and after the green revolution. The Bhakra Nangal project must have contributed substantially to the prosperity of these States. Along with of course the enterprise and hard working abilities of the people in these States. The high growth rates in crop outputs here have helped Indian to get rid of imports. These two States illustrate the proposition that industrialisation is neither necessary nor sufficient for real prosperity.

Maharashtra and Gujarat come next to Orissa, Punjab and Haryana. During the period 1960-61 to 1980-81 Maharashtra had a low per capita real income growth rate of just 1.26 per cent per annum. But during the 1980-81 to 1994-95 the per capita real income growth rate leaped to 3.86 per cent per annum. For the entire period of 34 years Maharashtra's per capita real income growth rate was 2.31 per cent per annum. During the second period specially, Maharashtra, more particularly Western Maharashtra witnessed considerable agricultural prosperity specially in sugarcane. The Bombay-Poona region also grew at a high rate in industry. The employment guarantee scheme supplemented incomes of large numbers of women in rural areas. Yet Maharashtra could have grown at a higher rate had capital been potentially not flowing out.

Gujarat also had a low growth rate of per capita real income of just 1.38 per cent per annum during the period 1960-61 to 1980-81.

But during the second period 1980-81 to 1994-95 its per capita income growth rate vaulted to 3.69 per cent per annum. For the entire period of 34 years it had the same per capita income growth rate of 2.31 per cent as Maharashtra. Gujarat's high growth rate in the second period was specially due to the massive capital investment in industries, assisted by the oil discoveries and the abundant use of natural gas, which freed the region from dependence on coal which is so distant to Gujarat. Large scale capital inflow has taken place from non-residents. Gujarat also is one of the few States which welcomes ordinary and skilled labour without any linguistic prejudice from all parts of India. Whatever the political squabbles, economic growth is unhampered in this State. Toynbee predicted very great economic future for Gujarat. With the completion of the Narmada project, Gujarat has a prospect of leaving Maharashtra and other States in India far behind in industrial prosperity.

Karnataka had a per capita real income growth rate of 1.34 per cent per annum during the period 1960-61 to 1980-81. But during the later period of 1980-81 to 1994-95 its per capita real income growth rate climbed up to 3.64 per cent per annum fifth in hierarchy to Tamil Nadu, Maharashtra, Gujarat and Rajasthan. For the whole period of 34 years Karnataka showed a growth rate of 2.26 per cent per annum. Karnataka has been welcoming entrepreneurs from all parts of India and the world. It has a rich reservoir of technical skill in Engineering and Electronics. If it can overcome its power and road shortages from a long run angle its prosperity in industry can match that of Maharashtra and Gujarat. It is in the West Coast and in the North Western districts that future high growth possibilities may exist for Karnataka.

Tamilnadu had a very low per capita real income growth rate of 0.23 per cent per annum during the period of 1960-61 to 1980-81. But it managed to obtain a growth rate of per capita income of 4.16 per cent per annum during the period of 1980-81 to 1994-95. This is the highest growth rate in per capita real income among all the States in this period. Tamil Nadu's transition from such a low growth rate to such a high growth rate is a most remarkable event in post-Independent India's economic history. For the whole period of 34 years Tamilnadu obtained a growth rate of 1.81 per cent per annum in per capita real income. Tamil Nadu's special forte is in its educated entrepreneurs and in its orderly and peaceful labour. The State enjoys also the benefits of lowest cost of living in India, thanks to the cross-subsidisation of food by the Government. It has to sustain in future its high rate of performance in per capita real income growth obtained during the second period.

Rajasthan obtained during 1960-61 to 1980-81 the lowest growth rate of per capita real income of 0.15 per cent per annum. But during the period of 1980-81 to 1994-95 it improved its growth rate in per capita real income to 3.69 per cent per annum. It seems that entrepreneurs from Rajasthan are turning their attention to their own State. Enterprise like charity begins at home. For the entire period of 34 years, its growth rate of per capita real income was 1.59 per cent per annum.

Kerala obtained a 1 per cent per capita real income growth rate in the first period. But in the second period it was able to move this up to 2.38 per cent. For the period of 34 years its per capita real income growth rate was 1.57 per cent per annum. This however underestimates the improvement rate in per capita real income because it abstracts from the effects of the large continuing inflow of remittances. Kerala is top in the human development index but in index of per capita real income growth it is far behind the top in this respect.

Andhra Pradesh obtained just a 1 per cent annual growth rate in per capita real income in the first period. But in the second period it was able to improve its per capita growth rate to 2.17 per cent. For the whole period the per capita real income growth rate was just 1.47 per cent per annum. Andhra Pradesh has yet to come up to the levels of achievement of Karnataka and Tamil Nadu. It has to make further efforts to reduce its population growth rate and to continue improving its yield growth rate in agriculture. It is here that Andhra is lagging. But it has prosperous segments specially in agriculture. But the surpluses are not flowing inadequate measure to investment in development of the State.

Assam had a meagre per capita real income growth rate of 0.58 per cent during the first period though it improved it to 2.64 per cent per annum during the second period. For the whole span of 34 years its per capita real income growth rate was just 1.42 per cent per annum. Assam was at the top in per capita real income at the time of Independence. Thereafter, it has been slipping down relatively. This is a matter of concern both to Assam and to the national economy. Manipur managed to obtain a per capita real income growth rate for the entire period of 34 years of 2.14 per cent per annum which is way better than that of Assam and of many other large States. In fact, Manipur's performance in economic matters has a lot to commend. Its excellent performance in national games is no flash in the pan. Among all the newly formed States in North East as well as Assam and West Bengal, Manipur has managed to take a rather big lead. Its achievement requires truly national recognition.

We now turn to Uttar Pradesh which had also a low growth rate of per capita real income of 0.68 per cent per annum during the first period. During the second period U.P. was able to raise this to 1.89 per cent. For the whole period the growth rate in per capita real income was as low as 1.16 per cent per annum. If Uttarakhand is formed U.P.'s performance level will go down further. Surprisingly West Bengal had one of the lowest per capita real income growth rates during the first period of 1960-61 to 1980-81. During the second period 1980-81 to 1994-95 it was able to improve this to 2.27 per cent per annum. But for the whole period of 34 years the per capita income growth rate was the same as that of U.P., i.e., just 1.16 per cent per annum. West Bengal was also among the top States in per capita real income at the time of Independence. Tripura for the whole period of 34 years performed better than West Bengal by obtaining a per capita real income growth rate of 1.43 per cent per annum.

Bihar obtained per capita real income growth rate of just 0.63 per cent per annum during the first period. During the second period it improved this to a modest 1.60 per cent per annum. For the whole period of 34 years Bihar had the lowest per capita real income growth rate of just 1.02 per cent per annum. Himachal Pradesh also had the same per capita real income growth rate for the entire period. Madhya Pradesh is at the bottom of the list with just 0.73 per cent per annum real income growth rate for the whole period of 34 years. Jammu & Kashmir had just 0.93 per cent per capita real income growth rate for the whole period of 34 years.

The States which are a matter of concern in regard to per capita real income growth rate are Bihar, U.P., West Bengal, Madhya Pradesh, Himachal Pradesh and Jammu & Kashmir. Only seven States in India after Independence have managed to double their per capita real income during the 34 years span for which data is available in the post-Independence period. These are, Punjab (2.72 times), Haryana (2.54), Orissa (2.42), Maharashtra (2.18), Gujarat (2.17), Karnataka (2.15) and Manipur (2.01). Probably if we take the entire post-Independence period Tamil Nadu might join the group. Together the population of these States would be just about 30 per cent in total population of India.

Conclusion

I have given above some indicators of our performance in the post-Independence India. The whole performance in different sectors is being reviewed in detail in the Saturday articles on the centre page of the *Hindu Business Line*. Interested parties are requested to go through these articles. Taking the whole period of 50 years we have no doubt done better than in the previous 50 years when we were under British rule. But there are a number of respects in which our performance has been well below expectations. We have fared poorly from a comparative standpoint in the world. In per-capita consumption of essential goods say in foodgrains our position today is the same as that during the early 30's. But we have improved our position in other commodities. In foodgrains our protein intake per-capita has declined. In elementary education we have been a great failure. In growth rates of product our position in the world has improved after mid 80's. But the future is uncertain because of the continuously degraded nature of our polity. The quality of our representatives has decayed. There is no vision nor statesmanship reflected in their words and actions. Their educational status has also gone down. Cheap popularism and narrow slogans have displaced long term outlooks and nationwide perspectives. A growing economy and a degrading polity cannot go together for long. The latter will pull down the former. We are still not able to discuss our problems in the light of the future in a true manner. One hopes and prays that the future will be better.

10

POVERTY ALLEVIATION IN INDIA: Its Various Facets

A.V. GOKAK

Before taking the plunge, it would be better to have an idea of the concept of poverty. Poverty is related to the income of an individual. The calorific value of the foodgrains which a person must consume to sustain himself is converted into the quantum of foodgrains which an individual ought to buy to sustain himself. This, in turn, is converted into monetary value to identify the income that would be needed to sustain the individual.

There is also the externality concept of poverty. The question of poverty is viewed when it starts affecting the general fabric of society. For instance, the slums create problems of hygiene and law and order and thereby provoke a discussion on the question of poverty. The drawback of this approach is that it tends to view human beings as a means to an end and is against the concept of human dignity.

Poverty is also very much linked with the concept of equality. It must, however, be remembered that the two are totally different concepts. If incomes of different income groups fall in the same proportion, the existing inequalities are not accentuated. However, the poverty of the persons belonging to the lower strata of society will get more acute under such circumstances. Further, a transfer of income from the top to the middle sections of society may reduce inequality, but makes no difference to poverty. The concept of an irreducible core of absolute deprivation, is central to the theme of poverty.

Poverty in India can be explained by a multiplicity of causes such as unequal distribution of land, lack of employment opportunities and the price factor specially the inflationary pressures. As the share of the rural poor in the marketed agricultural surplus is small and rural wages are rigid, a small change in prices can affect the rural poor very adversely. Peasant cultivators with small holding, landless labour and village artisans constitute the bulk of the rural poor in India.

There are divergent views on poverty estimates in the country. According to some of these estimates, the incidence of poverty has gone up. According to the Planning Commission, however, rural poverty declined from 54 per cent in 1972-73 to 51.2 per cent in 1977-78 and 40.4 per cent in 1983-84. It was estimated around 28 per cent in 1987-88. In the year 1993-94, it was estimated to have declined to 21.3 per cent.

Different strategies have been adopted in the country to tackle the problem of poverty since independence. It would not be out of place at this stage to recapitulate the strategies that were adopted from time to time for tackling the problem of poverty.

In the earlier years i.e. the 1950s, the emphasis was on land reforms and agrarian restructuring. It was felt a more equitable distribution of land may help to reduce the degree of poverty to a great extent.

In the 1960s, the emphasis shifted towards greater agricultural production. The planners and the policy makers seem to have been influenced by the *trickle down benefit theory*, which implies that rapid growth in agriculture even without major institutional reforms, would lead to a substantial reduction in the incidence of poverty. The protagonists of the Green Revolution who believed in the *trickle down benefit theory* had assumed that additional hired workers would be needed in the intensification of cultivation and multiple-cropping resulting from the high yielding varieties seeds. However, the assumptions did not materialise fully. The agrarian reforms were not sufficient to cope with the problem and the spirit behind the reforms could not be translated into action at the grassroots level. According to certain surveys, the lands distributed to the poor have been taken on lease by the richer sections in the rural areas. In South Korea and Japan, effective implementation of land reforms did play an important role in economic development as well as poverty alleviation. Japan's policy of raising agricultural productivity in South Korea, which was mainly due to its necessity to obtain increased food supplies on account of its industrialisation, acted as a catalyst in the period prior to the Second World War. After the Second World War, the occupation of South Korea by the American Army was helpful in ensuring enforcement of land reforms as it could resists the opposition of the rich landlords. The American Army played an important role in Japan too after the Second World War in this matter. Despite the influence of great personalities like Vinoba Ji, the land reforms could not be implemented in the proper spirit. The distribution of surplus land among the poor is still not complete because of protracted litigation.

The benefits of the Green Revolution were also not realised fully though the demand for labour increased on account of double cropping and the overall cropping pattern that emerged. More intensive use of irrigation and high yielding seed varieties, however, did not generate enough on-farm employment to reduce poverty among the landless agricultural workers and the households with inadequate land holdings of their own. The benefits of multiple cropping and the overall cropping pattern were offset by the increasing use of pesticides, chemical fertilizers and machines like tractors and harvestors. In the extreme case of Punjab and Haryana, there was, in fact, a fall in on-farm employment. The ratio of agricultural employment growth to the rate of agricultural output growth fell continuously from 0.7 per cent in 1970 to 0.5 per cent in early 80s and 0.3 per cent in late 80s. The breakthrough in production, moreover, was confined to a few areas only. The planners and the policy makers started realising that mere increase in output cannot bring about a change to the desired extent in a short time.

It was out of this realisation that the *target group approach* was introduced for the first time in the late 1960s, which continued in the 1970s, 1980s and 1990s as well. The First Five Year Plan aimed at reduction in inequalities of income, which is listed as one of its objectives. The Second Five Year Plan Document referred to a reduction in inequalities of income and wealth. In the Third Plan period, an important paper entitled "Perspective Development—1961-1987 Implications of Planning for an Immediate Level of Living "was prepared. This indeed was a forerunner to the direct attack on poverty in the Fourth Plan (1969-1974). Consequent to this shift in emphasis, programmes such as the "Small Farmers Development Agency" and the "Programme For Marginal Farmers and Agricultural Labourers " came into force. The emergence of the Tribal Sub-Plan in the early seventies and that of the Special Component Plan in the late seventies constitute important landmarks in the evolution of the target approach group.

During the period of the Fifth Five Year Plan (1974-1979), the concept of the "Minimum Needs Programme" was introduced. The objective of this programme was to improve the consumption levels of subsidised social services, especially for those families, who are below the poverty line. This was to be achieved through a network of certain essential services in an integrated and coordinated manner. The programme covered various services such as roads, water supply, electrification, housing, education for rural people, etc. It could be stated that the Fifth Five Year Plan introduced a qualitative change in the concept of poverty. Poverty came to be viewed not merely in terms of certain quantitative norms based on calorific intake for the subsistence of an individual but also in terms of certain qualitative norms relating to the provision of and access to certain basic facilities such as health, water supply, housing, etc.

While the *target group approach* continues even now, the philosophy of economic liberalisation, which was propounded in the course of Eighth Five Year Plan, has brought about a certain change in the approach to the question of poverty. The Government seem to be taking the view that removal of controls, which act as irritants to investment can give rise to a spurt in the quantum of investment, which in turn, would have the desired effect on the secondary and tertiary sectors of the economy. In other words, we are, to some extent, going back to the approach of the 1960s, though emphasis then was more on the Green Revolution than on removal of bottlenecks in investment and off-loading the burden and liabilities of the public sector. As the burden of subsidies of various types continued to mount, there was emphasis on reducing the magnitude of subsidies of various types specially the food and fertiliser subsidies. However, the political masters seem to have realised that it would be difficult to take such measures to the logical conclusion after their electoral debacle in some of the States recently. That is why the "face" of the reforms is currently being emphasised as much as their "pace". The *target group approach,* however, has not been dispensed with. In fact, the Government had introduced a number of schemes in the rural sector, which are target-oriented. In other words, emphasis, as of now, is on both, specific schemes geared to the needs of those who are below the poverty line and the need to accelerate economic development in general, which would also help in alleviating poverty through an appropriate strategy.

What has been the impact of the Five Year Plans on the rural poor in India ? Have their conditions improved or not ? These are legitimate questions, which nobody can ignore while discussing the problem of rural poverty. It can be stated generally that the people in rural areas are better fed and better clothed now as compared to the early 1950s. An increase in the output in agriculture has generated economic activity in the country-side and helped the rural poor to get both employment and food. The access of the poor to the various social services has also improved though these, especially the ones relating to health and education leave much to be desired in qualitative terms. It is also necessary to note that the death rate has gone down. While the decrease in death rate has contributed to what we call the population explosion, the very fact that we are facing the problem of population explosion would go to show that we have succeeded in improving the conditions of the poor through better medical and educational services. The successful pursuit of the programme relating to food security has also eased the problems of the rural poor.

These positive features need not, however, blind us to certain disturbing trends, which are discernible in our planned economic development. It is true that the Green Revolution has contributed to the increase in agricultural production. The overall growth rate between 1970-71 to 1990-91 has been of the order of 2.5 per cent per year. While the production of rice and wheat has increased, the production of pulses and such coarse grains as chickpeas and millets has shrunk in acreage and their production has stagnated. These staple foodgrains which are consumed by the poor suffer from two basic handicaps, these are grown on unirrigated lands and there has been little varietal improvement among them. These crops are grown on dryland farms which have lagged farther behind the regions where groundwater resources could be developed. Techniques for controlling soil erosion and retaining soil moisture and watershed management have yet to gain acceptance among the people concerned. The benefits of the Green Revolution have not extended to dryland farming. This has been an important deficiency in our strategy.

The increase in the production of rice and wheat has been mostly on account of the groundwater irrigation. Surface irrigation has not contributed in a substantial measure to the incremental production in agriculture. Tubewells serve a larger area than the canal systems in which the Government have made heavy investments. Tubewells are able to give assured supply of water round the year unlike the surface systems. The benefits of tubewells, however, have gone mostly to the larger farmers who have had the capacity to invest as well as access to credit facilities. Once in operation, these reduced the yield of the nearby traditional non-electrified wells in many areas. In areas where the water table went down, many of the earlier traditional wells had to close down their operations. The adverse effects on the watertable resulted in restrictions being imposed in the form of spacing between wells and on credit and electricity connections for the new wells. Thus, the richer farmers almost monopolised a natural resource, especially where a ban on new entrants was imposed. The groundwater was over exploited in States like Punjab and Haryana. In coastal areas, the over exploitation has had disastrous consequences in as much as the sea water has entered the tubewells making the water unfit for agricultural and drinking purposes.

The developmental process has displayed another characteristic which has proved to be detrimental to poverty alleviation. In their anxiety to raise agricultural productivity and usher in industrial growth, the planners diverted common areas to agricultural and industrial use. The common areas comprised forest lands and other non-agricultural lands which were reserved for meeting the common needs of the community. The forests, for instance, were used for meeting the requirements of fuelwood in villages and served as the source which provided fodder and medicines and also minor forest produce including fruits to the community. The utility of timber need hardly be stressed. Certain lands were reserved for purposes of grazing.

The traditional systems of collection of the materials from the "common properties" ensured their sustainability and were equitable. With the advent of the British Raj, the State started asserting itself and the common properties were axed to meet the needs of the Railways and industry. The process did not change in independent India. The rural poor were depending on the common properties to a considerable extent and the common properties met nearly two fifths of their daily requirements such as fuelwood, fodder, etc. The loss or deprivation of these properties has caused a great deal of hardship which is not reflected in the surveys of expenditure. As the materials were collected from the common properties, these were not purchased from the markets. The improvements in levels of household expenditure of the rural poor may thus overstate the improvement. The gains realised by the rural poor from increased agricultural productivity and wage employment have been offset by the impoverishment that they have suffered from in this manner. The adverse impact has been felt especially in certain areas where the diversion of "common properties" has taken place on a large scale.

Women have been the worst sufferers on account of the loss of common properties. They have to spend more and more time on collection of fuelwood. The agricultural wastes/residues and cowdung which could have been used as organic manure are now being used as fuelwood. Women's vulnerability to the loss of common property varies from region to region depending on how strong the gender bias is. The gender bias being especially strong in the northern north-western and eastern States, the position of women in these States is more serious. The worst scenario is witnessed where the gender bias is strong, degree of poverty is high and the common properties are inherently scarce. The conditions are relatively unfavourable on all these counts in Uttar Pradesh, Rajasthan and Bihar.

It is against this background that the question of poverty alleviation has to be considered. The policy makers and the planners have made use of the following strategies for poverty alleviation.

1. Public Distribution System
2. Wage Employment
3. Integrated Rural Development Programme

Public Distribution System

The availability of foodgrains at reasonable prices has got to be an important plank of the poverty alleviation programmes as a substantial portion of the income of the poor is spent on consumption of foodgrains. The Public Distribution System in India has succeeded in ensuring that the foodgrains are made available to the people staying even in the remotest corners of the country. It has surely insulated the poor from the rigours of inflation to some extent. However, the system is not free from its drawbacks, the important among which are as follows :

(a) There is no proper targetting. The system is not focussed on the poorer strata of society.
(b) The poor need coarse grains. The quantum of coarse grains procured, however, is negligible. This is mainly because the market prices of coarse grains are higher than the minimum support prices fixed for them by the Government.
(c) The procurement of rice is of superior groups which are

costlier as compared to the common group. It is, however, not very profitable for the farmer to cultivate "common rice". In fact, the extension work of the Department of Agriculture has also concentrated on the propagation of the superior groups of rice on account of their better returns. The area under common groups of rice has declined over a period of time both in Punjab and Haryana which account for the bulk of rice procurement. In fact, 90 per cent of rice procurement is accounted for by the superfine and fine groups of rice.

(d) The benefits on account of sugar which also figures in the public distribution system accrue mainly to the middle class.

These drawbacks are sought to be remedied by going in for concentrated efforts in the RPDS Blocks which are generally in the tribal areas and are coterminus with the Employment Assurance Blocks in which the scheme for giving assured employment to all able bodied persons in rural areas for a hundred days is implemented. The wages are also paid in kind to a certain extent. The storage capacity in these areas is also proposed to be increased.

The Public Distribution System is mentioned as an important plank of the strategy for poverty alleviation because the Government is subsidising the sale of foodgrains through it on a very large scale. The difference between the economic cost of foodgrains and the consumer issue price of foodgrains which is the subsidy on account of the Public Distribution System, is nearly Rs. 6000 crores and accounts for nearly 50 per cent of the food total Non-Plan subsidy. This subsidy would yield the desired results only if the consumer issue prices are lower than the market prices and are within the limits of affordability, especially for the rural poor. The high operating costs of the Food Corporation of India which are largely on account of the factors beyond its control such as the minimum support price for the farmer the statutory levies imposed by the State Government etc. may compel the Government to raise the consumer issue prices failing which there would be a very heavy burden of subsidy which the Government can ill afford. A radical attempt to restructure the Public Distribution System is called for. Though there has been considerable discussion on the subject, no concrete plan of action has emerged as yet. The need for restructuring the system is imperative as the lifting of foodgrains under the system in States that have a higher incidence of poverty is less as compared to that in States where the incidence of poverty is comparatively less.

Wage Employment

National Rural Employment Programme and the Rural Landless Employment Guarantee Programme were the main schemes, under which employment was provided to the rural poor, especially the rural landless agricultural labourers. The main aim of these schemes was to provide employment to the rural poor and also help in creation of assets for the community. These have recently been replaced by the Employment Assurance Scheme in the last two to three years. The annual expenditure on the two programmes totalled a sum of Rs. 32 billion, which was close to 0.3 per cent of the Gross Domestic Product (GDP). The two schemes were able to generate more than 500 million mandays of employment per year. Still this was equal to only 0.6 per cent of overall rural employment, which is important to many poor households but insignificant part of the total rural market.

The relevance and utility of wage employment programmes have to be viewed in their correct perspective. The Green Revolution did not generate additional on-farm employment to the desired extent. Increased mobility of the rural population on account of improvement in the network of communications was no doubt helpful in enabling the rural poor to commute to the work centres in urban areas. This by itself, was however, not sufficient to cope with the problem. The wage employment programmes in the rural areas, therefore, filled the gap.

The utility of the wage employment programmes has another important dimension as well. This has enabled a more equitable distribution of income in society, thereby making the income distribution less skewed. The increase in the purchasing power of the masses enables them to have better access to foodgrains. While referring to the role played by the Employment Guarantee Scheme in Maharashtra, Shri Amartya Sen, the noted Economist has observed that there can be starvation not only in times of famine but also in times when the production of foodgrains registers an increase. If the poorer strata of society have no access to the Public Distribution System or to foodgrains in the open market because of their meagre purchasing power, they can starve even when there is a perceptible increase in the quantum of foodgrains production. Citing the examples of Maharashtra, the noted Economist has described how Employment Guarantee Scheme in Maharashtra was able to shield the rural poor from the adverse impact of skewed distribution of income.

The available data go to show that the off-take from the Public Distribution System in States, viz., Bihar, Orissa, Uttar Pradesh, Madhya Pradesh which have a higher incidence of poverty is less as compared to the off-take in States, which have a lesser incidence of poverty. This can be explained by the lack of adequate purchasing power among the rural poor in the States, which have a higher incidence of poverty as also the inadequate infrastructure. Wage Employment Programmes would certainly be of great help in this regard. The Employment Assurance Scheme, which has been introduced in certain selected blocks all over the country should be able to give the necessary relief to the rural poor. However, evidence with regard to the lifting of foodgrains from the Public Distribution System in the EAS Blocks in the States with higher incidence of poverty both before and after the introduction of the EAS will have to be collected to ascertain whether the Wage Employment Programmes have had the desired effect.

A trend which has emerged as a result of the implementation of the Wage Employment Programmes is clearly discernible. The implementation of the Wage Employment Programmes in the countryside has definitely enhanced the bargaining power of the rural landless agricultural labour. The creation of employment opportunities in the countryside on account of Indira Awas Yojana, the Jawahar Rozgar Yojana and the Employment Assurance Scheme has registered an additional demand for labour. The increased availability of jobs in the rural areas has enhanced the bargaining power of the rural poor and they are not solely dependent on the employment provided on the farm and/or by the contractor and other traditional employers who are not getting labour with the same ease as before. In other words, implementation of the Minimum Wages Act is better ensured on account of the Wage Employment Programme. Not that the rural poor are being paid wages which are equal to the minimum wages prescribed under the law by the respective State Governments, by the contractors. That is very difficult to authenticate in the absence of reliable data. However, the qualitative assessment that one can make on the basis of discussions with responsible field officials is that rural landless agricultural labourers are now getting much more as compared to what they got prior to the implementation of these programmes.

In certain cases, the Wage Employment Programmes have worked almost as poverty alleviation measures by facilitating higher earnings of the poor. For instance, a road connecting forest villages in Madhya Pradesh with the nearby markets has enabled the authorities concerned to dispose of tendu leaves much more quickly thereby preventing the wastage, which was, at times, nearly to the extent of 20 per cent of the total collection of tendu leaves. Further, it was possible for the authorities to maintain in a much better manner the quality of tendu leaves, as the time lag between the collection and transportation of tendu leaves was reduced considerably on account of the network of roads. The better quality helped the authorities concerned to realise a higher rate in the auctions, which in turn improved the earnings of the tribals staying in the forest areas.

The Wage Employment Programmes serve another important purpose. These reduce intra-year variations in the earnings of landless agricultural workers in addition to raising their average earnings. These may not have any significant impact on rural poverty but certainly help in reducing the severity of poverty by enhancing incomes of the rural poor.

The Wage Employment Programmes however, have one major deficiency. These can be no substitute for the employment that is generated in the normal course as a result of economic development in all sectors of the economy. Wage Employment Programmes specifically evolved for providing employment, run the risk in the long run, of being dubbed as programmes for just *doling* out money. Another criticism, levelled against the Wage Employment Schemes is that these have erred in attaching more importance to the creation of social overheads like school buildings, Panchayat Ghars, roads etc., as against the creation of assets, which are directly productive like, say construction of irrigation works, watershed development, afforestation etc. While socio-economic infrastructure such as roads do not have to be altogether overlooked, because these can as in the case of the Madhya Pradesh forest villages, contribute to the productive processes. Assets, which are directly productive however, have a more decisive impact on output and employment and hence on alleviation of poverty and, therefore, deserve to be accorded a higher priority. Further, the Wage Employment Schemes have not resulted in the creation of any need-based skills but have only created job opportunities almost exclusively in the lean season.

Integrated Rural Development Programme

A third strategy which the planners resort to is that of implementing schemes that result in creation of income generating assets for the poor. The assets are handed over to the poor with the fond hope that the poor will make proper use of them and enhance their incomes.

The Integrated Rural Development Programme (IRDP) aims at achieving the objective indicated above. Provision of productive assets in the primary, secondary and tertiary sectors through financial assistance by way of Government subsidy and credit from the banks to the persons living below the poverty line is what it aims at. A rural family whose income is less than Rs. 11000 per annum and figures in the below poverty line list maintained by the Gram Sabha is entitled to get the benefit under the scheme. The expenditure on subsidy is shared between the Centre and the States in the ratio of 50:50. Subsidy is limited to 25 per cent of the project cost for small farmers, 33-1/3 per cent for the marginal farmers, rural artisans and agricultural labourers and 50 per cent for the Scheduled Castes and Tribes.

The implementation of this scheme has been the subject matter of a great deal of controversy and debate. The experience of the State Governments, however, indicates that there are several areas in which there is scope for improvement. The selection of the beneficiaries has been faculty in a large number of cases either on account of corruption or the lack of involvement of the Gram Sabhas in the selection process. The banks have not been very enthusiastic in giving loans because of the unsatisfactory repayment of the loans by the beneficiaries. The banking services are also inadequate, especially in the North-Eastern sector. There has, therefore, been inadequate credit mobilisation. As against the normative subsidy credit mobilisation ratio of 1:2, the actual ratio has been of the order of 1:1.77 on the average in the first three years of the Eighth Plan. The ratio was of the order of 1:1.87 in the Sixth and 1:1.98 in the Seventh Plan.

A survey at the national level has revealed that 71 per cent of the beneficiaries had their assets intact at the end of two years after the distribution of the assets. Remaining 29 per cent of the assets had either been sold, partly or fully perished or defective. Costly maintenance of the assets was an important reason for the remaining 29 per cent of the assets not being found intact. Emergency or unexpected developments which affected the financial position of the beneficiary adversely, was cited as another important reason for the same.

It was intended that specific schemes suited to the needs of the identified families should be devised with a view to distributing assets best suited to their needs. In actual practice, however, this became a milch animal and sewing machine programme. NABARD Survey of 1984 shows that 40 to 50 per cent of the investment as well as beneficiaries related to dairy, sheep and goats. Bullocks and camels with or without carts accounted for 20 per cent thereof. This happened because of the obsession with achieving the targets in a mechanical manner rather than the economic soundness of the investments made.

Concurrent evaluation at the national level by the IBRD shows that 24 per cent of the assets generated no income at all, 26 per cent of the assets generated less than Rs. 1,000 income and the remaining 50 per cent of the assets generated income of more than Rs. 1,000. A positive feature of the programme, thus, is that at least 50 per cent of the beneficiaries had income of more than Rs. 1,000 from the assets.

The most important question, however, is whether the scheme has enabled the beneficiaries to cross the poverty line. The fourth round of concurrent evaluation (1993) of the scheme shows that 14.81 per cent of the beneficiaries could cross the revised poverty line of Rs. 11,000, 50.4 per cent of the beneficiaries were able to cross the old poverty line of Rs. 6400 per annum as compared to 28 per cent in 1989.

Studies conducted by The Institute of Financial Management and Research indicate that 84 per cent of the sample households received incremental income. The survey conducted by NABARD showed that while 47 per cent of the sample households had crossed the poverty line, 82 per cent thereof had received incremental income. The Programme Evaluation Organisation's survey has indicated that 49.4 per cent of the sample households had crossed the poverty line, 88 per cent of them had received incremental income.

It would be seen that the scheme has helped the beneficiaries in receiving additional income. However, the effectiveness of the scheme in enabling the beneficiaries to cross the poverty line cannot be commented upon with the same degree of confidence. To sum up, the scheme has achieved greater success in raising the pre-assistance income of the beneficiaries than in enabling the people to cross the poverty line.

The conclusion that has been arrived at need not be a cause for worry. It is impossible for the poorest families to cross the poverty line in a couple of years. The process is bound to be gradual even after receiving the assistance under the IRDP. There are very many reasons for this. In the first place, the socio-economic conditions of the people below the poverty line are not identical. The position of a family with an annual income of Rs. 10,000 cannot be compared to that of a family with an annual income of say Rs. 5,000 or Rs. 6,000. Families below the poverty line may require different degrees of assistance depending on how below they are below the poverty line. Just as geo-physical conditions below the earth are different at various depths, so also the socio-economic conditions of the families which are below the poverty line also vary a great deal. The scheme however, provides for a uniform subsidy and loan without taking into account these niceties. It is the lack of this flexibility in providing the type of assistance that is required at various levels that is mainly responsible for the failure of the scheme in achieving its main objectives. The poorest of the poor may require a different kind of package altogether. They may, for instance, require a second dose of assistance after the initial assistance. The repayment schedule in their respect may have to be drastically revised.

All these aspects need to be gone into thoroughly. The absence of forward and backward linkages in the IRDP has already been commented upon. Their absence results in problems of marketing the products, which are produced with the help of the assets. The individual beneficiary is too poor and weak to organise the marketing of his product. The individual beneficiaries under the scheme being either marginal farmers or landless agricultural labourers many of whom have never known how to own and maintain an asset. The distribution of assets among them disturbs their normal life. Formation of groups has been recognised as an important strategy for overcoming this handicap. The products produced by the individual members of the groups can be sold by the group itself, which can undertake the initiative for marketing and selling. Such groups have been formed with the desired results in some parts of the country. In Assam, for example, power tillers have been distributed among many groups of farmers with a view to bringing more and more fallow land under cultivation. Use of power tiller has enabled the small and marginal farmers to reduce the time taken for tilling the land and has also helped them in taking double crops. The use of the power tiller has caught up as a gap between the land lying fallow and availability of power tillers is considerable. Most of the groups have lent the power tillers, which they have got with the help of bank loans to the farmers who do not possess them, on rent. The groups have been registered as cooperative societies and for the reasons indicated above, are making very good profits. The banks have been able to realise their dues and are enthusiastic in funding more and more such proposals. The formation of the group would, however, assume a great deal of cooperation among the members, which would require considerable motivation by the administrative machinery.

There is a very intense debate on the comparative merits and demerits of Wage Employment Schemes and income generation schemes like the IRDP. The merit of schemes like the IRDP lies in the fact that they enable the beneficiary to become independent and not be at the mercy of any employer. The Wage Employment Programmes would entail heavy public expenditure in the wake of the growth of population and additions to the agricultural labour force. The quality of execution of works under the Wage Employment Programmes also leaves much to be desired. On the other hand, the drawback of schemes like the IRDP is that these cannot cater to all segments of the rural poor below the poverty line. The IRDP will succeed only in cases where assisted families are marginally below the poverty line. For the rest of the beneficiaries falling below the poverty line, Wage Employment Schemes would have to be provided. If we do not provide wage employment to the poorer and poorest of the poor, the assistance given under the IRDP may not produce the desired results and prove to be infructuous investment. A judicious combination of the two schemes would, therefore, be inevitable for at least in the near future.

The evaluation criteria for the IRDP would also have to undergo a radical change. It will not be correct to judge the success of the scheme in terms of the number of families that have crossed the poverty line. It would be necessary, on the other hand, to evaluate its success on the basis of whether the assisted families have realised higher incomes than the non-assisted families, whether assisted families have progressively climbed to the next higher income bracket from the pre-programme income bracket and the cost, that is capital output ratio at which this has been achieved.

Social and cultural factors have an important bearing on the problem of poverty alleviation. These are especially important in relation to the demographic factor, which plays an important role in the development of the Indian economy. The problem of population growth has added to the poverty of this country. The participation of women in the process of development is a vital factor in this context. The adverse effects of certain developments in the country since independence, which have severely affected the conditions of women, have already been delineated. The involvement of women is absolutely essential in the implementation of programmes like social forestry, health and education. Experience shows that States where women have a favourable position in society, have succeeded better in controlling population. Kerala, which is not economically advanced and whose per capita income level is relatively low, has done remarkably well in this sphere. The most import favourable factor in Kerala is the position held by women in Keralan society which has a maternal tradition and a system of inheritance through the female line. In 1991, Kerala's total fertility rate was lower than that of Sweden and the USA. In Goa, the low degree of fertility has been achieved on account of the rapid economic modernisation and assimilation of Western ideas, including those based on women's equality.

It is, therefore, essential to ensure that women participate in the developmental programmes, which can be ensured only after their socio-economic status is enhanced. It is in this light that the significance of 73rd and 74th Amendments to the Constitution has to be understood. These amendments, which were long overdue would have a far reaching effect on both poverty alleviation and economic development in India in the long run.

The concept of poverty cannot be divorced from that of the Minimum Needs Programme, which was evolved during the Fifth Five Year Plan. It covers various facets such as elementary education, rural health, rural water supply, rural roads, rural electrification, housing assistance to rural landless labourers, environmental improvement of urban slums and nutrition public distribution and rural sanitation and domestic cooking energy are the newly added components.

All the components have to fulfil certain norms. The implementation of these programmes has no doubt made a difference in the living conditions of the rural poor. There is, unfortunately, no monitoring mechanism worth the name for evaluating the progress under it. Despite all the limitations and deficiencies, these programmes have contributed to the well-being of the poor. The results however, may not be commensurate with the efforts. This requires a deep probe.

In fact, the concept of poverty itself would have to alter radically in the wake of these developments. It need not necessarily be viewed in terms of income but also in terms of access to various social services. In India itself, the approach to poverty based on the food intake, i.e. the food approach in terms of the consumption of 2,300 calories of food per day by an individual is giving way to another approach based on certain minimum standard of living, which is called the Minimal Standard of Living Approach. Dr. Khusro for instance has tried to develop his own concept of the quality of life. The new trend is in line with the recent international trends. The UNO has also prepared a set of indices for assessing human resource development based on education, health and income. The concept of poverty needs to be encouraged and made more comprehensive on the lines of the UNO's concept. Such a course of action would be in keeping with the recent emphasis on the right to decent living. The Government of Madhya Pradesh have recently published very useful data on indices of human resource development such as employment, education, health, nutrition and employment of women. Such efforts need to be replicated. On the basis of such efforts, a new concept of poverty needs to be evolved.

If the incidence of poverty is to be judged, with reference to the extent of starvation, we have achieved considerable success. The famines are now a thing of the past and food production has increased substantially. Though, some qualitative improvement is necessary in the public distribution system, the poor are reasonably assured of foodgrains. The surplus food stocks in the country can be distributed among the rural poor through the rural works programmes. The National Sample Survey Organisation (NSSO) has reported in its 397th report, its findings regarding the perception of the rural poor regarding sufficiency of food in rural areas, the perception of 923 households per thousand households was that they got two square meals per day throughout the year. 70 households, on the other hand, felt that they got only two square meals in some months of the year, while 7 households felt that they did not get two square meals per day in some months of the year. In urban areas 973 households out of 1000 households felt that they had two square meals per day, 20 households felt that they did not get them even during some months of the year and

4 households felt that they did not get two square meals at all in some months of the year. At the all India level, the proportion of households not getting two square meals per day was less than 1 per cent in both the sectors. In Assam, however, the corresponding figure was 5 per cent in the rural sector and around 2 per cent in the rural sector of Bihar and Orissa. If the incidence of poverty were to be judged by the other indicators such as health, education, nutrition etc., there could be a different picture altogether. It is in this direction that greater efforts need to be made hereafter.

11

WORK PARTICIPATION, GENDER AND ECONOMIC DEVELOPMENT:
A Quantitative Anatomy of the Indian Scenario

ASHOK MATHUR

Introduction

The proportion of population which participates in economically productive work, subsequently to be referred to as the participation rate, is an important measure of effective utilisation of the available human resources. A higher degree of work participation by the population, *ceteris-paribus*, would be expected to enhance the level of per capita income and lower the incidence of unemployment in an economy. The extent of work participation in an economy depends upon a number of factors ranging over the supply and demand side determinants; age structure and health of population; pressure of population, particularly in overpopulated developing countries; rural *vis-a-vis* urban place of work; institutional system governing employment; social norms like system of inheritance and existence of joint family system *vis-a-vis* nuclear families.[1]

Many of the above influence in turn depend upon the stage of development of an economy. Over the long run, the process of development can, therefore, be envisaged to bring about transformation in the structure of the economy as well as changes in institutions and human attitudes which would have substantial implications for the extent of work participation. A study of the relationship between work participation, level of development and other determinants of work participation is thus an issue of significance. This study addresses three dimensions of this theme, using data from the Indian economy.

The article starts off by examining the influence exercised by development on work participation (section III). This theme has attracted considerable attention in literature in the context of work participation by women (Sinha, 1965; Boserup, 1970; Durand, 1975; ILO, 1978; Schuster, 1982, Agarwal, 1985). The present study, however, examines the relationship of development of work participation both for males and females in order to be able to compare the nature of response in case of the two genders. The next section takes a look at inter-temporal trend of work participation rates in the Indian economy, but the main contribution of this article lies in an intensive analysis of cross-sectional data.

At the second stage the article goes on to investigate the role of some important supply side determinants of male and female work participation rates, which have hitherto been neglected, together with some basic socio-economic and demographic determinants of work participation (sections IV-VI). For this purpose a multi-equation regression model has been made use of. The approach has been formulated keeping in mind some of the specific characteristics of female labour supply behaviour on which there has been considerable growth of theoretical literature (Mincer, 1962; Heckman, 1978; Heckman and Macurdy, 1980; Killingworth, 1983). The third part of the article is devoted to an intensive probing of one of the very important determinants of work participation, namely education, and its relationship to the level of development (section VII).

Many of these issues have been the subject matter of earlier studies. There are two directions in which the present article can claim to make an advance over the earlier works. The first of these pertains to the rural-urban dichotomy. Quite often this factor is incorporated by including the degree of urbanisation as a determinant of work participation. However, this procedure cannot fully reveal the nature of rural-urban differences in the behaviour of male and female participation rates. In this study the entire analysis runs along two parallel tracks, one for the rural and the other for the urban segment, as in case of Sahn and Alderman's (1988) study of Sri Lanka.

The second direction in which this study can claim to make an advance is in respect of the units of observation drawn upon for empirical cross-sectional analysis. Two types of approaches can be distinguished in the literature to examine the role of factors influencing the available supply of labour (*cf.* Ben-Porath, 1973). One is micro-level analysis based on attributes of individual households, obtained either through a sample survey (Standing and Sheehan, 1978; Bardhan, 1979; Behrman and Wolfe, 1984) or by retrieving individual level information collected while conducting a population census, as in certain parts of the monumental work of Bowen and Finegan (1969). The second approach is that based on a cross-sectional analysis of aggregated data for different regions. This chapter, as in many earlier studies, follows the second procedure (Nath, 1970; Gulati, 1975a or 1975b; Sinha, 1975; Reddy,1975; Tripathi, 1978; Krishnamurthy, 1982; Saxena, 1987; Raju, 1987; Sundaram, 1988). But most of these studies have used State level data, thus yielding a limited number of observations[2]. This encounters a dual problem—that of ignoring intra-State variations and many a time the absence of a high degree of statistical significance of many of the results. The present study, on the other hand, is based on district level data. The basic analysis of this study rests on the 1971 Census of population and district level data from other sources for the same year although the broad contours of national level inter-temporal trends cover the period from 1901 to 1991. The district level data for 1971 provided 306 observations,[3] thus making it possible to undertake much more intensive empirical analysis than possible on the basis of inter-State analysis.

The spinal chord of this study rests on a district-level index of development for 1971. The indicators chosen for this index encompass some of the key attributes of development. The process of development brings about important structural changes within an economy, it raises levels of productivity and is associated with enhancement of infrastructural facilities. Keeping these in mind, the district level index of development for 1971 is based on a set of nine indicators of development. Three indicators were taken to depict the state of development of the primary sector, namely agricultural productivity per hectare, percentage of cropped area that is irrigated and cropping intensity. Next, three structural indicators of development were used, namely, percentage of total workforce engaged in non-primary activities, percentage of population living in urban areas and percentage of workforce engaged in non-household industries to total industrial workforce. Finally, for social and infrastructural development another three indicators were used, namely overall literacy percentage, road mileage per sq. km. and bank deposits per capita.[4] These nine indicators were composited into an index of development for 306 districts in the form of the first principal component. In brief, the first principal component represents a weighted aggregate of the chosen indicators in which estimated weights attached to the indicators are such that the index of development derived through their linear aggregation yields a maximum sum of square of correlations with the individual indicators (for details see Herman 1960); Kundu (1980).

Participation Rates in the Indian Economy: A Bird's Eye View

Before coming to a cross-sectional analysis based on district level data, it would be worthwhile to take a fleeting view of inter-temporal behaviour of national level work participation rates[5] in the Indian economy since the beginning of the century. Table 11.1 puts together genderwise as well as overall participation rates from 1901 to 1991, based on decennial Population Census data. Estimates from 1901 to

TABLE 11.1: Inter-Temporal Trend of Participation Rates

Year	Males	Females	Overall
1901	60.8	31.7	46.4
1911	62.0	33.7	48.1
1921	60.4	32.6	46.9
1931	58.1	28.8	43.8
1951	53.9	23.4	39.1
1961	57.3	28.0	43.1
1971 (a)	52.5	11.9	32.9
(b)	52.7	14.2	34.2
1981 (a)	51.6	14.0	33.5
(b)	52.7	19.8	36.8
1991 (a)	50.9	15.9	34.1
(b)	51.6	22.3	37.5

Note: (1) 1991(a), 1981(a) and 1971(a) estimates are based on main worker concept. 1991(b) and 1981(b) estimates are based on main and 'marginal' workers while 1971(b) estimates are based on main and 'secondary' workers.

(2) 1981 estimates exclude Assam since no Census was conducted in that State during 1981, while 1991 estimates exclude Jammu & Kashmir since no Census was conducted in that State during 1991.

1961 are reproduced from Sinha (1982), while for 1971, 1981 and 1991 two sets of participation rates have been estimated. The participation rates for the different Census years cannot be easily compared with one another on account of inter-censal changes in the definition of workforce. Prior to 1961 workforce estimates were based on means of livelihood approach using income criterion for identifying an economically active person. From 1961 onwards the approach to workforce estimation is based on classifying persons into workers and non-workers on the basis of their activity status during a specified reference period. However, despite difficulties two broad conclusions can be derived.

First, the male participation rate has been consistently higher than the female participation rate and this gap has been widening. Whereas the male participation rate was less than twice the female participation rate towards the beginning of the century, it is well above twice for the more recent decades, indicating a faster growth of employment opportunities for males than for females.

Secondly, when we try to gauge the inter-temporal trend of participation rates for the period up to 1961, the workforce data for 1911, 1921 and 1961 are broadly comparable (Ambannavar, 1969 and 1975; Krishnamurty, 1982). If one ignores the 1931 and 1951 figures, which undercounted workforce by 10 to 16 per cent according to Ambannavar, it is evident that there was a continuous decline in the participation rate of both genders till 1961.

Interpretation of trends beyond 1961 is more difficult. The 1961 Census used liberal criteria for being counted as a worker. In case of regular employment, the reference period was 15 days prior to the count and a person who had worked for at least one out of these 15 days was counted as a worker. In contrast, the 1971 Census used a more restrictive concept of workforce. The major departure from 1961 was that a person was considered to be a worker only on the basis of his/her main activity. The reference period was one week in case of regular employment and preceding one year in case of non-organised activities. But only those persons whose main activity during this period was work could qualify as 'workers'. This excluded from workers those persons, largely females, who participated in economic activity but only as part time workers.

The 1971 Census Schedule did carry a question which sought information from a person who was classified as a 'non-worker' on the basis of main activity criterion as to whether he/she participated in some activity as a 'secondary worker'. As pointed out by J.N. Sinha (1982), the 'question of secondary work was not properly canvassed' and therefore, figures of 'secondary workforce' in 1971 Census are generally not considered to be very reliable. However, in table 11.1 two sets of participation rates have been given for 1971. Whereas set (a) gives estimates of participation rates on the basis of main workers, set (b) estimates of participation rates for 1971 include both main and 'secondary workers'. The 1961 and 1971 (set a) participation rates are not comparable on account of definitional change. Set (b) is better, though only slightly, from the point of view of inter-temporal comparability. Set (b) shows a considerable drop in participation rates in 1971 over 1961.

In order to get over this problem of comparability of 1961 and 1971 estimates, another approach was tried by Krishnamurty (1981). Using two alternative sets of age-sex-residence specific participation rates—one based on 1961 Census data and the other based on 1972/73 round of National Sample Survey—he applied these to the population estimates of 1971. This procedure also showed a decline in overall participation rate from 1961 to 1971.

The 1981 Census concept of work was very liberal, the criterion for inclusion as a worker being participation in at least some work during the last year. The workers so identified were classified into two categories—the main and the marginal workers. The 1991 Census follows concepts similar to 1981 Census. Thus, in the case of 1981 as well as 1991 Census one can formulate two concepts of participation rates—one based on main workers and the other, a more liberal one, based on main as well as marginal workers. Set (a) based on main workers concept can be used for comparison of 1991 and 1981 with 1971 set (a) while set (b) based on main as well as marginal workers can be used for a comparison of 1991 and 1981 with 1961 participation rates. If one compares 1961 with 1981 (b) and 1991 (b), there has been a continuing, though slight, decline in the male participation rate, but the female participation rate has taken an upward turn from 1981 to 1991. Set (a) estimates support a decline in male participation rate, but show the upturn in female participation rate to have started earlier on, that is, from 1971.

What does emerge from the inter-temporal trends discussed above is that for most of the present century a decline in participation rates of both genders accompanied a rise in the level of development of the national economy but the trend appears to have reversed over the past two decades in the case of the female participation rate. One of the important factors contributing to the declining trend had been a shift in the structure of population towards urban areas, which accompanies the process of development. Urban areas generally exhibit lower rates of work participation than the rural ones primarily on account of greater scope for 'informal employment, particularly of females, within the less regulated and household based rural work environment than in case of the urban segment.[6] Moreover, the proportion of student body is also larger in the urban segment and they are non-workers.

Some of these rural-urban and genderwise differences in participation rates are evident from Table 11.2, based on 306 districts data set for 1971. First, the disparity between male and female participation rates tends to be much greater in urban areas where the female participation rate was about one-seventh of the male participation rate as against that in rural areas where the female participation rate was about one-quarter of the male participation rate. Further, it is primarily the rural female participation which is much higher—almost double—compared to that of females in urban areas. In case of males the rural-urban gap (53.47 per cent—48.82 per cent) is much less. Secondly, inter-district variation in the extent of work participation is far higher in the case of female work participation than in the case of male work participation (Table 11.2, col. 2). Both these attributes point to much greater unutilised potential of human resources among females than among males.[7]

TABLE 11.2: Segmentwise Participation Rates and their Inter-District Variability (1971: 306 Districts Data Set)

	Average Segmentwise Participation Rates (Per cent)	Inter-District Co-efficient of Variation (Per cent)
(1) Rural Female Participation Rate	13.10	79.02
(2) Rural Male Participation Rate	53.47	12.80
(3) Urban Female Participation Rate	6.61	62.57
(4) Urban Male Participation Rate	48.82	9.03

Participation Rates and Development

Does development tend to reduce such unutilised potential of human resources? The initial impact of development on female work participation in fact is generally supposed to be negative, not positive. With the spread of development the institutional character of employment in the economy undergoes a change. In early stages a good portion of non-agricultural productive activity takes place in households where family members, females in particular, find it easy to combine their traditional duties with part-time participation in productive endeavour. But with movement to higher levels of development there is growth of organised wage-labour markets although such a process may be slow within the rural sector where tying down of labour through interlinked contracts for land and labour or credit and labour impedes the functioning of land and labour markets (Bharadwaj, 1989). The ultimate impact of such a transformation is to limit the scope of informal employment, which tends to constrain the size of the workforce, particularly of its female component.

Durand's international investigation (1975) emphasises the role of shrinkage in span of working age in contributing to the decline in work participation in the cases of both genders. Greater consciousness of the need for learning rather than earning in early years of life, combined with legislation prescribing minimum years of schooling, are important factors responsible for increase in the age of entry into workforce. At the other end of the age spectrum, spread of the organised sector activities means employment only up to a specified superannuation age, thereby lowering average exit age from the employment market.

Technological and structural change, on the other hand, can exercise a dual type of influence. On one side, many of the mechanical processes associated with modern industry provide limited avenues for employment of women. At the same time some of the fast-growing industries and many service-sector activities afford considerable opportunities for employment of females. The spread of education among women and acquisition of new skills, which accompanies rising levels of development, also goes to enhance their employability in the modern segment. Thus divergent forces come to operate upon the participation of women in work as one moves up the ladder of development.

What light does our district level investigation throw on this relationship ? Cross-sectional analysis for one point of time would be free of the problems posed by inter-temporal comparability of data. For the purpose of subsequent analysis two concepts of participation rates have been made use of in this study. First, there is the standard concept of participation rate, which measures the percentage of male (or female) workforce in the rural (or urban) segment to male (or female) population of the rural (or urban) segment of each district. The standard participation rates, $R_g(i)$, may thus be defined as :

$$R_g\,(i) = \frac{W_g\,(i)}{P_g\,(i)} \times 100 \tag{1}$$

where i indicates rural *(r)* or urban *(u)* segment of a district; g indicates gender, male *(m)* or female *(f)*; $W_g\,(i)$ indicates workforce of gender *(g)* in segment *(i)*; $P_g(i)$ indicates population of gender *(g)* in segment *(i)*.

The second concept has been formulated here specifically to take account of certain facets of the rural-urban dichotomy. This concept considers rural and urban participation rates in a slightly modified manner in order to take account of the fact that within a district some component of rural population may be participating in work but shifting its place of work from the rural to the urban segment as one moves up the ladder of development. In order to take account of this type of intra-district movement, the second concept, which may be called the 'modified' participation rate, contains total male (or female) population of a district as a whole in the denominator and can be expressed symbolically as :

$$MODR_g\,(i) = \frac{W_g\,(i)}{\sum_i P_g\,(i)} \times 100 \tag{2}$$

When districts are considered as a whole, the standard and modified participation rates obviously become identical. The modified participation rates have relevance only in the context of separate analysis for rural and urban segments.

Linear regressions of the standard or modified participation rate on the district level index of development I_d could give an idea of the direction of response of work participation to the level of development. However, some scholars, notably J.N. Sinha (1965: 1975), have suggested that the relationship of female participation rate to development is not a monotonically declining one but of a

U-shaped form. This can happen in view of divergent types of influences on female work participation that come to operate at higher levels of development, to which a reference has just been made. In order to test the hypothesis that there exists a tendency for the declining female participation rate to reverse its direction at higher levels of development, and to see whether a similar pattern holds true in the case of males, participation rates were expressed as a second order polynomial function of the level of development I_d.

The results for this type of polynomial model, when no bifurcation is made between rural and urban segments, are given by equations (3) and (4). The $\bar{R}$ values came out to be higher for the polynomial fit compared to linear regressions, particularly in the case of males. It may be observed from the first regression term in both equations that the initial impact of development on work participation

$$\text{Females: } R_f = 12.32 - \underset{(3.27)}{0.62^{***}} I_d + \underset{(1.31)}{0.015} \; I_d^2 \quad \bar{R} = 0.19^{***} \tag{3}$$

$$\text{Males: } R_m = 52.34 - \underset{(6.96)}{0.50^{***}} I_d + \underset{(5.51)}{0.023} \; I_d^2 \quad \bar{R} = 0.37^{***} \tag{4}$$

*** indicates significance at 0.01 level

is strongly negative not only for females but also for males as well. The sign of the second regression coefficient in both the equations is positive though its magnitude is small, thus confirming a U-shaped relationship for both male and female participation rates. But the U-shaped fit is in fact much better for males ($\bar{R}$= 0.37) than for females ($\bar{R}$= 0.19). The magnitude of the second regression term, as well as its '*t*' value, is smaller for females than for males, thus indicating a somewhat greater validity of the J.N. Sinha U-Shaped hypothesis for males than for females for whom it was originally formulated

The above results pertain to districts considered as a composite unit, without any bifurcation between their rural and urban segments. Equations (5)–(8) express modified participation rates as polynomial functions separately for the rural and urban segments. These functions were estimated for standard as well as modified participation rates. The relationships revealed a higher explanatory power in terms of modified participation rates and these alone are being given here. The superiority of relationships in terms of modified participation rates can be explained on account of the fact that movements in modified participation rates reflect not only the work participation effect but also incorporate intra-district shift in the structure of workforce from rural to urban areas as one moves up the developmental hierarchy of districts.

Females :

$$Rural : MODR_f(r) = 11.18 - 0.82^{***} I_d + 0.015 I_d^2 \quad \bar{R} = 0.27^{***} \quad (5)$$
$$(4.54) \qquad (1.42)$$

$$Urban : MODR_f(u) = 1.13 + 0.20^{***} I_d + 0.0004 I_d^2 \quad \bar{R} = 0.65^{***} \quad (6)$$
$$(11.22) \qquad (0.36)$$

Males :

$$Rural : MODR_m(r) = 43.92 - 2.06^{***} I_d + 0.14 I_d^2 \quad \bar{R} = 0.88^{***} \quad (7)$$
$$(25.38) \qquad (3.05)$$

$$Urban : MODR_m(u) = 8.43 + 1.56^{***} I_d + 0.009^{***} I_d^2 \quad \bar{R} = 0.89^{***} \quad (8)$$
$$(23.59) \qquad (2.31)$$

When we consider the segment-wise relationships of modified participation rates, the U-shaped behaviour is observable only in the rural segment (equations 5 and 7) and here also the relationship is stronger for males than for females. In the case of the urban segment the relationship is distinctively positive for males since both the regression coefficients are positive, indicating an accelerating rise in the modified male participation rate in relation to the level of development. In the case of urban females, while the coefficient of the first order term is positive, the second order term is very feeble. Thus both male and female participation rates may be lower in the urban segment compared to the rural ones (Table 11.3), but their response to rising level of development is positive and very different from that in the rural segment. This brings out a sharp dichotomy between rural and urban segments in respect of the relationship of work participation to development.

In order to gauge gender differentiation in the relationship of participation rates to development, male-female difference in the modified participation rates was regressed on the level of development in the form of a second order polynomial function. The resulting regression equations (9 and 10) are quite revealing. Both the relationships are highly significant but the nature of relationship is quite the opposite in rural and urban segments. In the rural segment

Rural Segment :

$$[MODR_m(r) - MODR_f(r)] = \underset{(6.60)}{32.74 - 1.24^{***} I_d} \underset{(0.05)}{-0.0005\ I_d^2} \quad \bar{R} = 0.45^{***} \quad (9)$$

Urban Segment :

$$[MODR_m(u) - MODR_f(u)] = \underset{(23.06)}{7.29 + 1.36^{***} I_d} \underset{(2.70)}{+ 0.009^{***} I_d^2} \quad \bar{R} = 0.89^{***} \quad (10)$$

the difference between male and female participation rates goes on narrowing down with a rise in the level of development, as revealed by the negative coefficients of both the first and second order terms. But in the urban segment both the regression coefficients are positive indicating an ever widening gap in the gender-wise participation rates. This is at least partly a consequence of the tendency for a higher pace of rural to urban migration in the case of male workers than in the case of female workers within districts at higher levels of development. This tends to push up the modified male participation rate in urban areas as one moves up the development hierarchy while suppressing it in rural areas.

TABLE 11.3: Causes of Non-Participation (Percentage of each Category of Non-Workers to Total Non-Workers)

Non-Worker Category	Rural		Urban		Total	
	Male	Female	Male	Female	Male	Female
(1) Students	28.58	6.74	44.73	19.34	32.19	9.29
(2) Household Duties	2.03	51.03	0.68	48.49	1.73	50.51
(3) Dependants	66.69	38.89	45.91	31.18	62.06	39.48
(4) Rentiers	0.06	0.02	2.76	0.34	1.07	0.25
(5) Beggars	0.04	0.02	0.46	0.17	0.44	0.18
(6) Inmates	0.01	0.001	0.37	0.05	0.13	0.02
(7) Others	1.63	0.02	5.05	0.42	2.39	0.27

Supply Side Factors and Socio-Economic Determinants of Work Participation

The Key Variables

We now turn to other factors which influence work participation. In searching for a comprehensive explanation of work participation it is instructive to view participation rates in terms of all categories of factors which prevent people from participating in economic activity and thus influence the supply of labour available for work. Gary Becker (1965) in his theory of time allocation points out that 'not only is it difficult to distinguish leisure from other non-work, but also even work from non-work'. However, notwithstanding the conceptual problems which have been well articulated by him, the Census classification of non-workers into seven categories is a useful one and it can be drawn upon as being indicative of the main causes of non-participation in work. These categories are: (i) Students; (ii) engaged in household duties; (iii) dependants; (iv) rentiers; (v) beggars; (vi) inmates of institutions/asylums; (vii) others.

All these categories do not necessarily reflect exclusively forces which influence the supply of workers. Two of these categories are likely to include non-workers on account of demand based reasons. The category 'dependants' includes persons who do not participate in work since they depend for their sustenance on other members of their family either on account of being too young or too old to work or some other inability. But this category is also likely to hide a substantial number of persons who become habitual dependants, that is those who might have got productively employed if adequate work avenue were readily available. This reason essentially reflects the existence of some Nurksian type disguised unemployment within category (iii). Similarly, the 'others' include those seeking work and is indicative of chronic unemployment (*cf.* Krishna, 1973; Sen, 1975).

Table 11.3 shows the relative importance of these seven causes of non-participation in the rural and urban segments at the all-India level in the form of percentage of non-working population in each of the seven categories to total non-working population of the respective segments. In the case of females, by far the most important reason for non-participation emerges to be household duties.[8] But in case of males the most prominent reason is 'dependency' followed by 'pursuit of studies'. The relative importance of 'students' is far greater in urban areas (44.73 per cent) than in rural areas (28.58 per cent) while in case of 'dependants' the percentage is much greater in rural areas, partly reflecting the pool of rural disguised unemployment.

A large number of factors have been considered as determinants of work participation in the literature (Bowen and Finegan, 1969; Standing and Sheehan, 1978). Factors like number of children per family can be suitably investigated only when a household questionnaire approach is used. The explanatory model used here includes prominent supply side determinants out of those listed above, key socio-economic determinants and three important demographic factors.

Among supply side determinants we have used three variables representing the three highest non-participation rates, namely 'dependency', 'household duties' and 'pursuit of studies'. The non-participation rates have been estimated as percentages of each type of non-worker to total population of the segment (rural/urban). Symbolically non-participation rate on account of cause *(m)* in segment *(i)*, that is, $NP_m(i)$, can be expressed as:

$$NP_m(i) = \frac{NW_m(i)}{\sum_m NW_m(i) + W_i} \times 100 = \frac{NW_m(i)}{P(i)} \times 100 \qquad (11)$$

where $NW_m(i)$ indicates non-workers in category m; i = rural *(r)* or urban *(u)*; m = 1,2,...7; W_i indicates workers in segment *(i)*; $P(i)$ is population of segment *(i)*.

In the socio-economic category five determinants have been drawn upon. Among these education occupies a very important place (Standing, 1976; 1981; Mitra, 1979; Benavot, 1989). Education enhances the range of jobs open to individuals, in addition to improving their earning prospects. The spread of education among different groups has been measured by literacy percentage, that is, the percentage of all educated persons within a group to total population of that group.

Next two socio-economic variables are based on specific characteristics of two social groups, namely the Tribals and the Scheduled Castes (SC). The tribal way of life is based on the spirit of collective community endeavour, thus involving a relatively greater degree of work participation among them. The Scheduled Caste (SC), on the other hand, represent a downtrodden group which had traditionally been associated with low level occupations. Since they belong to an economically weak section, economic compulsions among them may be forcing a higher proportion of SCs, particularly women and children, to seek work. These factors lie behind the participation rate among Tribals and SCs being higher than in case of population as a whole (Gulati, 1975a; K. Bardhan, 1985, Raju 1987). Keeping these attributes in view, the second socio-economic variable has been taken to be districtwise percentage of Tribal persons within rural and urban segments (Raza and Ahmad, 1989). The third variable is districtwise percentage of SCs in the rural and urban population.

The last two socio-economic variables are relevant only for the rural segment since they are related to agriculture. Higher cropping intensity would be expected to lead to greater absorption of labour for agricultural operations since it involves repeated cropping of the same land within a year. Hence the fourth variable is taken to be cropping intensity. Finally, cropping pattern is also supposed to be an important determinant of labour absorption capacity of agriculture (Boserup, 1970; Gulati, 1975a; Chopra, 1979; Chatterjee, 1984). Centain crops are labour intensive, particularly rice. Thus districtwise percentage of area under rice cultivation to gross cropped area is taken as the fifth socio-economic determinant, data for which were obtained from Ministry of Agriculture (1978).

This brings us to three demographic influences which hold a prime position in this context. First of these is the pressure of population on resources. In a labour abundant economy like India, its effect is likely to be adverse, particularly in the agricultural sector. This determinant has been incorporated in the form of population density per sq. km. The other two demographic factors are age structure and average household size, that is, members per household. They are taken to influence work participation not directly but primarily through their effect on the three supply side determinants discussed above, namely, 'household duties', 'dependency' and 'pursuit of studies'. For example, the extent of 'dependency' is affected to a considerable extent by the proportion of population below and above the working age group since they are least able to fend for themselves. Similarly the burden of 'household duties', particularly of females, may be expected to depend upon the population of young age needing attention of parents and upon the number of those who are too old, thus needing to be looked after.

The Relationship of Work Participation with Individual Variables

Before explaining the format of the model used to study collective influence of the above variables, it is imperative to examine correlations of individual determinants with the standard participation rates (Table 11.4). Among the supply side determinants, in case of females the most dominant and statistically significant negative influence is that of 'household duties'. The strength of the negative relationship is greater in rural areas. This negative relationship amply brings out the stress that Sundaram (1988) has laid on the role of 'domestic duties' and 'biologically determined burdens' in case of women in influencing women's participation in the traditionally accepted boundary of economic activity. It is also in conformity with Heckman and Macurdy's theoretical life cycle model of labour supply (1980), which underlines the part played by child bearing and child rearing in influencing female labour supply decisions. In the case of rural males the highest negative correlation among supply side determinants occurs in case of non-participation on account of being 'students' and in the case of urban males on account of 'dependency'.

Among socio-economic determinants, the correlation of tribal population percentage with work participation conforms to the expected positive direction and is significant at a fairly high level in case of rural males and females and urban females. But the correlation in the case of the SC percentage is insignificant for males while for females it is negative. For males this result is not surprising since the all-India participation rate of total male population (52.5 per cent) and of SC male population (54.1 per cent) are only marginally

TABLE 11.4: Correlations of Districtwise Participation Rates and Selected Determinants

Determinant Variables	Correlation Co-efficients of Participation Rates			
	Rural		Urban	
	Female	Male	Female	Male
(1) Pursuit of Studies	–0.10*	–0.33***	+0.07	–0.19***
(2) Household Duties	–0.61***	–0.12**	–0.32***	+0.14**
(3) Dependency	–0.12**	–0.20***	–0.17***	–0.38***
(4) Population Density	–0.40***	–0.42***	–0.24***	+0.05
(5) Tribal Population Percentage	+0.14**	+0.14**	+0.24***	+0.07
(6) SC Population Percentage	–0.37***	+0.05	–0.24***	–0.03
(7) Literacy	+0.32***	–0.46***	+0.20***	–0.09*
(8) Cropping Intensity	–0.39***	–0.13**	—	—
(9) Area under Rice	–0.02	0.06	—	—

*, **, *** indicate significance at 0.10, 0.05 and 0.01 levels respectively.

different. But in the case of females the all-India SC participation rate (17.4 per cent) is visibly higher than the participation rate of female population as a whole (11.9 per cent). Hence a negative correlation for females is contrary to expectations. One possible reason for it is that the proportion of SCs within total population (14.6 per cent) is not so large as to influence overall participation rate in the same direction as the SC participation rate.[9]

In case of literacy there has been a debate whether its relationship to female participation rate is negative or not (Standing, 1976). The inferences in case of India have mostly been based on cross-section of State level data and have not been conclusive (Nath, 1970; Gulati, 1975a; Sinha, 1975; Saxena, 1987). Table 11.4 shows that inter-district correlation between these two variables is significantly positive in case of rural and urban females. But in case of males it is negative. Thus this variable poses an enigma to which we turn in section VII.

The two agricultural variables, that is, the proportion of area under rice and cropping intensity both reveal a negative relationship to standard participation rates. This is the reverse of what would be expected. One possible reason for the reverse relationship of cropping intensity is that the level of agricultural prosperity and overall development by and large move in step with cropping intensity. And we have already seen that overall development and rural participation rates are negatively related in the initial stages. It is, therefore, possible that the expectation of a direct positive effect of cropping intensity on work participation is more than swamped by a negative influence operating via rising income levels in agriculture generated by higher cropping intensity.

An Explanatory Model

We may now outline the basic structure of the model through which collective influence of all the selected variables on standard participation rates has been investigated. Instead of using a single regression equation incorporating all the determinants, we have used a multiple equation regression model which better illuminates the channels through which level of development and other determinants influence work participation. Four separate sets of regression equations have been estimated, one set each pertaining to standard participation rates of males and females in rural and urban segments.

Each set consists of three equations, whose structure is outlined below

Set *i* :

$$R_g\,(i) = f(S_{i1}, S_{i2}/S_{i3};\ X_{i1}, X_{i2}, \ldots\ldots, X_{in}) \qquad \text{(i.1)}$$

$$S_{i1} = f(Y_{i1}, Y_{i2}, \ldots\ldots, Y_{im}) \qquad \text{(i.2)}$$

$$S_{i2}/S_{i3} = f(Y_{i1}, Y_{i2}, \ldots\ldots, Y_{i\,(m-2)}) \qquad \text{(i.3)}$$

where set $i = 1$ pertains to rural males; set $i = 2$ pertains to rural females;

set $i = 3$ pertains to urban males; set $i = 4$ pertains to urban females;

$R_g(i)$ is standard participation rate of set *(i)*;

$S_{i\,(1,2,3)}$ are the three supply side determinants of set *i*, which are endogenous to the system;

$X_{i(1\ldots.n)}$ are exogenous determinants of participation rate of set *(i)*;

$Y_{i\,(i\ldots.m)}$ are determinants of the endogenous supply side variables of set *(i)*.

The first equation of each set, that is equation *(i.1)*, attempts to explain the participation rate in terms of direct influence of the selected variables. In selecting the supply side determinants for the first equation of each set, it was felt that no equation should contain more than two non-participation rates as determinants since the supply side determinants taken as a whole would conceptually be expected to explain full variation of participation rates. For each set it was decided to select those non-participation rates having the two highest correlation co-efficients with the standard participation rate. Using this criterion, in the case of males non-participation rates on account of 'being students' and 'dependency' have been included as the two supply side determinants, both in rural and urban segments. In the case of females, on the basis of this criterion non-participation rates pertaining to 'household duties' and 'dependency' qualify as the two supply side determinants. However, in the final analysis non-participation rate on account of 'household duties' and on account of 'being students' have been included as the two supply side determinants for female participation rate equations. This was necessitated by the problem of multi-collinearity. Reasons of space constraint prohibit giving here a fuller explanation.

Population Density, Literacy and Tribal percentages appear as exogenous determinants in the first equation of all the four sets. Since cropping intensity reveals an unexpected negative relationship with rural participation rates, this variable has not been included. For the same reason SC percentage has also been dropped. In addition, it is imperative to incorporate region effect into the model. This is particularly so in the case of the female participation rate since their orientation towards work varies considerably among the regions. Ester Boserup (1970) had tried to explain a tendency towards higher participation in work by women in the South relatively to that in the North in terms of exposure of the Northern region to West Asian culture. Subsequently Leela Gulati (1975b) also drew attention to the fact that 'a sort of regional pattern can be observed in the participation in work'. The region effect has been introduced in our analysis by dividing the country into four regions[10] and using intercept dummies for the Eastern, Western and Southern regions. Further, regional slope dummies for Rice percentage have been used in the first regression equation of the rural sets since the prominence of rice in cropping pattern differs considerably among regions. In the case of the urban sets Rice percentage has obviously been dropped. Thus, the exact form of first equation which has four sets may be expressed as follows :

$$R_g(i) = (a_0 + a_1D^e + a_2D^w + a_3D^s) + b_1S_1 + b_2S_2/b_3S_3 + X_1 + X_2 + X_3 + (X_4 + D^e_r + D^w_r + D^s_r) + U \qquad (12)$$

where $R_g(i)$ is standard participation rate of set i;

a is intercept term for the Northern region;

D^e is intercept dummy for the Eastern region, that is, $D^e = 1$ for districts in the Eastern region and $D^e = 0$ for districts in all other regions;

D^w is intercept dummy for the Western region;

D^s is intercept dummy for the Southern region;

S_1 is non-participation rate on account of being 'students';

S_2 is non-participation rate on account of 'household duties';

S_3 is non-participation rate on account of being 'dependants';

X_1 is population density per sq. km.;

X_2 is literacy percentage;

X_3 is tribal percentage;

X_4 is proportion of gross cropped area under rice cultivation in the Northern region districts;

D_r are regional slope dummies for rice, the superscripts e, w and s representing Eastern, Western and Southern regions respectively. Northern region has thus been treated as the base region with reference to which the Dummy variables have been postulated;

U is the stochastic error term;

When $i = 1$ or 2 (i.e., in case of urban sets), delete variable X_4 and slope dummies D^e_r, D^w_r and D^s_r;
When $i = 1$ or 3 (that is, in case of male sets), delete variable S_2;
When $i = 2$ or 4 (that is,in case of female sets), delete variable S_3.

The next two equations of each set attempt to explain behaviour of the three endogenous supply side variables, namely, non-participation rates on account of 'household duties', 'dependency' and being 'students'. The explanatory variables used for this purpose are:

(i) average household size in the rural/urban segment of a district (H);
(ii) districtwise index of the level of development (I_d);
(iii) four age variables, $P_1(m)$, $P_2(m)$, $P_1(f)$ and $P_2(f)$, all representing non-working age groups. While $P_1(m)$ and $P_1(f)$ indicate the percentage of male and female population below 15 years, $P_2(m)$ and $P_2(f)$ indicate the percentage of male and female population above 60 years to total male and female population respectively. The 15-60 years group is taken to represent the working age group. These variables were estimated separately for the rural and urban segments of each district on the basis of 1971 Population Census data.

These exogenous variables exercise a direct influence on the endogenous supply side variables in the first instance and these supply side variables in turn exercise a strong influence on the participation rates.

All the three supply side factors are likely to be influenced by the level of development. Thus among the exogenous variables which appear in the second and third equations, the Index of Development I_d

appears in each set. But in respect of age variables and household size there is a difference among the sets. The burden of 'household duties' can be taken to depend upon the percentage of population below 15 years and above 60 years, both of males and females. Thus in the equation explaining 'household duties' S_2 there are four age variables, namely percentage of male population below 15, $P_1(m)$; percentage of male population above sixty, $P_2(m)$; percentage of female population below fifteen, $P_1(f)$; and percentage of female population above sixty, $P_2(f)$.

The extent ,of 'dependency' S_3 is influenced to a considerable extent by population below and above the working age group since that is the section of population—particularly the former one—which is unable to fend for itself. But in the case of any one gender, 'dependency' can be taken to depend on the percentage of population below 15 years and above 60 years of that gender alone. Thus in 'dependency' equations only these two age variables appear as determinants. And for the percentage of 'students' of any gender S_1, it is the percentage of population below 15 years of that gender which can be taken to exercise an influence on it.

Finally, household size H is obviously an important factor which may be expected to influence the quantum of 'household duties' S_2. Similarly, in larger sized households there is the possibility of greater degree of 'dependency' S_3, both because of the lower probability of everyone finding worthwhile employment in an overpopulated country (Todaro, 1976; Basu 1984: Ch.6) and also because large sized households can afford greater shelter to those belonging to the disguised unemployed category (Mathur, 1964). On the other hand, there is no obvious reason for household size to influence the proportion of students.

In the light of the above discussion, the exact form of the second and third equations of each set can be expressed as:

For Male Sets :

$$S_1 = p_1 + d_1 I_d + d_2 P_1(m) + V_1 \tag{13}$$

$$S_3 = p_2 + d_1 I_d + e_2 H + e_3 P_1(m) + \theta_4 P_2(m) + V_2 \tag{14}$$

For Female Sets :

$$S_1 = p_3 + r_1 I_d + r_2 P_1(f) + V_3 \tag{15}$$

$$S_2 = p_4 + k_1 I_d + k_2 H + k_3 P_1 (m) + k_4 P_2 (m) + k_5 P_1 (f) + K_6 P_2 (f) + V_4 \qquad (16)$$

where S_1, S_2, S_3, I_d have the same connotation as indicated earlier;
H is average household size;
$P_1(m)$ and $P_1(f)$ are percentages of male and female population below 15 years respectively;
$P_2(m)$ and $P_2(f)$ are percentages of male and female population above 60 years respectively;
V_k are stochastic error terms.

The Model Results

The Work Participation Equations

Within each of the four sets of regression equations there are two endogenous variables, but none of the determinant variables in equations 2 and 3 of each set appear as a dependent variable anywhere in the system. These sets of equations therefore are not subject to simultaneity bias. Each set forms a recursive system and consistent estimates of the regression parameters can therefore be obtained by applying OLS (Ordinary Least Squares) to one equation at a time.

The results of the estimated equations are discussed in two stages. First we present OLS estimates of the work participation equations. At the second stage OLS estimates of the endogenous variable equations are presented. But these estimates show only the direct effect of exogenous variables Y_i on the endogenous supply side variables S_i. Our main interest, however, lies in assessing the ultimate effect of these exogenous variables Y_1 on participation rates $R(i)$ through the channel of endogenous supply side variables S_i. For this purpose the estimated endogenous variable equations have been substituted in the estimated work participation equation within each set in order to obtain derived parameters which reflect the end impact of exogenous variables Y_i on the participation rates.

The OLS estimates of equation 1 of each set, which explain the respective standard participation rates, are given in Table 11.5. As may be seen from R^{-2}, the explanatory power of this equation is higher for the rural segment than for the urban segment, but in both segments it is highly significant. Judging by '*t*' values of regression coefficients, 'dependency' S_3 and 'pursuit of studies' S_1 emerge as the most

TABLE 11.5: Work Participation Equations

Determinant Variables	Regression co-efficients and *'t'* Values			
	Female		Male	
Intercept : North (a)	+ 32.50		+ 95.03	
Intercept Dummy : East (D^e)	+ 6.65**	(2.31)	+ 1.85**	(2.41)
Intercept Dummy : West (D^w)	+ 1.46	(1.15)	–0.04	(0.13)
Intercept Dummy: South (D^s)	+4.62***	(3.09)	–0.01	(0.02)
Pursuit of Studies (S_1)	–0.59***	(13.38)	–0.94***	(30.96)
Household Duties (S_2)	–0.68***	(21.71)	—	
Dependency (S_3)	—		– 0.89***	(37.42)
Population Density (X_1)	–0.01***	(3.85)	– 0.003***	(4.56)
Literacy (X_2)	+0.24***	(6.06)	– 0.01	(1.17)
Tribal Percentage (X_3)	–0.02	(1.22)	+ 0.01	(0.99)
Rice Percentage: North (X_4)	+ 0.13**	(2.35)	–0.01	(0.88)
Rice Slope Dummy : East (D^e_r)	– 0.30***	(4.31)	–0.03*	(1.87)
Rice Slope Dummy : South (D^s_r)	– 0.09	(1.50)	+0.02	(1.14)
Rice Slope Dummy : West (D^w_r)	– 0.03	(0.44)	– 0.04	(0.13)
$\bar{R}$	0.89***		0.95***	
F - Value ..	91.46 ***		240.69***	
URBAN SEGMENT				
Intercept : North (a)	+17.28		+ 72.42	
Intercept Dummy : East (D^e)	–0.59	(1.06)	– 1.12***	(2.88)
Intercept Dummy : West (D^w)	+ 1.45***	(3.05)	– 1.00**	(2.49)
Intercept Dummy : South (D^s)	+ 4.17***	(7.96)	+0.04	(0.09)
Pursuit of Studies (S_1)	– 0.30***	(5.67)	– 0.52***	(11.54)
Household Duties (S_2)	– 0.28***	(8.37)	—	
Dependency (S_3)	—		– 0.47***	(14.44)
Population Density (X_1)	–0.0002**	(2.23)	– 0.00003	(0.60)
Literacy (X_2)	+ 0.15***	(5.69)	– 0.04***	(2.79)
Tribal Percentage (X_3)	+ 0.10***	(3.66)	+ 0.03	(1.26)
$\bar{R}$	0.73***		0.71***	
F - value ..	42.05***		37.52***	

*,**, and *** indicate significance at 0.10, 0.05 and 0.01 levels respectively, t-values are given within parentheses.

significant determinants in the case of male participation rates. In the case of female participation rate, the most significant determinant is non-participation rate pertaining to 'household duties' followed closely by 'pursuit of studies'. The highly significant negative regression coefficient of population density X_1 underlines the strong depressive effect on work participation exercised by the pressure of population on land resources, particularly for the rural segment, for both genders.

The pattern of regression coefficients of literacy rate X_2 is broadly parallel to that discussed already with reference to zero order correlations. The regression coefficients of tribal population reveal a low degree of statistical significance except in case of the equation explaining the urban female participation rate.

Coming to the region effect, the three regional intercept dummies are prominent only in the case of female participation rate. In the case of the rural sector, the regional intercept dummies for female work participation are all positive. The intercept female participation rate is highest in the Eastern region followed by that in the Southern and Western regions, which reflects the relative ordering of their female labour absorptive capacity. The prevailing socio-cultural traditions, combined with the prominence of other labour absorbing crops besides rice, namely jute and tea, can be taken to account for the highest intercept value of female work participation in the rural segment of Eastern region. In the urban segment the highest positive and statistically the most significant intercept dummy occurs in case of the Southern region. These results reveal a higher overall orientation towards work participation of urban women in the Southern and Western regions.

In case of the regression co-efficient of percentage area under Rice X_4, this is positive and significant (0.05 level) in case of the female participation rate in the Northern region. Rice slope dummies for females are negative in other regions. The female labour absorption effect of rice cultivation therefore seems to be higher in the Northern region than elsewhere.

The Endogenous Variable Equations

The zero order correlations of the exogenous variables appearing in regression equations *(i.2)* and *(i.3)*, which explain behaviour of the three endogenous supply side variables S_i, are given in Table 11.6

while the OLS estimates of these equations are given in Table 11.7. However, in order to gauge the final impact of these exogenous variables on participation rates, the OLS parameters of respective endogenous variable equations *(i.2)* and *(i.3)* were substituted in work participation equations of each set *(i.1)*. The coefficients of the exogenous variables Y_i obtained through this substitution (Table 11.8) measure the ultimate total impact on work participation exercised by an exogenous variable through the channel of all the endogenous variables on which that particular exogenous variable exercises an influence.

TABLE 11.6: Correlation of Supply Side Variables with Exogenous Determinants

Exogenous Determinants	Rural Segment — Supply Side Variables					
	Household Duty		Dependency		Students	
	Male	Female	Male	Female	Male	Female
HH Size *(H)*	+0.08	+0.37***	+0.27***	+0.24***	—	—
Development (I_d)	+0.07	+0.14**	−0.11*	−0.14**	+0.23***	+0.17***
M<15 : P_1 *(m)*	+0.02	+0.07	+0.33***	—	−0.01	—
M>60 : P_2 *(m)*	+0.06	+0.17***	−0.06	—	—	—
F<15 : P_1 *(f)*	+0.05	+0.04	—	+0.39***	—	−0.07
F>60 : P_2 *(f)*	+0.03	−0.06	—	+0.17***	—	—
URBAN SEGMENT						
HH Size *(H)*	−0.10*	+0.23***	+0.28***	+0.14**	—	—
Development (I_d)	− 0.07	+0.14**	−0.17***	−0.22***	−0.03	+0.20***
M<15 : P_1 *(m)*	−0.08	+0.14**	+0.47***	—	+0.09*	—
M>60 : P_2 *(m)*	−0.13**	+0.28***	+0.39***	—	—	—
F<15 : P_1 *(f)*	+0.02	+0.02	—	+0.39***	—	+0.03
F>60 : P_2 *(f)*	−0.06	+0.21***	—	+0.13**	—	—

*, **, *** indicate significance at 0.10, 0.05 and 0.01 levels respectively.

The second task was to estimate the level of significance of these total impact co-efficients. For this purpose the Klein-Kamenta derivation (1953; 1971) based on partial derivatives of total impact

TABLE 11.7: The Endogenous Variable Equations

Dependent (Endogenous) Variables	Exogenous		Rural Segment Variables Regression		Co-efficients			
	I_d	H	$P_1(m)$	$P_2(m)$	$P_1(f)$	$P_2(f)$	$\overline{R}$	F
Male Students :	+0.53***	—	+0.09	—	—	—	0.22***	8.37***
S_1 (m)	(4.09)		(0.63)					
Female Students :	+0.47***	—	—	—	–0.16	—	0.17***	4.84***
S_1 (f)	(2.87)				(0.95)			
Female HH Duty :	+0.09	+9.52***	+0.11	+3.31***	–0.86**	–4.22***	0.45***	13.36***
S_2 (f)	(0.39)	(6.33)	(0.30)	(4.29)	(2.40)	(3.89)		
Male Dependency :	–0.29*	+2.43***	+0.65***	+0.09	—	—	0.36***	11.66***
S_3 (m)	(1.66)	(2.87)	(3.62)	(0.26)				
			URBAN SEGMENT					
Male Students :	+0.001	—	+0.09	—	—	—	0.07	1.21
S_1 (m)	(0.001)		(1.48)					
Female Students :	+0.43***	—	—	—	+0.23*	—	0.22***	8.09***
S_1 (f)	(3.98)				(1.84)			
Female HH Duty :	+0.42***	+1.68**	+0.16	+1.86***	+0.23	+0.40	0.35***	7.73***
S_2 (f)	(3.12)	(2.21)	(1.30)	(2.94)	(1.48)	(0.64)		
Male Dependency :	–0.12	1.42***	+0.47***	+1.46***	—	—	0.55***	33.21***
S_3 (m)	(1.46)	(3.10)	(6.22)	(4.49)				

*, ** and *** indicate significance at 0.10, 0.05 and 0.01 levels respectively. Figures within parentheses indicate 't' values.

co-efficients with respect to the component estimators, variance and covariance of the component estimators was drawn upon.[11] The 't' values of the total impact coefficients of the exogenous variables Y_i, based on variance estimates derived in this manner, are given within parentheses in Table 11.8.

The Impact of Development

We may first take a glance at the direct regression coefficients of the level of development I_d in endogenous variable equations (Table 11.7) and then at the final impact of I_d on participation rates through the channel of these endogenous variables (Table 11.8). In the former set of equations I_d has a highly significant positive regression coefficient in case of 'student percentage' S_1 equation pertaining to rural males and females as well as urban females. This goes to show that in the environment of more developed regions the habit of school enrolment, low dropouts and effectiveness of universal primary education programme, all tend to get firmly rooted.

TABLE 11.8: The Total Impact Coefficients

Exogenous Variables (Y_i)	The Ultimate Work Participation Impact			
	Rural Segment		Urban Segment	
	Female	Male	Female	Male
Development (I_d)	– 0.34*	– 0.30*	– 0.25***	+ 0.05
	(1.71)	(1.71)	(4.26)	(0.36)
HH Size (H)	– 6.42***	– 0.22	– 0.48**	– 0.67***
	(6.29)	(0.29)	(2.14)	(3.02)
M<15 : P_1 (m)	– 0.07	– 0.66***	– 0.05	– 0.27***
	(0.30)	(3.13)	(1.28)	(5.29)
M>60 : P_2 (m)	– 2.30***	– 0.08	– 0.53***	– 0.69***
	(4.21)	(0.26)	(2.79)	(4.29)
F<15 : P_1 (f)	+0.67**	—	– 0.14**	—
	(2.56)		(2.19)	
F>60 : P_2 (f)	+ 2.84***	—	– 0.11	—
	(3.83)		(0.63)	

*, **, *** denote significance at 0.10, 0.05 and 0.01 levels respectively. Figures within parentheses indicates 't' values.

I_d also reveals, though somewhat surprisingly, a highly significant positive regression coefficient in the equation pertaining to female 'household duties' S_2 in the urban segment. On the other hand, I_d has a negative regression coefficient in case of male 'dependency' S_3 equation in rural as well as urban segments, thus indicating that development tends to draw out hidden reserves of manpower into the world of work. Since all the endogenous supply side variables S_1, S_2, S_3 have a significant negative regression coefficient in participation rate equations, the total impact coefficient of I_d (Table 11.8) reflecting net effect of development on work participation through the above three channels, emerges to be significantly negative in all sets except in the case of participation rate of urban males. These results show the substantial negative effect of I_d on work participation through absorption of an increasing proportion of population as students at higher levels of development. The positive impact of development on female 'household duties' in urban areas tends to reinforce this effect. But the downward impact of development on 'dependency' is not large enough to offset the negative influence of I_d on work participation through the other two channels, except in case of the urban male participation rate.

Thus, in the rural segment the impact of development on work participation through the channel of supply side variables is in conformity with the results of direct relationship between development and work participation obtained in section III. But in respect of the urban segment the two sets of the results are not exactly identical. This is essentially a consequence of the fact that the direct relationship examined in section III reflects the effect of development on work participation operating through all possible channels whereas a total impact coefficient shows the aggregate effect of I_d operating through the channel of three supply side variables, which are very important but obviously not exhaustive.

The Impact of Demographic Factors

When we come to the regression coefficients of age variables in the endogenous variable equations (Table 11.7), three facets stand out prominently. First, males above 60 years exercise the strongest positive influence on the quantum of female 'household duties', both in rural and urban areas. Secondly, in the case of male 'dependency' equations, males below 15 [P_1 (m)] reveal a much more statistically significant positive regression co-efficient than those above 60 [P_2 (m)], thus indicating that the incidence of 'dependency' is primarily a function of the size of younger age group, particularly so in rural areas. Finally, the preponderance of either males or females below 15 years is not an important factor in determining the percentage of 'students' S_1 particularly in rural areas. Normally, the larger the proportion of children, the larger would one expect to be the proportion of students to population. However, this expectation is based on the implicit assumption that there is by and large a fixed relationship between the number of children and those enrolled as students. But in India, despite attempts at universalisation of elementary education, the actual situation leaves a lot to be desired, especially in rural schools. Consequently, in rural areas a significant positive relationship between the size of child population and the magnitude of student enrolment does not emerge. On the other hand, in urban areas where the habit of school enrolment is relatively well established, the regression coefficients are positive and significant.

The aggregate effect of age variables on participation rates though on the three supply side variables S_1, S_2 and S_3 may be gauged from the total impact coefficients of age variables (Table 11.8). The negative influence of the proportion of male population above 60 and below 15 on male work participation is statistically very strong is urban areas. In rural areas the negative impact on the male work participation rate is statistically significant in the case of the male population below 15 but not for the male population above 60.

In the case of female work participation in the urban segment, although all the four age variables have negative total impact co-efficients, it is statistically significant at a high level only for males above 60 (Table 11.8). In respect of female work participation in the rural segment, again it is only males above 60 which reveal a strong and significant negative total impact on female participation rate. For females below 15 and above 60, their total impact coefficients with regard to rural female participation rate are in fact positive. These results indicate that caring for the young and old aged population of males, but not of females, tends to enhance the quantum of female household work, thus reducing the female participation rate where the proportion of young and old males among the population is high. This is more evident in rural areas where a male dominated society and preferential treatment by females to male children are not uncommon.

Finally, regression co-efficients of 'household size' H in equations pertaining to female 'household duties' S_2 and male 'dependency' S_3 are positive and significant at a very high level, both in rural and urban areas (Table 11.7). Consequently the effect of 'household size' on work participation operating through these channels is strongly negative for females, both in rural and urban segments, and for of males in the urban segment (Table 11.8). The strong negative relationship of 'household size' to female participation rate is also borne out by Saxena's (1987) State level analysis based on the 1981 Population Census. However, an intensive household study in Child by Peter Peek (1978) found that whereas a negative relationship of household size to female labour participation existed in case of the modern sector, in the traditional sector the relationship was a positive one.

Education, Work Participation and Development

Finally, we now take up a more intensive investigation of the inter-relationship between education, work participation and development, whose full perspective cannot be captured if one stops at an analysis based on a single variable, namely literacy percentage (Mathur, 1990). In fact, an important result of the preceding analysis, namely a significantly negative relationship between the extent of literacy and male participation rate, is rather anomalous. Education exercises a dual influence on orientation towards work: it enhances employability and it increases the rate of earnings (Schultz, 1963; Becker, 1964; Mincer, 1974; Blaug, 1976). At a higher level of earnings, since the opportunity cost of non-participation in work increases, one would expect a higher—not lower—participation rate in case of educated manpower. How can one explain the above anomaly ?

There are two possible reasons for the gap between expectations and these results. First, since the educational process involves drawing a segment of the population away from employable status to the students category for purposes of human capital formation, when one takes a cross-sectional view of the aggregate picture, a higher incidence of education as reflected in the literacy rate may appear to be associated with a lower participation of population in work. This is another facet of the micro-level relationship between investment in human capital and the supply of labour available for work, which has formed the focus of models analysing inter-temporal allocation of time within an individual's life cycle between learning and earning

(Sheshiuski, 1968; Ghes and Becker, 1975; Heckman, 1976; Blinder and Weiss, 1976).

The above explanation also fits in with the fact that results of previous section revealed a positive relationship between literacy and the participation rate in the case of females, but a negative one in the case of males. As evident from Table 11.3, the proportion of males students is much larger than that of females and hence this 'withdrawal from labour market effect' appears to have been strong enough at the macro-level to lead to a negative repercussion of literacy on the participation rate of males but not of females.

The second reason could be the fact that literacy by itself is an inadequate measure of the degree of educational attainment. Literacy measures the percentage of all educated people, irrespective of the level of education, to total population. But a more disaggregative treatment of education is imperative. Thus separate rates of participation were estimated for segments of population with ten different levels and types of education for which the Census of Population gives information. $R_g(i,k)$,the participation rate for 'k'th level of education in segment i, for gender g, may be denoted as:

$$R_g(i,k) = \frac{W_g(i, k)}{P_g(i, k)} \times 100 \tag{17}$$

where i = rural (r) or urban (u); g = male or female; k = 1,2,3,... 10. The ten educational categories for which data have been used are :

> Illiterate (k = 1); just literate without any educational qualifications (k = 2); Primary passed (k = 3); Middle passed (k = 4);
> Matriculates (k = 5); Non-technical Diploma holders (k = 6); Technical Diploma holders (k = 7); Graduates (k = 8); Postgraduates (k = 9); Technical Degree holders (k = 10).

These participation rates for the country as a whole (Table 11.9) are portrayed in the accompanying graphs. In the graphs all the professional educational attainments, this is, k = 6, 7 and 10 are placed to the right of postgraduates although in terms of stagewise hierarchy and the number of years of education the diploma holder categories (k = 6, 7) would be below the postgraduate level. This has been done to bring out the contrast between the influence of general and professional education. Table 11.9 and graphs (Figure 11.1)

EDUCATION-WISE PARTICIPATION RATES

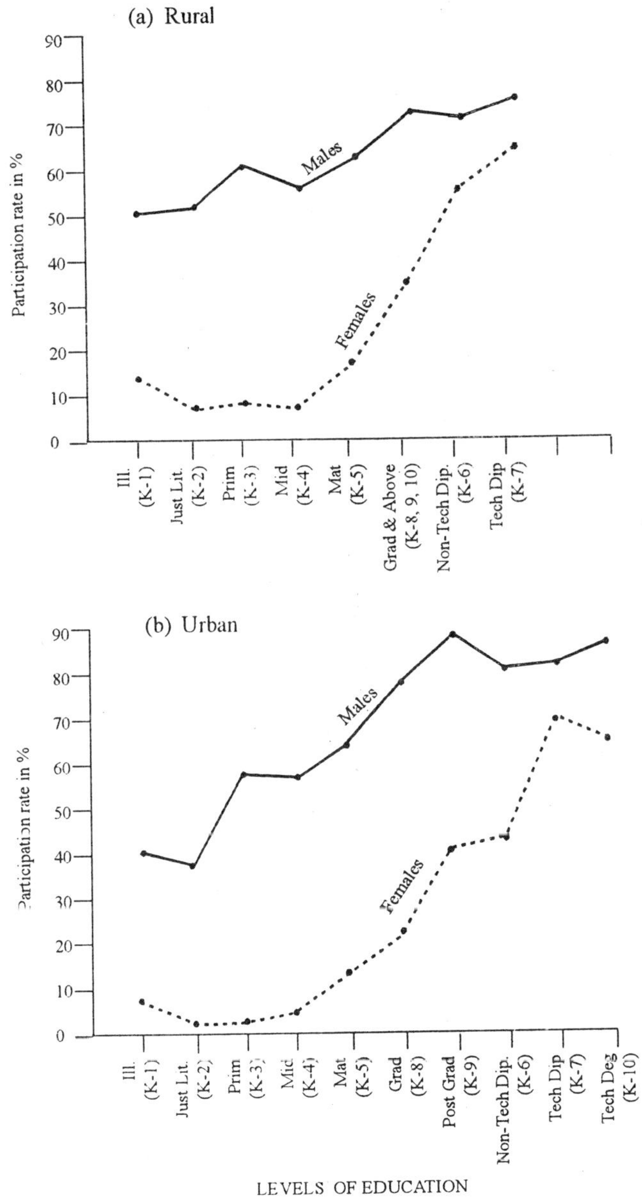

Fig. 11.1: Educationwise Participation Rates

reveal five main points :

(i) First, as one moves up the educational hierarchy, initially the participation rates fall, except in the case of rural males. But thereafter, the participation rates rise progressively. Thus the inverse relationship between literacy and participation rates observed on the basis of cross-sectional relationships, disappears when disaggregated educational participation rates are considered in a hierarchical manner.

(ii) Second, the increase in the participation rate in response to an increase in the level of education is much steeper for females than for males, particularly so in the urban areas. The last row of Table 11.9a shows that educationwise max-min gap in participation rates is much higher for females than in the case of males.

(iii) Third, the participation rates are distinctly higher in case of the professional education categories (k = 6,7 and 10) and their sub-categories (Table 11.9b). This underlines the significance of a properly job oriented professional education programme (Mathur *et al.*, 1978).

TABLE 11.9(a): Educationwise Participation Rates

Level of Education	Rural			Urban		
	Male	Female	M/F Ratio	Male	Female	M/F Ratio
	(1)	(2)	(3)	(4)	(5)	(6)
Illiterate	51.29	13.82	3.71	39.82	7.47	5.33
Just Literate	52.22	7.67	6.80	37.76	2.19	17.24
Primary	61.42	8.16	7.53	56.52	3.18	17.77
Middle	57.03	7.44	7.66	56.22	3.78	14.87
Matric	62.14	15.90	3.91	62.92	12.74	4.94
Non-tech. Diploma	71.72	56.46	1.27	78.54	42.60	1.84
Technical Diploma	75.37	65.50	1.15	82.50	66.68	1.24
Graduate	72.72	33.68	2.16	75.39	22.20	3.40
Postgraduate	—	—	—	85.93	40.93	2.10
Technical Degree	—	—	—	83.81	64.39	1.30
Max-min-Gap	24.08	57.83	—	46.05	64.49	—

TABLE 11.9(b): Professional Education Participation Rates (Urban)

	Male	Female
Engineering	82.34	28.38
Medicine	83.14	74.37
Agriculture & Veterinary	85.66	53.74
Teaching	89.59	65.97
Others	72.67	26.59

(iv) Fourth, the gap between male and female participation rates declines with increase in the level of education beyond primary/middle level (Table 11.9a cols. 3 and 6). Thus, a rise in the level of education does contribute to a reduction of the male-female differentiation.

(v) Finally, the male-female gap in participation rates is lower at all levels of education in rural areas than in urban areas.

We now return to the first theme, namely the direct relationship between development and participation rates, in order to observe the influence of education on this relationship. For this purpose education-wise modified participation rates were estimated for eight levels of education. Since Census data club together categories $k = 8$, 9 and 10 in rural areas, the same were clubbed together in case of the urban segment to obtain comparable categories. The modified participation rate for education level k, in segment i, gender g, can be expressed as :

$$MODR_g\,(i,k) = \frac{W_g\,(i,\,k)}{\sum_i P_g\,(i,\,k)} \times 100 \qquad (18)$$

$i = (r)$ and (u)

Two points emerge quite clearly from linear regressions of education wise participation rates on the districtwise index of development (Table 11.10) First, as in case of the general participation rate, whereas in rural sector most of the educational participation rates reveal a negative relationship to the level of development, in urban segment all relationships are positive. The patterns of negative regression coefficients of rural participation rates reflect a tendency for greater intra-district migration from rural to

TABLE 11.10: Relationship of Modified Educational Participation Rates and Level of Development (Regression Results)

Level of Education	Gender	Rural			Urban		
		Co-eff. of I_d	t value	R	Co-eff. of I_d	t value	R
Illiterate	Male	–1.98	1.74	–0.10*	+1.24	1.45	+0.08
	Female	–0.65	3.42	–0.19***	+0.18	12.26	+0.56***
Just Literate	Male	–2.28	11.58	–0.56***	+0.88	8.49	+0.44***
	Female	–0.16	1.52	–0.09	+0.05	4.15	+0.23***
Primary	Male	–1.84	10.22	–0.51***	+1.77	20.91	+0.77***
	Female	–0.27	1.84	–0.11*	+0.10	8.51	+0.44***
Middle	Male	–2.08	13.15	–0.60***	+1.88	17.39	+0.71***
	Female	–0.59	5.18	–0.29***	+0.05	3.28	+0.19***
Matric	Male	–2.46	13.39	–0.61***	+1.94	11.98	+0.56***
	Female	–0.63	6.30	–0.34***	+0.21	3.89	+0.22***
Non-technical	Male	–0.89	2.01	–0.12**	+2.03	8.07	+0.42***
Diploma	Female	+0.72	1.23	+0.07	+1.38	5.14	+0.28***
Technical	Male	–0.30	6.73	–0.36***	+2.08	5.99	+0.33***
	Female	+0.26	0.56	+0.03	+2.26	4.77	+0.26***
Graduate & above	Male	–2.76	12.77	+0.59***	+1.69	8.51	+0.44***
	Female	–0.28	1.69	+0.10*	+0.22	1.35	+0.08

*, ** and *** denote significance at 0.10, 0.05 and 0.01 levels respectively.

urban areas as we move up the ladder of development. This tendency is quite pronounced in the categories of 'Graduates and above' and 'Matriculates'.

Secondly, in the case of the urban segment the magnitude of the positive influence of development on urban participation rates, as shown by the regression coefficients, rises progressively as we move up from 'just literate' towards 'Graduates and above'. It is the highest in case of 'Technical Diploma' holders. The magnitude of this influence is visibly lower for females than for males in most educational categories. However, this gender gap is much narrower in case of the professional categories. Thus the positive impact of development on work participation does appear to get strengthened by advancement in the level of education and by the process of urbanisation.

A Resume

The propensity of women to participate in economic activity is generally considered in the literature to be influenced by the level of development in a negative direction. The cross-sectional analysis of this chapter shows that this view needs to be qualified on two counts. First, the tendency of work participation to decline shows signs of being reversed at higher levels of development in case of both genders. Second, the relationship of work participation and development as also gender differentiation is widely divergent as between the rural and urban segments. The U-shaped tendency is a characteristic of the rural segment whereas in the case of the urban segment the relationship is a distinctly positive one.

When we look at the inter-temporal trend during the present century, the male participation rate shows a continuing declining trend right up to the 1991 Census. But the female work participation rate reveals a reversal of the downward trend after 1971, thus pointing to a U-shaped behaviour.

An investigation of the role of factors which influence work participation has been carried out in three stages, using a recursive system of regression equations. In the first stage participation rates are explained in terms of three factors which influence the supply of labour and a few socio-economic variables. Whereas, in the case of female work participation regression coefficients reveal 'household duties' to be exercising the most significant negative influence, in the case of male work participation 'dependency' rate carries the most significant regression coefficient. Among other factors, the most significant influence is that of population density, whose adverse effect on absorption of labour in worthwhile work opportunities is clearly visible in the rural segment.

In the second stage the supply side variables representing three causes of non-participation in work have been explained in terms of the level of development, household size and age structure. Female 'household duties' have been found to be influenced positively in a significant manner by average household size and specifically by the old age component of the male population, whose care presumably occupies a considerable portion of female time. 'Dependency' is influenced positively to a much more substantial degree by the size of young age component than by the size of old age component. Development on the other hand exercises a negative influence on 'dependency', which indicates the potential of development in drawing out hidden reserves of manpower into the orbit of work. 'Pursuit of studies' as a cause of non-participation emerges to be much more strongly influenced by the level of development in a positive direction than by the proportion of school going age group. This reveals the demonstration effect which development can exercise in bringing children within the fold of education.

The ultimate repercussion of these factors on work participation through the channel of three supply side variables has been assessed at the third stage. The results show that work participation rate of females is influenced significantly in a negative direction by 'household size' and by the proportion of old aged males, especially in the rural areas. On the other hand, the male work participation rate is affected significantly in a negative direction by the proportion of males below 15 years, both in rural and urban areas. Finally, the impact of development on work participation exercised through the channel of the three supply side variables emerges significantly negative in the case of rural male as well as rural female participation rates and in the case of the urban female participation rate, but not in the case of the urban male participation rate.

One of the variables among the socio-economic determinants which reveals an intriguing relationship to work participation is the level of literacy. A part of the explanation for its negative macro-level relationship to the male participation rate can be found in repercussions of the process of human capital formation on the supply of labour available for work. The second direction for unravelling the role of education followed in the study lies in undertaking a dis-aggregative analysis of education. This line of investigation shows that influence of the level of education on participation rates is a positive one and it is more pronounced in case of females than in case of males.

NOTES

1. For a lucid discussion of many of these factors, one may refer to Standing (1981).
2. There are some exceptions to this, for example, Kamala Nath's paper (1970) makes a foray into the realm of district level analysis.
3. The two hill States of Himachal Pradesh, Jammu-Kashmir, very small States and Union Territories are not covered here. At the time when work on this paper was started, the requisite district level data were available for 1971 and not for the next population Census year, that is, 1981. This explains the reason for analysis of this paper being based on 1971 rather than 1981 data.
4. Estimates of district level agricultural productivity per hectare were obtained from the work of Alagh and Bhalla (1979). For remaining variables data were obtained from a mimeographed volume of Planning Commission (1974) which complies at one place substantial district level data for 1971 published by diverse statistical agencies of the Government of India.
5. The participation rates are estimated as percentage of workforce to population
6. Punjab and Haryana are two exceptions to this. For detailed discussion of Statewise participation rates; see Sinha (1982) and Krishnamurthy (1982, 1984).
7. For details based on 1961 and 1981 data, see Kamla Nath (1968), Sinha (1982) and Krishnamurthy (1982). Estimates of segmentwise participation rates based on 1991 Census data are given below:

	Total Workforce	*Main Workers*
Rural Female Participation Rate	27.06	19.07
Rural Male Participation Rate	52.43	51.29
Urban Female Participation Rate	9.73	8.62
Urban Male Participation Rate	48.96	48.43

8. It may, however, be borne in mind that household work is categorised as non-work only by force of convention and it can be argued that household work by females is as essential a component for smooth functioning of any society as any other duly recognised form of productive work (*cf.* Uma Devi, 1987; Banerji and Sen, 1987; World Bank, 1991);
9. The percentage figures given in this paragraph are based on 1971 Population Census data. According to 1981 Population Census SCs formed 15.8 per cent of total population., Their participation rates were 52.6 per cent for males and 18.5 per cent for females based on main worker concept and 53.7 per cent and 24.5 per cent respectively on the basis of main plus marginal worker concept of

workforce.

10. The districts have been delineated into four regions as follows : (a) Northern Region—Punjab, Haryana and UP; (b) Eastern Region—Assam, Bihar, West Bengal, Orissa and Eastern Districts of Madhya Pradesh where tribal component is high; (c) Western Region—Gujarat, Maharashtra, Rajasthan and the remaining districts of MP; (d) Southern Region—Andhra Pradesh, Tamil Nadu, Karnataka and Kerala. Madhya Pradesh which lies in the middle of India, was bifurcated on the basis of rural characteristics, following a suggestion made by Saraswati Raju based on her detailed study of Madhya Pradesh (1987).
11. The general formula used for the purpose of obtaining variance of a composite estimator $\hat{\rho}$, as given by Kamenta [1971: 444] is:

$$Var(\hat{\alpha}) \approx \sum_{k} \% \frac{\partial_k f^2}{\partial_l \beta} Var(\hat{\beta}_k) + 2\sum_{j<k} \frac{\partial f}{\partial \hat{\beta}_k} \frac{\partial f}{\partial \hat{\beta}_j} Cov(\hat{\beta}_j, \hat{\beta}_k)$$

$$(j, k = 1, 2, 3, \ldots\ldots\ldots, k;\ j<k)$$

where $\hat{\rho} = f(\hat{\beta}_1, \hat{\beta}_2, \ldots\ldots \hat{\beta}_k)$

In the case of our problem $\hat{\rho}$ indicates a total impact coefficient and $\hat{\beta}s_k$ refer to the estimated regression coefficients in equations (i.1), (i..2) and (i.3) on the basis of which a particular α is derived. Since equations (i.2) and (i.3) are taken to be independent of (i.1) ex-hypothesi, all covariance terms other than those based on regression coefficients belonging to equation (i.1) have been reduced to zero.

REFERENCES

Agarwal, Bina 1985, ' Work Participation of Rural Women in the Third World : Some Data and Conceptual Biases', *Economic and Political Weekly,* Vol. II, Nos. 51 and 52; A155 - A164.

Alagh, Y.K. and G.S. Bhalla, 1979, *Performance of Indian Agriculture: A Districtwise Study,* New Delhi: Sterling.

Ambannavar, Jaipal P., 1969, 'Comparability and Adjustment of the Indian Working Force Data, Censuses 1911-61'. *Artha Vijnana,* Vol. XL, No. 4, pp. 521-40.

Ambannavar, Jaipal P., 1975, 'Changes in Economic Activity of Males and Females in India: 1911-61', *Demography India,* Vol. LV, No. 2, pp. 345-63.

Banerji, Anita and Raj Kumar Sen, 1987, 'Role of Women in Economic Development'. *The Indian Economic Association, Annual Conference Volume,* Jaipur.

Bardhan, Kalpana, 1985, 'Women : Work, Welfare and Status, Forces of Tradition and Change in India', *Economic & Political Weekly,* Vol. XX, No. 50, pp. 2207-20 and Vol. XX, No. 51, pp. 2261-69.

Bardhan, Pranab K., 1979, 'Labour Supply Functions in a Poor Agrarian Economy, *American Economic Review,* Vol. 69, No. 1, pp. 73-83,

Basu, Kaushik, 1984, *The Less Developed Economy,* Oxford: Basil Blackwell.

Becker, Gary S., 1964, *Human Capital,* New York: Columbia University Press.

Becker, Gary S., 1965, 'A Theory of the Allocation of Time', *Economic Journal*, Vol. LXXV, pp. 493-517.

Behrman, J.R. and B.L. Wolfe, 1984, 'Labour Force Participation and Earnings Determinants for Women in the Special Conditions of Developing Countries', *Journal of Development Economics*, Vol. 15, pp. 259-88.

Ben Porath, Yoram, 1973, 'Labour-Force Participation Rates and the Supply of Labour', *Journal of Political Economy*, Vol. 81, pp. 697-704.

Benavot, Aaron, 1989, 'Education, Gender and Economic Development: A Cross-National Study', *Sociology of Education*, Vol. 62, pp. 14-32.

Bharadwaj, Krishna, 1989, 'The Formation of Rural Labour Markets : An Analysis with Special Reference to Asia'. World Employment Research Programme Working Paper (WEP 10-6/WP 98), ILO, Geneva.

Blaug, Mark, 1976, 'The Empirical Status of Human Capital Theory: A Slightly Jaundiced Survey'. *Journal of Economic Literature*, Vol. 14, pp. 827-55.

Blinder, Alan S. and Yoram Weiss, 1976, 'Human Capital and Labour Supply: A Synthesis', *Journal of Political Economy*, Vol. 84, pp. 449-72.

Boserup, Ester, 1970. *Woman's Role in Economic Development*, London: George Allen & Unwin.

Bowen, W.G. and T.A. Finegan, 1969, *The Economics of Labour Force Participation*, Princeton NJ: Princeton University Press.

Chatterji, Ruchira, 1984, 'Marginalisation and the Induction of Women into Wage Labour: The Case of Indian Agriculture', World Employment Programme Research Working Paper (WEP 10/WP, 32), ILO, Geneva.

Chopra, Kusum, 1979, 'Female Work Participation in the Three Crop-Regions of India: An Intertemporal Study of Rural India', Occasional Paper No. 19, Centre for the Study of Regional Development, Jawaharlal Nehru University, New Delhi.

Durand, John D., 1975, *The Labour Force in Economic Development*, Princeton, NJ: Princeton University Press.

Ghes, Gilbert R. and Gary S.Becker, 1975, *The Allocation of Time and Goods Over the Life Cycle*, New York. Columbia University Press.

Gulati, Leela, 1975a, 'Female Work Participation: A Study of Inter-State Differences', *Economic & Political Weekly*, Vol. X, No. 15, pp. 35-42.

Gulati, Leela, 1975b, 'Occupational Distribution of Working Women: An Inter-State Comparison, *Economic & Political Weekly*, Vol. X, No. 43, pp. 1692-1704.

Herman, H.M., 1960, *Modern Factor Analysis*, Chicago : Chicago University.

Heckman, James J.,1976, 'A Life-Cycle Model of Earnings, Learning and Consumption', *Journal of Political Economy*, Vol. 84, pp. S11-S44.

Heckman, James, J., 1978,'A Partial Survey of Recent Research on the Labour Supply of Women', *American Economic Review*, Papers and Proceedings, Vol. 68, No. 2, pp. 200-12.

Heckman, James, J. and Thomas Macurdy, 1980, 'A Life-Cycle Model of Female Labour Supply', *Review of Economic Studies*, Vol. XLVII, pp. 47-74.

ILO, 1978, *Women at Work: An ILO News Bulletin*, No. 586, Geneva.

Kamenta, Jan, 1971, *Elements of Econometrics*, New York: Macmillan.

Killingworth, Mark R., 1983, *Labour Supply*, Cambridge: Cambridge University Press.

Klein, L.R., 1953, *A Textbook of Econometrics*, Evanston, IL : Row, Peterson.

Krishna, Raj, 1973, 'Unemployment in India', *Economic & Political Weekly*, Vol. VIII, No. 9, pp. 475-84.

Krishnamurthy, J., 1982, 'Population and Employment', in United Nations, *Population of India: Country Monograph Series*, No. 10, New York, pp. 217-32.

Krishnamurthy, J., 1984, 'Changes in the Indian Workforce', *Economic & Political Weekly*, Vol. XIX, No. 50, pp. 2121-28.

Kundu, Amitabh, 1980, *Measurement of Urban Processes: A Study in Regionalisation*. Bombay: Popular Prakashan.

Mathur, Ashok, 1964, 'The Anatomy of Disguised Unemployment', *Oxford Economic Papers*, Vol. 16, No. 2, pp. 161-93.

Mathur, Ashok, 1990, 'Human Capital, Spatial Disparities and Economic Development in India', *Manpower Journal*, Vol. XXVI, No. 3, pp. 1-39.

Mathur, Ashok, Raza, Moonis and G.S. Bhalla, 1978, 'Vocationalisation of Education in India: A Regional Perspective', mimeo, Report on a research project sponsored by the National Council of Educational Research and Training, New Delhi.

Mincer, Jacob, 1962, 'Labour Force Participation of Married Women: A Study of Labour Supply', in H.G. Lewis (ed.), *Aspects of Labour Economics*, Princeton, NJ: Princeton University Press.

Mincer, Jacob, 1974, *Schooling, Experience and Earnings*, New York: Columbia University Press.

Ministry of Agriculture, 1978, *Indian Agricultural Statistics*, Vol. II, Government of India, Delhi.

Mitra, Asok, 1979, *The Status of Women, Literacy and Employment*, New Delhi: Allied Publishers.

Nath, Kamla, 1968, 'Women in the Working Force in India', *Economic & Political Weekly*, Vol. III, No. 31, pp. 1205-13.

Nath, Kamla, 1970, 'Female Work Participation and Economic Development: A Regional Analysis', *Economic & Political Weekly*, Vol. V, No. 21, pp. 846-49.

Peek, Peter, 1978, 'Family Composition and Married Female Employment: The Case of Chile', in Guy Standing and Glen Sheehan (eds.), *Labour Force Participation in Low-Income Countries*, ILO, Geneva.

Planning Commision, Multilevel Planning Division, 1974, 'A Statistical Profile: Districts of India', mimeo, New Delhi.

Raju, Saraswati, 1987, "A Socio-Geographic Analysis of Female Participation in Labour Force in Urban India: Madhya Pradesh as an Example', *Asian Profile*, Vol. 15, No. 3, pp. 247-66.

Raza, Moonis and Aijazuddin Ahmad, 1989, *An Atlas of Tribal India*, Delhi: Concept Publishing.

Reddy, Narasimha, D., 1975, 'Female Work Participation: A Study of Inter-State Differences—A Comment', *Economic & Political Weekly*, Vol. X, No. 23, pp. 902-5.

Sahn, David E. and Harold Alderman, 1988, 'The Effects of Human Capital on Wages and the Determinants of Labour Supply in a Developing Country', *Journal of Development Economics*, Vol. 29, pp. 157-83.

Saxena, Pradeep K., 1987, "Regional Disparities in Female Work Participation Rate in India', Seminar on 'Development of Women as a Human Resource', Institute of Applied Manpower Research, New Delhi.

Schultz, T.W., 1963, *The Economic Value of Education*, New York: Columbia University Press.

Schuster, I., 1982, "Review Article: Recent Research on Women and Development', *Journal of Development Studies*, Vol. 18, No. 4, pp. 511-35.

Sen, Amartya, 1975, *Employment, Technology and Development*, Delhi: Oxford University Press.

Sheshinski, E., 1968, 'On the Individual's Life Time Allocation Between Education and Work', *Matroeconomica*, Vol. 20, pp. 42-9.

Sinha, J.N., 1965, 'Dynamics of Female Participation in Economic Activity in a Developing Economy', World Population Conference, Belgrade, Vol. IV, UN Publication No. 66, XIII, 8.

Sihna, J.N., 1975, 'Female Work Participation: A Comment', *Economic & Political Weekly*, Vol. X, No. 16, pp. 672-74.

Sinha, J.N., 1982, '1981 Census Economic Data', *Economic & Political Weekly*, Vol. XVII, No. 6, pp. 195-203.

Standing, Guy, 1976, 'Education and Female Participation in the Labour Force', *International Labour Review*, Vol. 114, No. 3.

Standing, Guy, 1981, *Labour Force Participation and Development*, ILO, Geneva.

Standing, Guy and Glen Sheehan (eds.), 1978, *Labour Force Participation in Low-Income Countries*, ILO, Geneva.

Sundaram, K., 1988,'Inter-State Variations in Workforce Participation Rates of Women in India: An Analysis', ARTEP Asian Employment Programme, ILO, New Delhi.

Todaro, Michael P., 1976, 'Urban Job Expansion, Induced Migration and Rising Unemployment', *Journal of Development Economics*, Vol. 3, pp. 211-25.

Tripathi, B.L., 1978, 'Female Work Participation in Rural Areas', *Indian Journal of Labour Economics*, Vol. 21, April-July.

Uma Devi, 1987, 'Role of Women in Economic Development', Keynote Paper, *The Indian Economic Association*, Annual Conference Volume, Jaipur.

World Bank, 1991, *Gender and Poverty in India*, Washington, DC.

INDEX